THE COFFEE CAN
INVESTOR

THE COFFEE CAN INVESTOR

A Stock-Picker's Journey to Build Generational Wealth

NEERAJ KHEMLANI

Columbia Business School
Publishing

Columbia University Press
Publishers Since 1893
New York   Chichester, West Sussex
cup.columbia.edu

Cataloging-in-Publication data are available from the Library of Congress.
ISBN 978-0-231-22106-1 (hardback)
ISBN 978-0-231-56352-9 (epub)
ISBN 978-0-231-56542-4 (PDF)

Cover design: Noah Arlow

GPSR Authorized Representative: Easy Access System Europe, Mustamäe tee 50,
10621 Tallinn, Estonia, gpsr.requests@easproject.com

LEGAL DISCLAIMER

As a reminder to readers and investors, the information provided in this book is for informational purposes only, not financial advice. Past performance is not indicative of future results. No specific outcome or profit is guaranteed in connection with your reliance upon this content. There is always a risk of loss of some or all your capital when investing, and it's important to consult a financial advisor and conduct your own thorough research before making investment decisions.

For Heather, Samantha and Ian

Thank you for your love and the songs you sing; your empathy and insatiable wanderlust; your strength and determination to make an impact.

CONTENTS

THE COFFEE CAN

INVESTOR

INTRODUCTION

A Midwestern Dad on a Mission

Matt Ankrum is a Midwestern dad on a mission (figure 0.1). He wants to fill a coffee can with stock investments—the same way pioneers in the Old West used to store their valuables—and then gift it to his daughters a couple of decades from now. It's part moonshot, part time capsule. But the goal is nothing short of a vehicle to build and pass on *unimaginable wealth.*

A Kansas City father of three high school and college-aged young women and a longtime portfolio manager, Matt Ankrum spends his free time taking his daughters Peyton, Morgan, and Pierce to movies such as *Barbie* and *Wicked*, discussing Royal Family gossip, and teaching them investing and overall life lessons (figure 0.2).

During the workday, Matt has spent much of his time identifying and researching something called 100-baggers, or US stocks that have multiplied more than a hundred times in value over a few decades. You would recognize Business to Consumer (B2C) companies that achieved this feat, such as Amazon or Nike, and think that they were the majority of such 100-baggers. But his findings show quite the contrary—since 1980, *68 percent of the 100-bagger stocks in the US were actually Business to Business (B2B) companies.* In other words, they are companies that sell professional and essential products to other businesses rather than to consumers; companies most people have never heard of, such as Fastenal, a nuts-and-bolts supplier to construction sites. He is now using the clues that surfaced from his research, along with long-standing principles from his investing idols—including Warren Buffett and the late Charlie Munger—to choose potential future 100-bagger stocks for his girls.

0.1 Matt Ankrum, 2010, in Denver, Colorado.

0.2 The Ankrum girls in 2022: Peyton (left), Pierce (middle), and Morgan (right).

His plan is simple but audacious: to invest $5 million, or 20 percent of his investable assets, across ten to twenty different stocks that he believes could become future 100-baggers . . . and wait. That $5 million could eventually grow into $500 million. In essence, he's building what could become *a half a billion dollar coffee can for his three daughters*, and he's agreed to share his story—as well as his stock picks—so readers everywhere can learn from his insights and understand what he believes is required for a company to endure for the long term. For someone like me, an author who doesn't have $5 million laying around, Matt's picks still represent a completely scalable opportunity. A $1,000 investment could become $100,000; $10,000 could someday become $1 million; and so on. It's something I kept in mind as I contemplated making an investment in those same stocks for my kids.

From my early days as a *60 Minutes* producer to my most recent role as president and cohead of CBS News & Stations, I have looked to Matt for decades for his point of view on corporate America, Wall Street, and the economy. When he shared his analysis on 100-baggers with me, I knew he was onto something big— largely because I spent twelve years at Hearst, a company that quietly shifted its media investment priorities from B2C (think newspapers and magazines that consumers read) to B2B companies (think data and information that businesses need to succeed). And when he told me about the coffee can, a metaphor for a long-term basket of stocks he and his wife are investing in for their girls, I knew I had to share their story with the world.

This is part *Rich Dad, Poor Dad* (with Matt educating his daughters and readers about long-term quality investing) and part *Good to Great* (with Matt's exclusive research into 100-bagger stocks from 1980 to 2000)—but with real skin in the game. Matt is putting his money where his mouth is and sharing his investment picks and ideas for anyone to learn from or scrutinize. At a moment when the Magnificent Seven (Microsoft, Apple, Alphabet, Amazon, Meta, Nvidia, and Tesla at the time of writing) have become so large (with market caps in the trillions) that they are all unlikely to multiply in value one hundred times again, investors like me are hungry for new long-term stock ideas that can compound for decades to come.

I've organized this book to first tell you about Matt Ankrum and his humble beginnings, and then take you into how he first learned about coffee can investing. I then explore with him the power of compounding (Einstein called it the eighth Wonder of the World) as well as concentration (having a portion of your investments in a concentrated portfolio of stocks). You will then learn about his research of previous 100-bagger stocks and what they have in common, qualitatively as well as quantitatively. The heart of the book are individual chapters on his stock picks for his daughters' coffee can—the fascinating businesses Matt believes have potential to be future 100-baggers. Remember, he invests hundreds of thousands of dollars into each of them. More important, you will learn Matt's process for identifying what he considers to be enduring companies. And, ultimately, you will see how he tells his daughters what he has done for them, and how they respond to the idea of one day receiving a portfolio that could be worth up to half a billion dollars.

This is an accessible book based on sound, easy to understand principles and insights into the companies of tomorrow. It will appeal to anyone who dreams of one day being able to retire comfortably and passing on life-changing wealth and wisdom to their children and grandchildren. Quite simply, this book—for his family, my family, and perhaps your family—is the ultimate lottery ticket.

CHAPTER 1

THE BOY FROM BELOIT

Matt Ankrum thinks of himself as the least sexy person on the planet. But trust me, you're about to fall in love with him . . . and his story—an unequivocal example of the American Dream in action. He hails from Beloit, Wisconsin, a working-class town located some ninety miles northwest of Chicago and about an hour southwest of Milwaukee. The community proudly lays claim to manufacturing automobile speedometers and inventing something called "Korn Kurls," which resemble Cheetos and are said to be the original puffed cheese snack. Back then, the younger generation had some fun with the city's cheese heritage (and accompanying odor), selling T-shirts at local rest stops that asked: "Did you fart or are we in Beloit, Wisconsin?" For people passing through the city, it was probably most famous for having the world's largest can of chili (with beans!) right next to the Hormel Chili Plant along Interstate 39 (figure 1.1).

More recently, Beloit has experienced a revival through continued contributions and investments into the community by Diane Hendricks, the owner of ABC Supply, a private business-to-business wholesale distributor of roofing supplies to contractors and builders across the country. Today the Beloit executive is ranked number 1 on "America's Richest Self-Made Women" *Forbes* list, with a net worth of $21.9 billion.[1] (To put that into perspective, she is far ahead of Oprah, who is ranked number 14, with a net worth of $3 billion.)

The son of a mechanic (Charles) and a part-time school nurse (Jonel), Matt Ankrum came of age in a blue-collar community in the seventies and eighties (figure 1.2). "We didn't have much money when I was growing up. I never felt like we were in want of anything as we always had food on the table, a roof over our

1.1 Hormel Chili Can in Beloit, Wisconsin.
Source: Freddie L. Wright

1.2 Matt Ankrum (back right) with his parents (Jonel and Chuck in front) and siblings, Melody and Chris.

heads, and clothes on our back," recalls Matt. "However, looking back, we never had anything fancy. I wore Keds shoes—yes, the ones with the massive soles— and since my dad was a mechanic, he would buy old, ugly cars and make them run forever. When I would complain that we needed a better car so as not to be embarrassed, my dad would quip: 'if your girlfriend is picking you based on your car, she really isn't that into you. Plus, this builds *character*. Everything was about 'building character' with my dad."

Matt worked odd jobs—lots of odd jobs—since the age of twelve, including mowing lawns, keeping score for a men's softball league, cutting pizza at Little Caesars, delivering mail for the USPS, and dropping boxes on the night shift (10 P.M. to 6 A.M.) for Frito-Lay.

"At one summer job at Outboard Marine Corp, I was tasked with counting little piece parts, putting those in small boxes, putting those small boxes into bigger boxes, and then putting all those boxes onto a pallet. I did this for eight hours a shift," said Matt. "The whole goal was to get faster and faster at counting and packing, so we could move more piece parts. It was brutally mind-numbing work. At lunch one day I was sitting with a coworker, probably in his mid-thirties at the time. I asked how anyone could do this day after day, it seemed to turn your brain into mush. He looked at me and said that he had been doing this for twelve years and abruptly left. I knew I had to get a real education and do something better with my life."

The University of Wisconsin was Matt's ticket out of Beloit, and his father didn't want him to take it for granted. "When I went off to college, after my mom and dad helped me move in, as I was closing the car door for them to drive away, my dad casually remarked, 'I hope you don't flunk out.' I was flabbergasted, but I knew it was one of his 'classic reverse psychology' moves."

It was the only motivational rocket fuel Matt would ever need. He went on to graduate at the top of his class (GPA 3.9) and was awarded the Distinguished Student Award at the undergraduate business school, before getting an MBA with honors at the University of Chicago. He started his career in investment banking but quickly realized he didn't want to be a middleman shopping potential deals to decision-makers at other companies. Instead, he wanted to make his own investment decisions and chose to become a mutual fund manager. He got his Chartered Financial Analyst (CFA) designation after completing a three-part exam over at least three years that tests the fundamentals of investment tools, valuing assets, portfolio management, and wealth planning. About half the people who take the test any given year fail; Matt was one of the 18 percent who passed all three exams in the three consecutive years he took them.

He climbed the ladder at Janus, the mutual fund company in Denver, during the early explosive years of the internet and became one of the firm's top stock analysts, responsible for more than $10 billion dollars of investments. He then went to Lateef, where he comanaged $5.5 billion of assets on behalf of high-net-worth families and institutions—an experience that offered Matt a chance to look into the eyes of the people entrusting him to invest their capital. He had a brief side journey driving strategy at the University of Phoenix because he wanted to get into the weeds of day-to-day business operations and because he believed in the mission of democratizing education. And later he even had the obligatory failed start-up in the small business fintech space. But he always came back to stock picking, now focused purely on long-term investing.

Overall, he models his investment style—and lifestyle—after the understated duo in Omaha, the greatest investors of all time: Warren Buffet and the late Charlie Munger. Living a modest if not thrifty life, focusing on long-term investing, and working not from America's coasts but instead from the Midwest, Matt became a quiet, stable pillar of his community and profession.

Love and family are two things Matt never took for granted. "My Dad rarely told me he loved me unless I said it first. And I knew he did, but he was more handshakes than hugs." Matt's brother Chris almost drowned as a child when he fell below the ice of a large drainage ditch in Beloit. He now lives in Kentucky. Matt's twin sister Melody stayed in Wisconsin, working in HR for the city government of Appleton. Matt is close with his siblings, but geography and careers have them leading largely separate lives.

Matt's focus on career ascension left him little time to find a life partner. That all changed when he met Maury Murray, a woman who captured his heart and who came from a family of exciting Irish entrepreneurs (who started and owned everything from a haberdashery, a grocery, and a jewelry store that supposedly once sold a black diamond to Elvis, to a beer distribution company that they eventually lost when her uncle died). But in typical Matt fashion, he only proposed after five years of quiet internal deliberations on whether she would be the right one (figure 1.3). "I guess you could say I take a long time to commit, but when I do, I commit for the long-term," he says about his wife . . . as he does his portfolio of investments.

1.3 Wedding photo of Matt and Maury Ankrum in Ireland.

They got married in Ireland at a castle called Adare Manor and then had three smart and beautiful daughters, all with Irish middle names (figure 1.4). They moved from Denver to Kansas City, and the girls are now in high school and college. Peyton "Adare" (named after the castle in Ireland where her parents were married) is the oldest daughter, who is studying psychology at Northwestern University.

Morgan "Ashford" (named after the sister Irish castle to Adare) is at the University of Wisconsin, and since a young age she has wanted to open a MedSpa—essentially a medical facility for beauty (facials, Botox, etc.). Matt is teaching

1.4 Matt and Maury Ankrum with their three young daughters, 2009, on the University of Denver campus.

her how to create a business plan so she can come out swinging when she graduates from college. She's learning the difference between fixed and variable costs, researching the average salary for an aesthetician, and trying to build a business that can stand the test of time, not to mention throw off hundreds of thousands of dollars in annual net profits. According to Maury, she has helped others struggling with acne and also practices facials on Matt . . . after waxing his eyebrows, of course.

The youngest, Pierce "Areland" (named after Ireland but spelled with an "A" because, well, they ran out of castles starting with an "A") was on the best high school debate team in Missouri, which is ranked seventh nationally (figure 1.5). Maury said Matt is routinely found mapping out and diagramming arguments with Pierce on white boards strewn throughout the house. The two of them will spar for hours, and he also works with her on her "poker face."

"He is very much a Girl Dad," the youngest, Pierce, says. "He knew all the different Disney princesses when we were young. He's gone to the American Girl store. He knows about all the drama we face at school. He knows we like to talk about the Royal Family, and so he will do research. Now he sends us articles

1.5 Morgan, Pierce, and Peyton in Greece, 2023.

on Megan Markle. He wore pink to take us to *Barbie*. He watched the *Golden Bachelor* with us. He doesn't belittle anyone or anything. He doesn't mansplain. That's very cool."

"The only argument we have with him is our car," says Morgan. "It's old and has two damaged panels. We put magnetic band aids on each side of the car to

1.6 The car named "Wilbur Andy," with magnetic band aid, 2022, Kansas City.

cover some of it up. It's cute, and kids at school recognize our car. But it also pools water on the passenger side floor when it rains. My dad was driving a fifteen-year-old car himself, and only when it completely broke down did he replace it. He truly does believe in saving money. But if not for Mom, we would not have furniture in the house. We're not flashy. I'm going to a public university. Education was first and foremost for us. We've even come to like our car. We now call him Wilbur Andy the Acura . . . who has asthma!" (figure 1.6).

"Dad gets really excited about stocks," says Peyton. "When I was fifteen or sixteen, he said you should always have two kinds of income, one from your main job, and the other from investing. Nobody else was talking to us about it. He is an educator at heart. He would talk to our investing club at St. Mary's in high school. He still talks to students there every month even though I've graduated from that school."

"His main idea is to hold stocks for a long time," Peyton explained. He would remind us that we shouldn't buy it unless we're willing to own it for at least ten

1.7 Peyton and Pierce at the Berkshire Hathaway Annual Meeting in 2023, Omaha, Nebraska.

years. Day-trading is bad. He is more a Warren Buffett kind of guy. He quotes him and Charlie Munger every two days. We went to Omaha with him one spring (for the Berkshire Hathaway annual meeting). It was very cool—a whole other world, a ton of people (figures 1.7 and 1.8). You could tell my dad was so excited to be there."

1.8 Matt Ankrum at the Berkshire Hathaway Annual Meeting in 2023, Omaha, Nebraska.

"And when Charlie Munger died, I knew something terrible had happened because Dad texted me while I was in the gym," Pierce remembers. "It was so sad that such an incredible person and investor passed away."

Matt gave each of his girls $10,000 to start buying stocks and to kick-start their investment education. They are responsible for researching their ideas. Matt will routinely tell them their Google searches are not good enough and encourage them to read annual reports. They each have a digital portfolio to track their investments, and Matt will casually share his own ideas with them as part of routine family chatter.

"When I first started, I put money in beauty companies, naturally, like Estee Lauder," says Pierce. "But that hasn't gone so well (because their business in China tanked). Also, I bought some Disney stock, but that hasn't done well either. I have bought some of the companies my dad is buying. Those have done a lot better! Our dad is an investment genius."

His daughters have no idea that at the age of fifty-five Matt has already accumulated tens of millions of dollars and no longer has to work . . . but still does. From his home office in Kansas City, he feels he has one last thing to prove as well as one more thing to teach his girls: the ultimate way to invest. The once poor boy from Beloit, who grew up near a giant can of chili, who went further than most of the people around him, has methodically hatched a plan to leave his girls someday with what can only be described as unimaginable wealth, far greater than what he has already accumulated. And the wealth would be hidden inside a different kind of can, a coffee can.

CHAPTER 2

COFFEE CAN INVESTING

Robert Kirby was not the kind of guy Matt Ankrum would normally idolize. In his free time, Kirby was into extreme sports. In 1979, his racing team finished ninth in Le Mans, a harsh test of endurance where competitors race cars for twenty-four hours straight at average speeds of more than one hundred miles per hour.[1] Kirby raced a Porsche 935 and competed in Le Mans four times in total, pushing himself and his machines to their limits. In 1984, he won the national championship of the Sports Car Club of America.

In the office, however, the dashing race car driver was completely risk averse. A graduate of Stanford and the Harvard Business School, Kirby spent decades as a top executive managing billions as a senior retirement and institutional investment fund manager at the Capital Group in Los Angeles. He also served on President Reagan's five-person Brady Commission, which investigated the causes behind the October 1987 stock market crash.

He and the commission ended up recommending that the Federal Reserve become a "supercop," overseeing financial market regulation, coordinating "circuit breakers" such as trading halts on stock, and disclosing the identities of buyers and sellers of securities.

When he died at the age of eighty in 2005, the only thing the *Los Angeles Times* said about his investment philosophy was this: "Somewhat conservative in his investing philosophy, Kirby advised clients to buy stock as if they were buying the company and to hold the stock over many years. He preferred investment in solid, staid companies rather than flashy high-tech upstarts."[2]

THE ORIGIN OF THE COFFEE CAN

Matt Ankrum knew of Kirby not from the *Los Angeles Times* but from his published work in *The Journal of Portfolio Management*, a quarterly academic magazine for finance and investing nerds that also bestows the "Quant of the Year" award. It covers topics such as asset allocation, performance measurement, market trends, risk management, portfolio optimization . . . and in 1984, it featured an article by Kirby called "The Coffee Can Portfolio." He wrote:

> The Coffee Can portfolio concept harkens back to the Old West, when people put their valuable possessions in a coffee can and kept it under the mattress. That coffee can involved no transaction costs, administrative costs, or any other costs. The success of the program depended entirely on the wisdom and foresight used to select the objects to be placed in the coffee can to begin with.
>
> The idea was brought home to me dramatically as the result of an experience with one woman client. Her husband, a lawyer, handled her financial affairs and was our primary contact. I had worked with the client for about ten years, when her husband suddenly died. She inherited his estate and called us to say that she would be adding his securities to the portfolio under our management. When we received the list of assets, I was amused to find that he had secretly been piggybacking our recommendations for his wife's portfolio. Then, when I looked at the total value of the estate, I was also shocked. The husband had applied a small twist of his own to our advice: He paid no attention whatsoever to the sale recommendations. He simply put about $5,000 in every purchase recommendation. Then he would toss the certificate in his safe deposit box and forget it.[3]

In other words, every time Kirby told the husband to buy a stock for his wife, he would dutifully buy her the equity. He would also quietly buy $5,000 of the same stock for himself with his own money. Then, when Kirby would call the husband to sell a stock for his wife, he would dutifully sell her shares, but he wouldn't sell it from his own holdings—instead keeping them forever in a safety deposit box the way old fashioned westerners did in a coffee can.

Kirby wrote, "Needless to say, he had an odd-looking portfolio. He owned a number of small holdings with values of less than $2,000. He had several large holdings with values in excess of $100,000. There was one jumbo holding worth over $800,000 that exceeded the total value of his wife's portfolio and came from a small commitment in a company called Haloid; this later turned out to be a zillion shares in Xerox."

Kirby went on to talk about strategies to beat the market. He said mutual funds charge too much in fees and trade too often, and index funds represent too many individual stocks. With the coffee can approach, he subtitled the paper, "You can make more money being passively active than actively passive."

"It would be fun and interesting (and maybe very rewarding) to have someone come along and give the idea a try," Kirby wrote to end his article, enticing others to continue the experiment someday.

After Matt read Kirby's story, he understood the sheer beauty of coffee can math. Stock losses, in Kirby's example, were capped at the $5,000 initially paid for each stock, but the upside on the winners, over time, was infinite. Some turned to $100,000 or more and one, in this case Xerox, was worth $800,000, for a 160x return.

Matt wondered, what if he took up Kirby's invitation to build his own coffee can? But instead of filling it with average stocks that have potential short-term upside and hoping a couple of them overperform years later, what if he tried to consciously fill it with as many overachieving stocks as possible? Stocks such as Xerox that could multiply over a hundred times in value—stocks known in the trade as 100-baggers. But how would Matt identify stocks that could be future 100-baggers? It was time for him to go big game hunting.

CHAPTER 3

THE EIGHTH WONDER OF THE WORLD

Referred to as 100-baggers, these rare, beautiful, majestic creatures roam in the background of the financial jungle. If you push past the leaves, past opening and closing bells, the daily financial headlines, the jobs and quarterly earnings reports, the analysts upgrades and downgrades, the federal reserve announcements, and even the United States presidents going in and out of the Oval Office, you can see 100-baggers quietly growing in value in the background. These are companies whose stock price has astonishingly multiplied over one hundred times, usually compounding in value year after year over a couple of decades (such as the Xerox example in Kirby's coffee can story). If you invested $1 in them, it would eventually be worth $100. If you had invested $10,000, it would now be worth $1 million. If only you knew their ultimate trajectories when they were just starting their climbs.

KNOWLEDGE IS POWER

Matt Ankrum has been reading obscure articles and books for decades. It's part of his daily regimen and a lifestyle purposely modeled after the late and legendary investor Charlie Munger, who said he and Warren Buffett would spend 80 percent of their day reading or thinking about what they have read.

"You'd be amazed at how much Warren reads—at how much I read," Munger once said. "My children laugh at me. They think I'm a book with a couple of legs sticking out."[1] Munger believed the best investment was in yourself, and you could develop into a lifelong learner through voracious reading and compounding your learnings. "Spend each day trying to be a little wiser than you were when you woke up. Day by day, and at the end of the day—if you live long enough—like most people, you will get out of life what you deserve."[2]

It's why Matt made time to read things like Kirby's article. And he made another big step forward in his plan to build a coffee can the day he discovered a book from 1972 titled *100 to 1 in the Stock Market: A Distinguished Security Analyst Tells How to Make More of Your Investment Opportunities* (figure 3.1). That distinguished analyst was Thomas Phelps, who was a reporter turned investor, logging years at the *Wall Street Journal* and *Barron's* before becoming a partner at

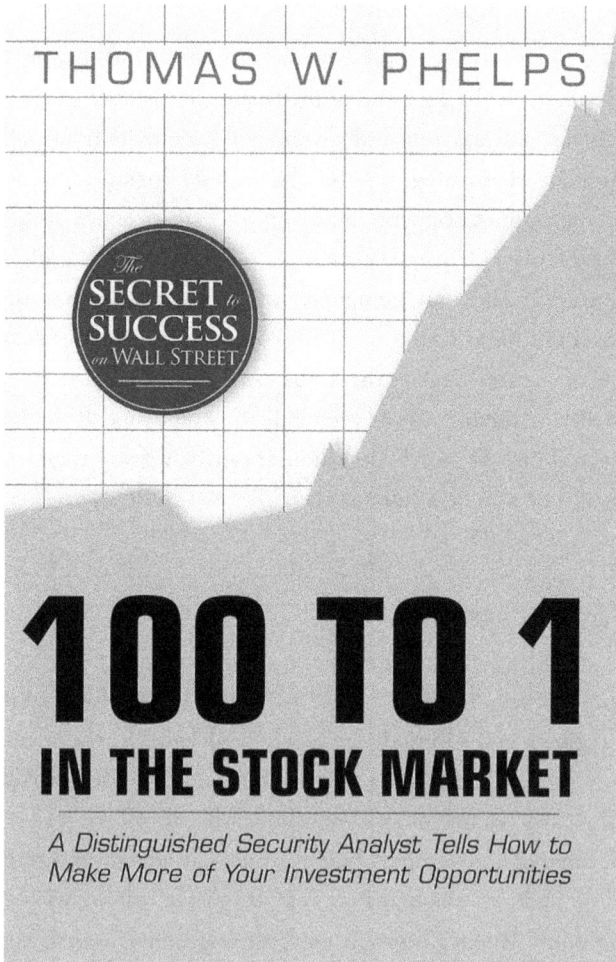

THOMAS W. PHELPS

The **SECRET** *to* **SUCCESS** *on* **WALL STREET**

100 TO 1
IN THE STOCK MARKET
A Distinguished Security Analyst Tells How to Make More of Your Investment Opportunities

3.1 Book Cover of *100 to 1 in the Stock Market.*

a brokerage firm, and then heading a research department at a Fortune 500 company before ultimately becoming a partner at Scudder, Stevens, and Clark. It's not the kind of book you would ever see on the bestseller list. And when Phelps died in Nantucket in1992, the *New York Times* didn't even mention his book in his obituary.[3]

For those who did read his book, they learned that Phelps identified hundreds of 100-bagger stocks from 1932 to 1971—bunches of them available to buy each year. In other words, in the history of capital markets, 100-baggers are more common than we think.

Timing wasn't critical either. "It was not necessary to pick the one right stock or the one right time to invest. Starting with 1932, a different stock could have been bought in each of thirty-two different years, and every dollar invested would have grown to $100 or more by 1971," Phelps wrote. "What nonsense it is to say that Opportunity knocks but once. That beautiful lady has been banging incessantly on Everyman's door for more than a quarter century."[4]

For fifty years the book has developed a small but growing cult following in the finance community (including investor/writer Christopher Mayer who also admirably wrote about 100-baggers a decade ago).[5]

THE IMPORTANCE OF PATIENCE

The main message Phelps's fans took away was to buy right and hold on and avoid the temptation of selling for the wrong reasons. Phelps said he made this mistake once in 1954 because he sold his Polaroid stock to pay a steep doctor's bill of $7,415. Less than twenty years later the stock he sold was worth $843,000.

Selling to pay the doctor's bill is one scenario, but the more common one is losing faith in a good company when the market reacts to short-term news. After identifying the right companies, he urged investors to focus on the business and its key metrics, not just the company's stock price. "Investors have been so thoroughly sold on the nonsensical idea of measuring performance quarter by quarter—or even year by year—that many of them would hit the ceiling if an investment advisor or portfolio manager failed to get rid of a stock that acted badly for more than a year or two."[6]

"To make money in stocks, you must have vision to see, courage to buy and patience to hold," Phelps said, quoting George Fisher Baker, who was known as the

Dean of American Banking and who died in 1931, the third richest man in America after Henry Ford and John D. Rockefeller. "Patience is the rarest of the three."

The internet has only made being patient much harder. In the 1950s, the average investor held onto stock for eight years. You had to call your broker to buy and sell stock. Today, with online trading platforms and no commission fees, holding periods continue to trend shorter. In 2022, the average investor held shares for only 5.5 months.[7] And when you look at the impact of meme stocks and social media, herd mentality and loss aversion drive day trading to whole new levels. All this movement in and out of stocks also punishes traders with higher capital gain taxes.

The real power of patience that Phelps was referring to is the power of compounding. For a stock to multiply a hundredfold, it must compound its value year after year, usually for decades, at very high rates (see table 3.1). If a stock can compound at a rate of 16.6 percent a year, it will take three decades to become a 100-bagger. If it grows at a higher rate, at say 20 percent, it will take less time, or twenty-five years. And so on.

The awesome power of compounding has been written about for centuries. There is an ancient story about an Indian king who loved chess so much that he offered the inventor of the game any wish as a reward. The sage inventor said he wanted one grain of rice that then doubled with each square across the board's sixty-four squares: 1 grain, 2 grains, 4, 8, 16, and so on. The exponential power of compounding isn't obvious at first. The true impact is felt at the end of the doubling cycle. That's when the king realizes that he will never be able to pay off his debt.

Today, if you were to assign a dollar value to a single grain of rice (say $0.000027 per grain), and double it every day for sixty-four days, it would take nine days to be worth a single penny.[8] It would then be worth $58,000 after

TABLE 3.1 The power of compounding

Percent Return	Years to 100-Bagger
14	35
16.60	30
20	25
26	20
36	15

thirty-two days or halfway through the sixty-four-day cycle. It then seems to magically accelerate, worth $1 million just five days later at thirty-seven days; $100 million in forty-three days; $1 billion in forty-seven days; more than Warren Buffett's net worth of $146 billion in fifty-four days; more than Elon Musk and Jeff Bezos's combined net worth of $638 billion in fifty-six days; more than all of US GDP of $27 trillion in sixty-one days; and ultimately worth $250 trillion after sixty-four days.

EXPONENTIAL COMPOUNDING, THE EIGHTH WONDER

You never thought rice could amount to something that expensive, but compounding is irrational. Our minds don't process things that are exponential, says Matt. We tend to think on a linear basis. An investment that compounds over decades grows into something most of us can't fathom. It's why Albert Einstein called compounding the eighth wonder of the world! "He who understands it, earns it . . . he who doesn't . . . pays it," Einstein said.[9] And it's also why Charlie Munger said, "The big money is not in the buying or the selling, it's in the waiting."[10] You essentially gain increasingly higher returns for the same amount of work or initial investment.

That exponential phenomenon can be clearly seen across the life cycle of a 100-bagger stock, far exceeding the performance of the stock market in general. When a stock grows 16.6 percent a year, its price multiplies one hundred times in thirty years. It is known as a 100-bagger stock. The stock market in general grows 10.8 percent a year, resulting in a stock whose price has grown 21.7 times in thirty years, or 78.3 times less than a 100-bagger. And the steepest part of the curve is at the end of the timeline (figure 3.2).

That steep growth in the latter half also translates into net worth. Look at Warren Buffett. At the age of forty-three, his net worth was $34 million, and he used some of his capital to purchase See's Candies for $25 million.[11] He didn't become a billionaire until he was fifty-six. Today, at the age of ninety-four, he is worth almost $150 billion.

In essence, the coffee can approach rescues us from our own bad habit—the deep-rooted desire to trade stocks rather than to invest in the companies behind them. It also means that your initial investment must be in a stock, or better said, in a business that can endure the test of time.

A stock that has increased over 100x (+10,000%) from its purchase price
in 30 years, which results in a 16.6% annual return

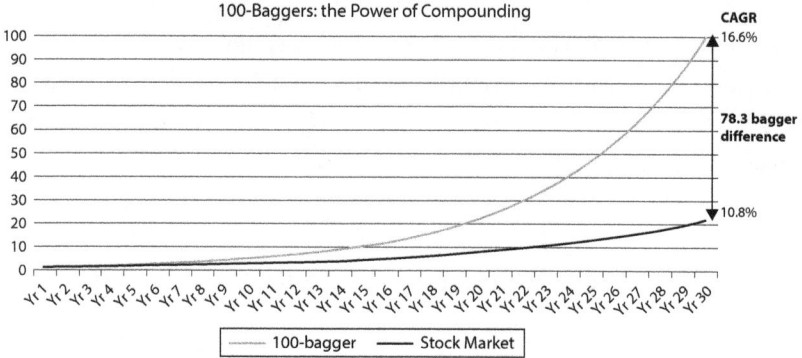

100-Baggers: the Power of Compounding

CAGR

16.6%

78.3 bagger
difference

10.8%

Yr.1 Yr.2 Yr.3 Yr.4 Yr.5 Yr.6 Yr.7 Yr.8 Yr.9 Yr.10 Yr.11 Yr.12 Yr.13 Yr.14 Yr.15 Yr.16 Yr.17 Yr.18 Yr.19 Yr.20 Yr.21 Yr.22 Yr.23 Yr.24 Yr.25 Yr.26 Yr.27 Yr.28 Yr.29 Yr.30

------- 100-bagger   ——— Stock Market

Secondary definition: a dream stock to own as it delivers exceptional alpha over an extended period of time without excessive work required

3.2 Definition of a 100-bagger stock.

This is when Matt decided he needed to put on his proverbial lab goggles and do his own quantitative analysis of more recent 100-baggers . . . to see what if anything these stocks have in common and then use those clues to help him predict and buy tomorrow's 100-baggers.

CHAPTER 4

MATT'S 100-BAGGER STUDY

G etting accurate historical information on every stock in a structured digital format is tricky; robust public records only became available in 1980. Matt thus decided to target his research on any company that had an initial public offering (IPO) from 1980 to 2000 and whose stock increased more than 100-fold from the initial price. (He stopped in 2000 because it usually takes a few decades for a company to hit this benchmark. That's why you won't see Google, Facebook, or other companies that went public after 2000 in his study.)

He wanted to focus on companies that are still actively traded, and he excluded any companies with no financial information or penny stocks that could skew the results because of the law of small numbers. He also wanted to make sure his 100-baggers achieved their compounding goal in thirty years (their price must have compounded more than 16.6 percent a year). In other words, he didn't want to include companies that took half a century to get there at a much slower speed. He also focused on domestic companies because of the challenge of getting data from stocks internationally.

At first Matt thought this would be a relatively easy screen, the equivalent of a quick sorting exercise. But the project exploded in complexity as he kept pounding away on his Thomson Reuters Eikon financial data platform. He then went directly to the database providers because he kept asking more questions and needing more answers. Finally, when the analysis was done and the smoke cleared, his trusty bat computer spit out a list of fifty companies. He then researched each one individually and even met with the management teams of some of them.

4.1 100+ baggers included in Matt's study.

The Hall of Fame list is a beautiful mosaic of corporate logos and business success (figure 4.1). The recognizable names include Nike, Apple, Cisco, Starbucks, Adobe, Intuit, Oracle, Amazon, Nvidia, Home Depot, Dollar Tree, and Monster Beverages. However, the names you know and love are not the majority of the companies he identified. The majority actually fall into another group that I consider a major headline hiding in plain sight (more on that in a minute). Matt then showed me the same companies broken down by the half decade in which they went public (figure 4.2).

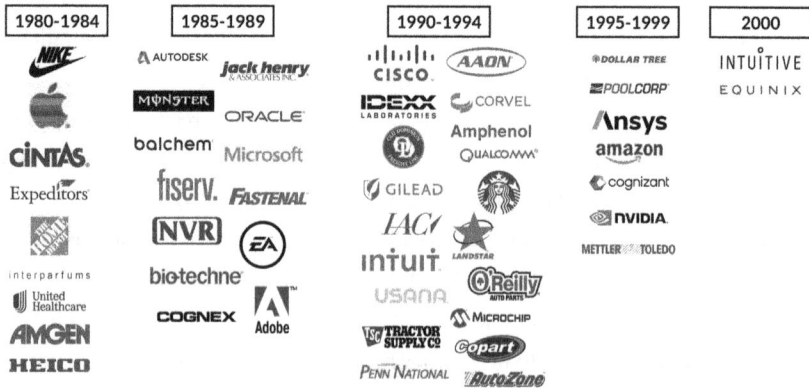

4.2 100+ baggers in Matt's study by IPO year.

4.3 100+ baggers in Matt's study by industry.

Two things become apparent. First, some of these names have been around for a long time. But, more important, Matt says, is "that in every five-year period, you had many companies born that eventually went on to grow in value 100-fold. There are always new names, which means there are always opportunity to find new 100-baggers." He then showed me the same names sorted by industry (figure 4.3).

The list ran the gamut. "Everyone thinks it must just be technology or software, but the 100-bagger list also includes retail, manufacturing, health care, business services, and others," said Matt. I couldn't help but start looking up companies that I had, frankly, never heard of before. Business services company Old Dominion started with one truck and is now a leader in the freight business and has a real impact on the global supply chain. The manufacturer AAON makes heating, ventilation, and air conditioning equipment and is headquartered in Tulsa, Oklahoma. The Tractor Supply Company, a retailer, caters to farmers and ranchers and is a source for agriculture and gardening supplies, not to mention animal feed, fencing, and even clothing! So many companies were quietly creating value for so long, and I had never heard of them. How I wished they had been part of my Yahoo! Finance stock portfolio as a young man!

Now let me take you deeper into some of Matt's observations of what a lot of these companies have in common—both on a quantitative and qualitative basis. He shared them with me, and now I share them with you for the first time.

On the Quantitative Side:

- **Growth was a critical driver** for achieving 100-bagger status. These companies were, on average, delivering north of 20 percent revenue growth every year, year after year—some two decades after their IPO.

  According to Matt, "Starbucks was the quintessential compounder as it grew its sales annually at 22.5 percent (for twenty years after IPO). The top-line growth was driven by company-owned store growth of ~21 percent (company-owned stores grew from about 165 at IPO to 7,857 twenty years later), and revenue per store compounded at a little over 2 percent during this twenty-year period."

  20 percent is a massive hurdle for any company to achieve in one year, let alone every year for two decades. Each year, as the revenue base grows, 20 percent growth hurdles become harder and harder to achieve—quickly disqualifying most runners from even finishing the race. On a relative basis forty years later, as these companies have matured they are now growing at approximately 12 percent, which is still 50 percent greater than the S&P according to Matt (figure 4.4).

  Cisco was another one of the great growth stories in his study. "It was the most valuable company in terms of market cap in 2000," said Matt. "It was the biggest benefactor of the world going digital and the internet coming on. They were essentially in the 'picks and shovels

Growth was a critical driver to achieving 100-bagger status

Compound annual growth rate (CAGR)

	5 Yrs post-IPO		10 Yrs post-IPO		15 Yrs post-IPO		20 Yrs post-IPO	
	Average	Median	Average	Median	Average	Median	Average	Median
Net Sales	42.3%	32.9%	32.0%	27.1%	25.8%	23.8%	21.9%	20.7%
EBITDA	39.1%	37.3%	29.4%	29.4%	25.3%	23.9%	21.2%	21.3%
EBIT	43.0%	36.3%	30.1%	28.9%	26.9%	24.5%	22.8%	23.4%
EPS	41.2%	33.1%	29.8%	24.7%	26.7%	22.6%	23.2%	21.1%

(excludes companies with negative operating metrics in IPO year)

100-Bagger companies delivered high, sustainable growth over the period

4.4 Consistent, high growth rates helped companies achieve 100-bagger status.

business,' selling routers to everyone building out the infrastructure of the internet. They had a good acquisition strategy and kept buying more and more companies, and their business grew at a 37.4 percent CAGR over a twenty-year period." Eventually the bubble burst and most of the companies that prematurely overbuilt the internet's infrastructure scaled back its purchases from Cisco, but it didn't stop it from achieving 100-bagger status.

- **Operational excellence** plays a factor. On average, earnings before interest and taxes (EBIT) margins improved 25 basis points every year for twenty years (figure 4.5). That's like taking a company from a 10 percent margin to a 15 percent margin. It may sound small, but you've actually improved your margin by 50 percent. Those high margins translate into lots of cash. Incredibly, ten years after their IPO, 44 percent of the companies had more net cash on the balance sheet than their total market cap at their IPO. Twenty years after their IPOs, these companies had an average EBIT margin of 26.5 percent, up from the 12.4 percent average at the time of the IPO.

Intuit, which built digital personal finance tools, was known for its operational excellence, said Matt:

They had two big advantages. First, they were in software, which means they built it once and sold it a million times. That's a real scale advantage as they spread their development costs across a growing

Annual improvement in bps

	5 Yrs post-IPO		10 Yrs post-IPO		15 Yrs post-IPO		20 Yrs post-IPO	
	Average	Median	Average	Median	Average	Median	Average	Median
Gross Margin	(40.8)	18.3	(9.7)	12.9	15.1	20.6	13.3	19.5
EBITDA Margin	34.0	53.9	29.6	27.4	36.0	25.9	26.8	28.7
EBIT Margin	28.8	27.8	21.2	19.3	36.3	29.2	26.5	24.8
Net Income Margin	53.6	40.2	28.3	17.9	37.7	20.2	30.0	21.2

(excludes EQIX, ISRG, AMGN and GILD due to highly negative margins at time of IPO)

100-Bagger companies generated steady margin improvement with focused execution

incredibly, 10 years after their IPO, 44.0% of the companies had more net cash on the balance sheet than the market cap at its IPO

4.5 Margin improvement plays a vital factor.

customer base. Second, they bought TurboTax and built QuickBooks for small businesses, and they were able to cross sell the products. In the end, they were able to knock out their competition and raise margins over time.

The company, Matt explained, grew its margins 98.6 basis points a year for twenty years (from 10.7 percent to 30.6 percent). Sorry team Redmond, but nobody is ever going to even remember Microsoft Money!

- **Return on Tangible Assets** (ROTA) was a dazzling 29.7 percent twenty years after the IPO (figure 4.6). ROTA is calculated by dividing profit by the tangible assets (such as machinery, buildings, and equipment). Basically, it measures how efficiently a company uses its assets to generate profits. Before your eyes glaze over, you should know that this is a key metric Warren Buffett uses to evaluate companies: "A good business is one that earns a high rate of return on tangible assets, and the very best businesses are the ones that earn a high rate of return on tangible assets . . . and grow," said Warren Buffett in an interview with *Fortune* in 2014.[1] In other words, as they grow and accumulate more cash, they can deploy more capital at similarly high returns and become what Buffet calls a *compounding machine*. That deployment of cash can be used to grow faster or get into new markets or acquire other companies. And the higher the ROTA, the higher the quality of the business. Matt considers companies with a ROTA over 15 percent a decent business, 20 percent a good business, 25 percent a great business, and 30 percent an exceptional business.

In his study, Matt singled out Ansys, which was bought out by chip design software maker Synopsis for $35 billion. Ansys sells engineering simulation software for semiconductors, medical devices, and satellites. "Once they got to be the leader, they had high margins, low capital intensity, and a faithful and loyal customer base," said Matt. "That

Returns realized

	5 Yrs post-IPO		10 Yrs post-IPO		15 Yrs post-IPO		20 Yrs post-IPO	
	Average	Median	Average	Median	Average	Median	Average	Median
ROTA	24.4%	21.1%	23.2%	19.8%	28.3%	24.6%	29.7%	28.9%

4.6 The quality of the business was paramount to realizing 100-baggers.

allowed them to invest their cash pile into a long list of acquisitions of technologies that benefited their customer base and grew the overall business. Twenty years after their IPO, their ROTA was 54.4 percent."

When Matt looked at all the quantitative metrics—strong growth, margins, and returns—he noticed there were many ways to achieve 100-bagger status. In other words, multiple paths to victory—sort of like watching cable news anchors Bill Hemmer, John King, or Steve Kornacki talk about presidential candidates' various routes to winning electoral votes on election night. He was able to bucket the fifty companies into different categories with compound annual growth rates (CAGRs)—which he obviously had fun naming—to illustrate his point (figure 4.7).

The "Pure Turbos" on the left side are companies that grew revenue the fastest (with revenue CAGRs greater than 20 percent), but no real margin improvement over time. The "Rock Stars" in the middle were companies that grew revenue at a 17 percent CAGR and were simultaneously able to improve their margins 25 basis points a year. Both got to the same place—into the 100-bagger winner's circle. Per Matt's research, both groups got the lion's share of attention from the financial press. But the next group, what he calls "Stealth Superstars," which had slower revenue growth (12–17 percent CAGRs) and margin improvement (15 basis points a year) than the "Rockstars," also managed to achieve 100-bagger status. Those companies are not as glamorous and are harder to spot, but those who discover them are usually well rewarded. "The Rockstars and the Turbos are like the pretty and smart people at a

4.7 Multiple paths for companies in the study to become a 100+ bagger.

party. They were always going to win anyway," Matt said. "The Stealth Superstars are not as popular, but they know how to compound over the long term too. They're just flying below the radar!"

"Time Delivered Marvels" started their growth later in the cycle. Apple, for example, boomed after Steve Jobs came back to the company. Heico, as you will soon read about, started its climb when a family bought control of the company.

- **For Exceptional Companies, Valuations Matter, But Less So in the Long Term**. Although most 100-baggers benefited from an increase in valuation, it was a smaller contributor to investor returns than the quality of the underlying business. Matt was thrilled to see this prove out in his study because it confirmed one of Charlie Munger's most famous quotes:

Over the long term, it's hard for a stock to earn a much better return than the business which underlies it earns. If the business earns 6 percent on capital over 40 years and you hold it for those 40 years, you're not going to make much different than a 6 percent return—even if you originally buy it at a huge discount. Conversely, if a business that earns 18 percent on capital over 20 or 30 years, even if you pay an expensive looking price, you'll end up with a fine result. So, the trick is getting into better businesses.[2]

Matt added, "Valuations wasn't a big driver for the 100-baggers in the study. At the end of the day the returns of the business drove the returns of the stock. If you hold a stock for six months or one year, the valuation you paid has a huge impact on your returns. But if you hold for a long enough time horizon, the returns of the business will drive the value you receive, not the valuation you paid."

On the Qualitative Side:

- **Around 58 percent of the companies were family/founder run**. "It wasn't blood, but fanatic missionary drive and willingness to adjust to changing customer needs executed consistently over a long period of time," said Matt. "Extensive stock ownership impacted mindset and tenure as well."

Matt noted that Heico is a family run business, even though they didn't start the company. While studying at Columbia University in the late 1980s, when leveraged buyouts were fashionable on Wall Street, Victor Mendelson came across Heico, which sold one thing (an engine combustion chamber). According to Forbes, he and his brother, Eric, felt the management team and board should have been doing more. They went to their father, Larry, to supply them with capital.[3] Together, in 1990, they bought $3 million of stock, enough for them to take control of the company. Over time, Matt said the family did three things: (1) introduced more parts and got FAA approval for each of one of them; (2) manufactured the parts more efficiently, so they could sell them for less than what the original manufacturers charged; and (3) acquired other parts companies they needed to expand their portfolio. Today the company also sells parts to the US military and has a market cap of over $30 billion; in the summer of 2024, Warren Buffett bought over a million shares in the company, valued at more than $185 million.[4]

The other powerful characteristic of management in Matt's study was that they were resilient. Nearly every company suffered at least one "existential event" that required the company to pivot and adapt to the threat and come out stronger. On the surface of it, it sounds implausible, until Matt starts rattling off a few examples that somehow our memories have repressed:

- Microsoft was sued by the Department of Justice, looking to break up the company for being a monopolist.
- Amazon saw a 95 percent drop in stock price from December 1999 to September 2001, driven by fear it was going to go bankrupt.
- Starbucks's stock was essentially flat from March 2000 to January 2003 due to fears it had saturated the market and there was no growth left.
- Interparfums, which manufactures and distributes perfumes, had to do a complete restructure from 1996 to 1998 to refocus the company on its core profitable fragrances.

"Whether it was a real or perceived existential threat, the management teams of these companies had to lead their teams through the challenge and come out stronger," said Matt.

- **Counterintuitively, companies that also made strategic acquisitions** in addition to relying on organic growth fared better in the long run. All too often when evaluating companies, outside analysts will ding management teams for acquiring growth instead of just growing organically. That shouldn't be the case, according to Matt. A smart management team knows how to grow organically as well as how to acquire strategically important assets that enable the company to realize even higher growth rates. Only 18 percent of the companies in his study became 100-baggers because of nearly pure organic growth.

  Matt points to Copart, the car auction company, as one example of a good acquirer. "They essentially consolidated the salvage auction market. When your Oldsmobile Cutlass Calais hit its end of life, you can sell the car and its parts to them. Others can buy the car because they can repair it . . . or use it for the parts." He says the company then layered an inventory management system and auction platform on top of all the physical auction locations they acquired over the years and offered online customers everywhere a chance to source and buy cars from all its outposts. To date, Copart is a 380-bagger. Another example is Cintas, which was in the uniform cleaning business, servicing hotels, factories, and hospitals. They acquired other uniform companies as well as business services companies in other sectors that were also needed by the same customers. "Cintas is a consolidator that brings more value to the customer," said Matt. To date, Cintas is a 600-bagger!

- **Primary sources of competitive advantage**: It was evident that transformative innovation was a defining characteristic of the 100-baggers. For example, Intuit, as we learned earlier, revolutionized accounting through software. Competitive advantages, such as "Switching Costs" (i.e., making a product so sticky that customers don't want to leave), were seen in companies such as Intuitive Surgical, which offers revolutionary new surgical approaches to surgery that require training doctors and staff as well as big upfront costs, making it hard to switch. "Scaled Economies" (i.e., companies with large customer bases that allow it to buy supplies with volume discounts) was seen at AutoZone, which rapidly consolidated the auto parts shop industry and implemented its inventory and people management systems to create massive buying power that could not be matched by competitors. Only one company demonstrated the early benefits of network effects—in which each new entity to join the network added value to every other member of the enterprise—and that was Expeditors International. "In the past, if you wanted to ship something from London to Des Moines, you would have to hire a boat from London to New Jersey, then get it on a train to Kansas City, and then on a truck to Des Moines. You had to call each segment of the chain to see if they had space on their vessel for your package," said Matt. "Freight forwarders such as Expeditors International said they would do it all for you. All you had to do was tell them that you needed to ship something from London to Des Moines, and they would figure it all out. The more parts of the supply chain they had relationships with, the more powerful their service became to customers."

These and other business model attributes or powers helped these companies create moats—a term Warren Buffett popularized to describe a business's ability to maintain its advantage over competitors to protect long-term profits as well as its share of the market.[5] In ancient times, a moat prevented thieves from entering a castle and stealing a royal family's riches!

- **Predictability matters.** Consistent operating results were relatively uniform across the study even if the stock price wasn't (figure 4.8).

  Matt loves it when the stock price of a company that is compounding its way to be a 100-bagger takes a hit. "I get giddy because I know these companies are not going away," Matt says. "They are not overleveraged (saddled with too much debt), and they have enduring, sustainable businesses. The best investors want the market to go down . . . so they can buy more of the companies they respect."

- **Nearly three-fourths of all the companies had recurring or repeatable revenue**, making them more like predictable Swiss watches! In television companies, for example, some of their revenue comes from locked-in, recurring revenues from distributors such as Comcast or DIRECTV . . . and some of their revenue comes from advertising, which starts from zero at the beginning of each year and creates uncertainty. Most of the revenue in the successful companies in Matt's study is a result of recurring or repeatable revenue, and very low churn. Management doesn't have to start from ground zero each year. Instead, they can focus on growing and taking the business to a new level.

Share Price v Operating Results

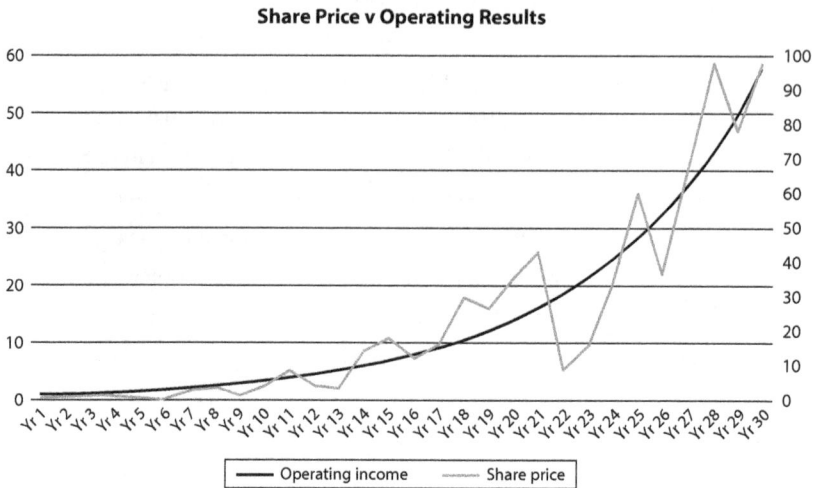

Share price moves can be harrowing and will test investor's conviction, but the consistency of the operating results and returns was generally quite uniform across the study, demonstrating the sustainability of the businesses

4.8 Most of the businesses had consistent, predictable results even though the stock price did not reflect it.

Fiserv is a company that provides technology to the financial services sector, a good example of a company with strong recurring revenue. He said they sign 5+ year-long contracts with financial institutions that locks them into Fiserv's technology and solutions. "It has allowed Fiserv to acquire new capabilities that banks need to serve their customers and then sell these features into their captive customer base, which further creates more 'hooks into the customer.' It is so difficult to leave Fiserv because its solutions power everything the financial institution does."

THE MAJOR HEADLINE HIDING IN PLAIN SIGHT

Of the companies on the study's list, 68 percent were B2B companies! We are all used to thinking about investments in companies of consumer products. We see them every day and have individual opinions about them and their products. The ones that offer *essential* products and services to consumers that they can't live without year after year (i.e., Apple) do well in the stock market—very well.

B2B comprise 68% of total companies in the study

4.9 Most of the companies in the study were Business to Business companies. Only a few were Business to Consumer companies.

But we rarely think about the Business to Business stocks, the kinds of companies that make essential products and services for other businesses (figure 4.9).

IDEXX Labs makes diagnostic and software products to ensure the safety of pets and livestock, as well as dairy milk and clean water. Amphenol makes electronic and fiber optic connectors for the military-aerospace, automotive, industrial, and broadband sectors. Bio-Techne makes proteins and reagents, and Mettler Toledo makes precision weighing instruments, with both sets of products sold to scientific research laboratories all around the world. Even Microsoft, the most well-known, has derived most of its revenue from B2B customers—first from being bundled into computers in the early years and now from offering cloud services. If these kinds of businesses don't get you excited, just take a look at their performance this century!

Matt graphed how the collection of essential B2B stocks identified in his study performed (number of baggers over time) versus the S&P (see figure 4.10).

It's not even a close contest. B2B stock performance is driven by consistently growing earnings and cash flow. It's also important to note that buyers didn't have to time their purchase of these stocks to a single event or headline . . . and they didn't have to wait thirty years to start seeing real gains.

These companies tend to be "unsexy," in Matt's parlance, unassuming companies with unassuming names that very few people talk about at dinner parties . . . the kinds of companies that Matt loves and will certainly include in a healthy proportion, alongside a couple of B2C companies, in his coffee can!

Q1 2000 - Q3 2024

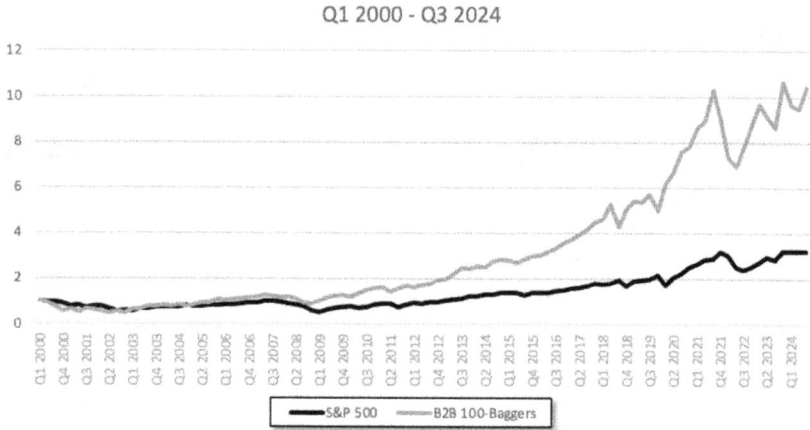

4.10 Business to business 100-baggers versus the S&P 500.

Consider Fastenal, for example. It refers to itself as a supply chain solutions company, an industrial parts distributor. Even the description is boring. Basically, it's a company that got its start by selling nuts, bolts, and screws. Even so, it has Oscar-worthy stock performance—yet despite that, it is unlikely that anyone on the management team has ever been invited to a *Vanity Fair* after-party.

When the late Bob Kierlin and his four cofounders started it in 1967, he wanted to call the company Lightning Bolts, but his partners didn't like the name. Probably too flashy. In a brainstorm session, one partner, Steve Slaggie, said that the products they were selling would be *fastening all* kinds of things . . . and that led to the name Fastenal.[6] Decades later, the product mix is more diverse. The Winona, Minnesota company's stores, according to Reuters, stock about 690,000 products in about a dozen different categories.[7]

In the no-nonsense worlds of heavy equipment, manufacturing, maintenance, operations, repair, and construction, getting all the right parts and supplies to build a new office building or do maintenance on a jet engine is difficult but critical. For these customers, Matt said, Fastenal became the trusted source by delivering the right parts on time and with any required service (i.e., "How do I install this?" or "There is a blockage, can I get this exact part but 3 inches smaller and at an angle?")

"Fastenal's customers care about service and support. The price the customer pays for a Fastenal product is *de minimis* relative to the overall cost of the project," Matt said. "Therefore, if Fastenal can always enable the customer to run smoothly and not be held up by a small part, Fastenal becomes invaluable—dare I say essential—to the customer."

Deliveries and on-site vending machines go a long way toward making that happen. The business model then becomes less about being the low-cost provider and more about charging a fair price for high-end service. Historically, fasteners, screws, and bolts were low-margin pieces. But no matter how low the price, the only driver for customers is that they get their team back to work using really expensive equipment without delay. It wouldn't matter that the screws cost 200x the best price because they still only make up about 1 percent of the total cost. Thus the service (right part, on time, plus any extra help required) is the most important driver of the value proposition for the customer. The company generates approximately 50 percent gross margins as a result, which is unheard of in this industry.

Fastenal's secret sauce is empowering their branch managers to deliver the best-in-class service required by their customers, never have a job stoppage or slowdown, and to price it for the market needs. Each branch manager can tell you what every part is used for and how it should be applied at a job site, and they know the cost of each part and have the autonomy to price the part as they see fit. Per Matt's analysis:

> This model works because the branch manager is deeply educated at "Fastenal University" *and* knows that he/she doesn't get a bonus if they don't generate a 47 percent+ gross margin and it is all on incremental growth (i.e., last year's success doesn't pay this year's bill). They need to grow, which means they need to get more customers and more of existing customer's total business. The incentive structure allows them to make very good money but not from some short-term gamble/promotion, it is about building lasting trust and value with their customers and getting paid to grow Fastenal's business with them.

Matt used to talk to the CEO about growth and asked Bob to model out the impact of each new store. "It was amazing how predictive Fastenal's model was—hire a branch manager, plug them into the system, educate them on the

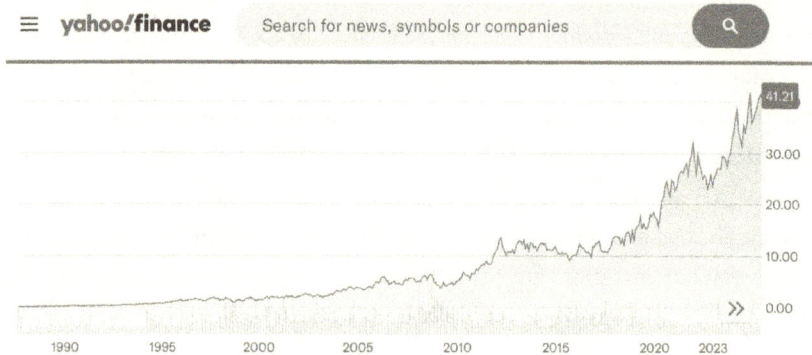

4.11   The Fastenal stock chart, 1990 through 2023.
Source: Yahoo Finance.

parts, service, and incentive plan, give them a territory, and let them run. It was like magic—wash, rinse, repeat. Year after year. The markets are massive ($1 trillion+), so Fastenal had plenty of room to run."

Fastenal has 3,300 stores and in-market locations. Matt found that the company has generated $7.6 billion in free cash flow, paid out $6.9 billion in dividends, and bought back $1.1 billion of its stock through 2023. The stock chart over time is up and to the right, getting steeper as the decades march on (see figure 4.11).

When he was a young analyst in 1998, Matt remembers that a single fund—the Janus Enterprise Fund—owned nearly 8 percent of the whole company:

> We loved the Fastenal management, felt there were tremendous barriers to entry and that the company could continue to grow for decades. But in April 1998, after my due diligence checks, we believed Fastenal would miss numbers. We sold the stock. In the short run, we were justified: the stock went down 55 percent. Investors were on edge because there was also perceived existential threat that Amazon would go into industrial supplies. However, that didn't happen. In fact, Amazon is now a big customer. And Fastenal has gone up 19-fold from the price we sold the stock versus the S&P 500 (up 4.3-fold), outpacing the index (including dividends) by approximately 500 bps per year for twenty-six years. That is a lot of Alpha we left on the table. That one investment likely would have placed our fund in the top quartile for the thirty-year period.

Today Fastenal represents not only the kind of B2B company Matt wants to invest in for his coffee can, but also how his strategy has evolved over time:

> The most meaningful change to my approach is that I now more deeply understand the power of compounding and how few truly great companies there are. This has led me to spend all my time in search of these amazing businesses and, when I find one, to buy and hold on as long as I determine the company maintains its competitive advantages and has real growth opportunities with the right management team. These are the mistakes that hurt the most—we were right, but then we chose action over inaction. We let the fear of a market drop shake us out of a great investment (short-term mentality). We didn't act like owners of a business; we acted like renters of pieces of paper. Worse, we never bought back in even though we knew it was an amazing company.

To understand why Matt's investment strategy made intuitive sense to me, I need to go back to how we met.

CHAPTER 5

SHIBBOLETH

I first met Matt in Denver in 1999 when I was visiting my then girlfriend and now wife, Heather Cabot. She was the education reporter at KUSA, the NBC television affiliate, and she was covering the horrific tragedy and aftermath of Columbine, the deadliest school massacre in Colorado history. I was an associate producer at *60 Minutes II*, the Wednesday spinoff of the Sunday show, and living in New York (figure 5.1). For years I had been covering foreign affairs—from Russia to the Balkans to Haiti—but I was becoming more interested in how the internet was going to change media, business, and the world. Heather introduced me to Matt. The moment I met the Janus analyst we hit it off, and over the decades I have come to rely on his sound guidance and pragmatic point of view whenever my reporting intersected with his domain expertise: Wall Street, corporate America, or the economy in general. When he told me at the end of 2023 that he was analyzing 100-baggers, I was intrigued. When he told me 68 percent of them were B2B stocks, I knew he was onto something.

After meeting Matt during the heady days of the internet, I became a producer at CBS News, moved to the Sunday edition of *60 Minutes*, and helped the team negotiate and then create content for a digital *60 Minutes*—a branded product for Yahoo!, which was one of the big three internet portals (along with AOL and MSN). I then left to go work for Yahoo!, eventually running the business and product of Yahoo! News as well as overseeing editorial for Yahoo! Finance. Those were wild days, with at least 50 percent profit margins and complete creative experimentation and reinvention. I was also leading the team creating original video for Yahoo!: producing the first streaming interviews with a sitting president (George W. Bush), interactive primary debates (i.e., selecting to just see Hillary Clinton face off against Barack Obama on a single subject such as health

5.1 Author as a young producer at CBS News, *60 Minutes II*, in 2004.

care or the war in Iraq), fantasy football shows, and music concerts (with Cold Play!). Yahoo! had so much scale that it had the most popular news and media websites, and at its peak it was worth $125 billion.

Having experience with both traditional and new media, I was soon recruited by Hearst, a private media company in New York, to be a digital advisor to then CEO Frank Bennack (the legendary media investor and operator who presciently bought Nabisco's 20 percent share in ESPN in 1990). I worked with different operating groups that were tackling very big questions: How would legacy media adapt and grow in the digital age? What would be the best business models? What kinds of new businesses should we invest in? How should we evolve our content and products? Free newspaper websites, for example, had trouble competing with the scale of the large internal portals. Even as the company started moving toward the digital subscription model we are all familiar with today, the profit contributions were not at the same size and scale as yesterday's print business. Instead, the Hearst corporation saw opportunity within its small portfolio of B2B media businesses run by Rich Malloch. They had higher margins, and both revenue and profits were growing. Let me explain.

Consumer media was going through a cosmic upheaval. The legacy structural advantages of owning a printer the size of one city block by one city block or a TV license and station in a local market meant few competitors, but the internet democratized public media creation and opened the door to many more competitors and creators. Newspapers were incredible businesses until classified ads went to Craigslist. Magazine sales plummeted as customers went down cashier lines with their faces buried in social feeds on their iPhones instead of sampling the print magazine rack. Eventually, Hearst's magazines became more like ecommerce sites that allowed readers to purchase the products they were reviewing. And as magazines became more like stores, physical stores became more like old fashioned magazines, creating elaborate showcases for their latest products. Even Hearst's cable network partnerships with Disney (ESPN and A&E Television Networks), which I was later overseeing, started to see subscriber losses as consumers moved away from television to streaming channels.

As consumer media worked through decline and then reinvention and now through a period of rebundling, the B2B Media divisions at Hearst were steadily growing in importance. Most other media companies took their intellectual property from movies and television and leveraged them for additional revenue in theme parks or video games. Hearst—historically known as a magazine company with titles such as *Cosmo* and *Good Housekeeping*—instead diversified by investing into database and information companies that provide "critical content" to transportation, health care, and financial companies that they need to conduct their daily operations. Motor, a Hearst B2B company (with the obligatory nondescript name), supplies automotive repair data to body shops all across the country; CAMP provides maintenance tracking for twenty thousand private planes; Zynx Health provides doctors treatment information based on the most up-to-date medical research. None of this content is meant for consumers; it is used by businesses. There is no advertising involved, no flashy upfront parties. These are purely subscription, recurring revenue, sticky businesses with minimal churn—because a client company can't do its business without this content. The CFOs of these businesses would also tell me how annual price increases coupled with a growing client base virtually guaranteed sizable revenue growth each year. No sweat!

And the CEOs are more like the successful but anonymous bowler-hat wearing businessman whose face is obscured by an apple in Magritte's *The Son of Man* painting than the creative media executives splashed about in the tabloids.

(Trust me, I know!) In 2023, Fitch, the B2B credit ratings agency, was the largest single business at Hearst, overtaking the profit contributions from any one of the company's consumer holdings, including Hearst's share of any one of its cable television partnerships with Disney.[1] Overall, under the strong and pragmatic leadership of the current president and CEO Steven Swartz, who accelerated corporate investment into these kinds of B2B media businesses, Hearst hit historic profit highs in 2022 and 2023—setting itself apart from many other media conglomerates. At the end of 2024, Hearst announced that it would grow top-line revenue to almost $13 billion, with more than half of its profits coming from B2B media assets for the first time.[2]

So, when Matt said he was studying and wanted to invest in B2B companies with essential products, it was as if he had uttered a shibboleth or secret password that only a very few would easily understand. While Hearst executives were accelerating their efforts to acquire more *private* B2B companies (spending $3 billion on them in the last two years alone), Matt was saying that he wanted to be investing in *public* B2B companies because they had a strong chance of becoming 100-baggers. This was too much of a coincidence. He might as well have said, "Open Sesame!"

CHAPTER 6

DIWORSIFICATION

With his historical analysis in hand, Matt started contemplating how many stocks should be in his coffee can. One hundred? Twenty? One? Once again he studied some of the greats. Their portfolios tell an instructive story about focusing on quality not quantity. (Although many of the investments in this chapter are focused on B2C companies, they provide the kinds of *essential* products and services Matt looks for in great companies.)

Matt first turned to the writings of Nick Sleep, another one of his investment idols. Sleep and his business partner Qais Zakaria are not well known, particularly because they largely avoid interviews. Instead, they do most of their talking through their revealing investor letters, which they released a few years ago and showcase an incredible track record. Between 2001 and 2013, Sleep's fund, the London-based Nomad Investment Partnership, returned 921.1 percent and had an annual return of 20.8 percent versus 6.5 percent annual returns by the MSCI world index.[1]

What may be even more astonishing is that his fund ultimately focused on just three stocks: Berkshire Hathaway, Costco, and Amazon. With the benefit of hindsight, it's not difficult to understand why he chose the first and last holdings, but Costco? Why Costco? What did Sleep see there that would have him concentrate so much of his investment in a retailer that sells products in bulk?

He considered Costco to be a perpetual growth machine. The company offers customers products they want at very low costs, and they never mark up a product more than 14 percent. That then creates a flywheel effect: low prices lure shoppers, which generates more revenue, which allows Costco to self-fund the opening of more stores, which gives the company the market power to negotiate lower prices from suppliers, and the savings are passed on again to the consumer—and on and on the wheel turns. Costco gives customers access to this cost-saving flywheel for a mere $60 annual membership fee.

"The answer lies in analyzing not the effects and outputs of a business but digging down to the underlying reality of the company, the engine of its success," Sleep wrote in his December 31, 2004, letter. "That is, one must see an investment not as a static balance sheet but as an evolving, compounding machine." Sleep coined a new term for Costco's business model: "scale efficiencies shared." It was also Costco's moat. He wrote:

> In the office we have a white board on which we have listed the (very few) investment models that work and that we can understand. Costco is the best example we can find of one of them: scale efficiencies shared. Most companies pursue scale efficiencies, but few share them. It's the sharing that makes the model so powerful. But in the center of the model is a paradox: the company grows through giving more back. We often ask companies what they would do with windfall profits, and most spend it on something or other, or return the cash to shareholders. Almost no one replies "give it back to customers"—how would that go down with Wall Street? That is why competing with Costco is so hard to do. The firm is not interested in today's static assessment of performance. It is managing the business as if to raise the probability of long-term success.[2]

The company could self-fund revenue growth of 14 percent each year. Today it has 871 warehouses worldwide, and for every $1 in profit Costco was passing on $5 in savings to its customers.[3] It's a business model that's very hard to disrupt.

If the model sounds familiar, it's because it is. Amazon does the same thing online, passing along savings and offering free delivery with a subscription to Amazon Prime.

A MEETING OF THE MINDS

In *The Everything Store: Jeff Bezos and the Age of Amazon*, Brad Stone discusses a 2001 breakfast meeting that Bezos once had with Jim Sinegal, founder and then CEO of Costco. Sinegal explained the Costco business model to Bezos: it was all about customer loyalty. The low prices drive loyalty, and the loyalty drives membership fees.

The Monday after that meeting Bezos met with his senior managers and announced that Amazon.com would immediately be cutting prices of books, music, and videos by 20 to 30 percent. Later, during a quarterly conference call with analysts, he observed, "There are two kinds of retailers: there are those folks who work to figure how to charge more, and there are companies that work to figure out how to charge less, and we are going to be the second, full stop."[4]

Although Bezos has never publicly credited Sinegal for inspiring any of Amazon's decisions, at an offsite later that year he and his team drew Amazon's version of the flywheel. In its case, lower prices lead to more traffic, which then attracted more commission-paying third-party sellers to list their products on the website, which drove prices down. Also, the more customers, the more it could spread its cost structure across more people, further driving prices down.[5]

BACK TO THE (FUTURE) THREE INVESTMENTS

And so Sleep made Amazon his third investment . . . and he never wavered. Even in 2008, when the markets collapsed after the subprime mortgage crisis and Amazon's overall retail sales went down 10 percent, Sleep didn't sell. Despite the overall drop, the largest single shopping day of the year was still up 16 percent versus the same day the year before, and Sleep knew the business would continue to grow in the long term. By 2009, Amazon revenue was up 60 percent, and Nomad Investments—built on the three stocks of Berkshire Hathaway, Costco, and Amazon—was up 71 percent. Sleep closed his fund in 2014 at the ridiculously young age of forty-five. His personal wealth continued to triple in the first five years of his retirement.[6]

"Sam Walton did not make his money through diversifying his holdings. Nor did Gates, Carnegie, McMurtry, Rockefeller, Slim, Li Ka-shing, or Buffett. Great businesses are not built that way," Sleep wrote in 2009. "Indeed, the portfolios of these men were, more or less, 100 percent in one company and they did not consider it risky! Suggest that to your average mutual fund manager."

Jeff Bezos could be on that list too. As for his Amazon stock, Matt says, it became a 927-bagger in just 25.8 years. Looking back, Bezos said his company succeeded because of the decision to keep pricing low and deliveries quick:

I very frequently get the question: "What's going to change in the next 10 years?" And that is a very interesting question; it's a very common one. I almost never get the question: "What's not going to change in the next 10 years?" And I submit to you that that second question is actually the more important of the two—because you can build a business strategy around the things that are stable in time. . . . [I]n our retail business, we know that customers want low prices, and I know that's going to be true 10 years from now. They want fast delivery; they want vast selection.

It's impossible to imagine a future 10 years from now where a customer comes up and says, "Jeff, I love Amazon; I just wish the prices were a little higher." "I love Amazon; I just wish you'd deliver a little more slowly." Impossible.

And so, the effort we put into those things, spinning those things up, we know the energy we put into it today will still be paying off dividends for our customers 10 years from now. When you have something that you know is true, even over the long term, you can afford to put a lot of energy into it.[7]

True for Bezos, True for Costco . . . and true for Sleep and his stock concentration. But is this type of concentration the anomaly? Even with three stocks, Sleep was banking hard on a single shared business model between two of them (Amazon and Costco). Charlie Munger eventually joined the board of Costco. Did he and his partner Warren share Sleep's philosophy on concentration?

"At the Berkshire Hathaway shareholder meeting in 2013, Warren Buffett said he's owned 400 to 500 stocks during his life and made most of his money on 10 of them," according to Morgan Housel, author of *Psychology of Money* and *Same As Ever*. Charlie Munger added: "If you remove just a few of Berkshire's top investments, its long-term track record is pretty average."[8]

But haven't we grown up being told to diversify our investments? You know, put 60 percent of our investments in equities and 40 percent in bonds. As you get older, move to a larger percentage of bonds . . . and along the way avoid mutual fund fees while buying low-cost index funds such as the S&P. Isn't that the basic advice we all receive? Yes, that's true, says Matt, as an ideal construction for a *purely passive* portfolio. Most people don't have the time to research individual stocks, and this passive approach has performed relatively well.

How well? Has the S&P performed well enough to be called a 100-bagger? The index started in 1957. Since then, it is a 133-bagger, with a compound annual growth rate of 7.58 percent. This is, of course, a wonderful return on a stock (or index in this case), but not quite a true 100-bagger as Matt defines it. Remember, Matt's bar for a 100-bagger is to achieve the feat in thirty years. The S&P became a 100-bagger in 2023, taking sixty-six years to get there.

THE CHAPTER TITLE, AT LAST

But owning a portfolio of 500 stocks does have some limitations. Munger called it "diworsification."

"A lot of people think that if they have a hundred stocks, they're investing more professionally than they are if they have four or five. I regard this as insanity. Absolute insanity," said Munger. "I find it much easier to find four or five investments where I have a pretty reasonable chance of being right that they're way above average. I think it's much easier to find five than it is to find a hundred. I call it diworsification—which I copied from somebody. I'm way more comfortable owning two or three stocks which I think I know something about and where I think I have an advantage."[9]

Matt says some portfolio managers buy a lot of stocks because they believe they are derisking the overall basket: "The more stock you add, the worse the performance. The reason you add more names is because you become less confident. Say you have a fund with 500 equal weighted names. That means each one is 20 basis points (one-fifth of 1 percent) of the portfolio. If one goes bust, I didn't kill myself. If one doubles, it adds 20 basis points. That's the point. I don't want to take on too much risk. There is no deep conviction about any one business. Ask your fund manager, 'What's the ticker symbol of the 137th stock in your portfolio?'"

If you looked at Berkshire Hathaway's $266 billion stock portfolio in 2024, it held stakes in forty stocks. But 71 percent of its stock portfolio was invested in only five stocks. And the biggest holding was Apple.[10]

Charlie Munger has often said: *"Take a simple idea and take it seriously."*

Most stock investors take Apple seriously too. In fact, you have seen "concentration" come back in fashion with retail investors, especially around tech stocks. Apple, Alphabet, Amazon, Meta, Microsoft, Nvidia, and Tesla are now monikered the "Magnificent Seven." At the end of 2023 the *Wall Street Journal* wrote, "Within the MSCI All Country World Index—a benchmark that claims to cover about 85 percent of the global investable equity market—the combined weighting of the Magnificent Seven is larger than that of all the stocks from Japan, France, China, and the UK."[11]

The Magnificent Seven accounted for more than half of the S&P index's performance in 2024.[12] They have all achieved 100-bagger status, and their combined market caps, as of the start of 2025, represent a third of the entire S&P index.[13] Given their monster performance and ongoing dominance, particularly in a world of artificial intelligence, why wouldn't Matt simply put all the companies that make up the Magnificent Seven into his coffee can and call it a day? He has owned some of them for a long time, and they are still growing, but these trillion-dollar-plus companies are likely too big to multiply one hundred times again.

Matt did a simple mathematical analysis. "If you take a company worth $1 trillion and grow it at 16.5 percent a year for thirty years (what you require to be a 100-bagger), while growing the rest of the market at its average of 9 percent, a single company—just one—will end up representing a whopping 20 percent of the entire US market cap. Theoretically, that could happen, but the odds are extremely low." It's the same thing I often heard from Hearst's Chairman William Hearst and Executive Vice Chairman Frank Bennack, who would say when discussing cable companies in their heyday: "Keep in mind, trees don't grow to the sky."

Buffett has trimmed his holdings in Apple over time, hinting that the selling was for tax reasons, but as of March 2025, it still dominates a quarter of his stock holdings. Part of the attraction for Buffett is likely the company's reputation for returning capital to shareholders. Apple has repurchased $674 billion of its own stock since 2013.[14] And on top of that, it's also a dividend paying company. Even if the company's growth slows, Buffett continues to own a greater portion of the company's future earnings and cash flow . . . and is collecting hundreds of millions of dollars in dividends a year.[15]

So, although it may make sense for investors across the globe to continue to ride the Magnificent Seven's success in the near and midterm, those companies are not necessarily good candidates for Matt's coffee can of potential 100-baggers . . . a few decades from now.

TIMING THE STOCK PICKS

Instead, Matt is looking for companies that are just beginning their journeys. Not trillion dollar companies, but smaller ones that are between $500 million and $20 billion in market cap (with a sweet spot of $1 billion to $10 billion). They, of course, still need to have strong business models with strong moats—the kinds of companies Buffett would like in spirit, but just smaller than the kinds of companies needed to move the dial on a Buffett-sized portfolio.

Matt agreed with Buffett, Munger, and Sleep on concentration versus diversification for his coffee can. Plus, for Matt, the reality is that there aren't hundreds of great companies at any given time that can compound at high rates for decades. Matt believed less would be more and decided he would spend the year researching and identifying ten to twenty stocks, leveraging the learnings from analysis of his 100-bagger study. His confidence for holding these companies for the long term would be resolute, unless they lose their competitive advantage or face a true existential threat they can't overcome (i.e., an unforeseen technology shift, etc.). If something like that were to happen, he would divest and shift those funds to further concentrate on the remaining stocks or add new 100-bagger candidates. He would also stack the deck with companies with essential products, both on the B2C and B2B sides, but probably overweighted on B2B.

The final question would be how much money to invest? If the stock picks were all good and multiplied one hundred times, $1,000 would turn into $100,000; $10,000 could turn into $1 million; and $1million could turn into $100 million.

After a career in investing, Matt felt sure about his game plan and decided to put 20 percent of his investment portfolio in the coffee can strategy. (That's good news for me because I am still largely invested in index funds and bonds. In other words, it's not an all or nothing strategy. I, too, could participate.) At the age of fifty-five, he no longer needs to work, but he still does . . . and believes he will be alive long enough to see how many of his stock picks turn into 100-baggers in two to three decades. So he decided to go for it: he would invest $5 million across his stock picks; $5 million could eventually grow into $500 million. In essence, he wanted to build what could become a half a billion dollar coffee can for his girls.

Sometime later I got a call from Matt. "Neeraj, exciting news, I've bought the first stock for the coffee can!"

CHAPTER 7

FLUGELBINDERS

Matt doesn't choose stocks lightly. He's constantly screening the entire market for companies with successful performance metrics as if he's drafting players for a fantasy baseball team. Each new screen adds a new range of filters: from size to sector to a whole array of ratios and indicators floating in an alphabet soup of financial abbreviations. *High EPS (earnings per share)* and *Low P/E (price to earnings) ratios* may be the more recognizable ones; terms such as *High ROTA (return on tangible assets)* may be more arcane but are substantially more important to Matt.

And when the screen is ready, he prints up the list of three hundred or so potential companies that made it past his initial prerequisites, and he sits down excitedly, clicking his pen, ready to do battle. He starts scratching names off the list, like a teacher grading an exam full of mistakes, shaking his head and commenting along the way. Watching him do this is like listening to someone quietly revealing their tastes with each elimination of a company, sharing hard-earned lessons learned over decades that have been reduced to a mental shorthand for avoiding landmines. Just listen to the reasons he gives:

> I only screen in countries that have a good or fair legal system in place. Don't ever spend time on Nigerian companies. Right now, I'm also not investing in Chinese names either because they don't have the governance that I need; they're also not next door to me for me to easily visit; I strike those off my list.
>
> I look at companies ideally $20 billion or less in market cap.
>
> Return on assets needs to be greater than twelve.
>
> Net debt to EBITDA is less than four, free cash flow conversion is high.
>
> Eliminate industries like movies—they are hit businesses, utilities (slow growth), financial companies that offer commodity services (no moat), cyclical

transportation companies (make money in up cycles, lose money in down cycles), and energy companies.

Why eliminate energy companies? I ask, interrupting his flow.

Because energy companies make money on the price of oil. That's why I don't necessarily own them. It is totally reliant on a commodity that is out of its control. I tend to boil it down to the core and try to eliminate anything management can't control. I want a company and a management team that has as much control over the company's future as possible. No surprises. My value add is what I do to take companies off that list.

I interrupt again. Matt, do you worry that artificial intelligence will make stock pickers obsolete?

AI may take out some investors, but they will work together down the road. The bots don't have the gained experience yet. For example: "God, I know that company and they have a terrible management team and people leave there all the time."

From the three hundred names, twenty are left without ink scratched through their ticker symbols, survivors of a brutal elimination contest on par with the call-in portion of Jim Cramer's *Mad Money* show. But that was only the first round.

With the names I didn't cross out, I need to know more about what they do. I start pulling all their financial metrics to better understand the quality of the business, its growth, margins, and the consistency of its free cash flow. I look at it over ten years. Are the numbers getting better? Is it a smooth climb? Is it a seemingly predictable, consistent business? From there I have whittled it down to three to five names, and that's when I start my deep research, truly learning about the company.

What Matt does next is to check for what he calls the 4Es (that only get stronger with time):

- Essential Product and/or Service
- Excellence in Operations, Growth and Returns

- Enduring Power/Competitive Advantage(s)
- Entrepreneurial Management

In Matt's opinion, anyone can do computer screens for stocks and look for certain quantitative metrics. Looking for the 4Es, however, is where he spends most of his time. He needs to feel confident about the long-term trajectory of the company: "A stock is a function of future opportunities and how much cash flow a company throws off over time, and that is a result of growth and sustainability. Essential products, excellence in operations (growth and returns), and entrepreneurial management all help contribute to a company's enduring power. And that's what I am looking for."

Matt is essentially panning for gold. He whittles down stock lists like these all the time. Keep in mind that there are fifty-eight thousand publicly traded companies in the world. He is looking for reasons *not to buy* a stock before he even begins to start to look for reasons *to buy* a stock (the 4Es). Most of the time, 99 percent of the time, he doesn't find something actionable. Every quarter he dusts himself off and starts the process all over again. He goes back, adjusts the filters, and screens a new list. He starts the whittling down again. He starts modeling and looking for the 4Es. He reads everything, and when I say everything, I mean everything he can get his hands on about a single company. Years' worth of earnings reports, 10-K and 10-Q reports, investor relations presentations, conference call and management call transcripts—all to understand how the company is evolving, to see what management said in the past and whether they delivered on what they said, year in and year out. He will read similar reports from the company's competitors, sell side or short reports from analysts to see if they add or challenge his thinking on the company, and any trade press or books about the company. From there, Matt will start talking to other human beings, from the company's management or investor relations teams, to competitors, and customers, as well as vendors.

"We do the hard work," he says, trying to demystify his process. "We do the really hard, boring work!" Matt believes you do more work before you buy the stock than afterward . . . because afterward you are monitoring the company to see if it sticks to its plan and is growing the way you thought it would (regardless of its stock price). "And when you find it, when you find that one, you get very excited because you just found the ultimate company, the ultimate investment. I love to feel that way," Matt says with pure joy.

The first time I felt that joy in Matt's voice was when he called me to tell me he had made one of his first purchases for the coffee can. The suspense was killing me. Matt presents his ideas with great care: telling me about the company, its products, its management, the compounding financials, the competitive landscape, and how it is deliberately working to create real value in the long term. When he gives me a deck, it's as if he's sharing a piece of origami, something that is so precious that it might as well be a piece of art. But it's less about the presentation and more the sheer respect he has for a well-crafted business and his desire to share what makes it so special. After he ends a thoughtful presentation of the company's mechanics and ambitions, he shares with me a single page where he boils down everything attractive about the company to the three most important numbers behind his decision to invest in them. It's as if he just created a personalized baseball card for them. More on that later. First, without further ado, the company he bought was:

Diploma PLC.
Ticker symbol: DPLM.L

Know it? Probably not. In fact, I would be shocked if you *had* ever heard of it. It's a London-based business that supplies highly technical products and services in life sciences, seals, and controls. If you are a geek like me, you'll enjoy hearing about what they do.

Anyone who has watched *ER*, *Grey's Anatomy*, or *The Pitt*, knows surgeons can put tube-like instruments with cameras down into our bodies to see what's going on. It's called Endoscopy. Well, Diploma PLC's Life Sciences division partnered with Fuji to commercialize a camera that uses artificial intelligence and deep learning to not only detect a polyp but help doctors characterize if it is cancerous or not . . . in real time.[1]

It's part of a much larger life sciences division that supplies and services surgical devices and clinical diagnostic instrumentation for operating rooms, hospitals, and laboratories. They work side by side with surgeons, pathologists, laboratory scientists, and health care professionals to deliver innovative products from third party, midsize suppliers in a complex regulatory environment. Many of their clients have signed exclusive deals with Diploma to supply them with a range of products they can then distribute to hospitals.

Diploma's Seal Division supplies seals, gaskets, and related fluid-sealing products to . . . well, it seems to everyone. Their end markets include everything from food and beverage, to automotive and marine, to mining and industrial companies. If you don't know, gaskets seal a connection between two components that have flat surfaces; whereas seals are used between engine parts, pumps, and shafts that rotate. Seals tend to be flat and round; gaskets are cut into different shapes, so they fit the components they are sealing. Selecting an appropriate seal design and material depends on the operating conditions of the application such as temperature, speed, type of lubricant, vertical or horizontal orientation, grease retention, contaminant exclusion, liquid separation, pressure differentials, installation restrictions, and so many other factors (figure 7.1). If this business reminds you of Fastenal, it should. Remember, they specialize in fasteners such as screws, nuts, and bolts and work closely with their clients. And if you are a Tom Cruise fan, this will remind you of the movie *Cocktail*, where Tom's character Brian Flanagan, a bartender eager to become a wealthy businessman, says he wants to become insanely rich by inventing his version of a Flugelbinder—the fictional name for the plastic tips that go on the end of shoelaces. Well, seals may be just as much a sleeper hit as Flugelbinders, and Diploma is the company responsible for getting clients the right one . . . right away.

7.1 Stacks of seals produced by Diploma.

The last division of Diploma is Controls, which supplies everything from adhesives for electronic control units in cars to waterproofing compounds for the connections of fiber optic rollouts. They are also big in wires and cabling. I'm not just talking about the cable wire that provides last mile connectivity to your home or office so you can watch your favorite television show or security camera feed, but the kinds of cables and wires that go into race cars and fighter jets, as well as the low-voltage wires that go into data centers (the super-hot rooms that are full of computer servers that handle the internet traffic happening "in the cloud"). Diploma sends out specialists and engineers to create bespoke solutions.

Many of these capabilities came to Diploma through acquisitions, but they weren't always good at the art of buying companies. For many decades in their one-hundred-year history, they bought industrial companies in areas that were in secular decline (i.e., building parts, specialty steel, etc.). In 1996 they brought in a new CEO, Bruce Thompson, to reboot their acquisition efforts. He came in and sold ten businesses and used the proceeds to acquire better, more resilient businesses that would add value to the entire enterprise. "Once bitten, twice shy," said Charlie Huggins, an analyst who covers Diploma, in an interview with Business Breakdowns.[2]

The reorganized company is now highly diversified by geography, sector, and market. It's a value-add distributor of technical products and services in the US, Europe, Canada, and Australia. It is made up of dozens of companies across high growth sectors all running independently in a decentralized corporate structure—which leads to a highly agile, entrepreneurial culture. The company had high teen percentage profit margins and a return on capital of 20 percent for the last few decades. "Diploma is one of the best acquirers I've ever come across," Huggins said, adding, "In my view, Diploma is one of the highest quality businesses listed on the UK stock market. I think it is under the radar for most investors."

THE HARD NUMBERS

Matt, as we know, is not like most investors. His work on Fastenal helped him see the potential for Diploma rather quickly. As I foreshadowed, he likes to boil down the opportunity to three key sets of numbers that showcase the strength of the company. Here they are, and I will explain each of them.

KEY NUMBERS TO UNDERSTAND DIPLOMA'S BUSINESS

5–7%	32.6%	5 TO 20

5–7%: Across its companies, Diploma has been growing its revenue organically by 5 percent annually, and in the last three years it has accelerated organic growth to 7 percent.

But then it acquired new companies that have pushed overall revenue growth to 23 percent over the last three years. As Matt revealed in his 100-bagger study, acquisitions were a key part of growth for so many companies on the list.

Diploma also has a higher profit margin (18–19 percent) than most distributors (sub 10 percent) because of all the high-level service they provide their clients. Most middlemen businesses get squeezed on both sides. The work Diploma does is a real value-add; they can charge more for it, and because they don't manufacture the products, they don't need to spend a lot of money to make a lot of money.

32.6%: This leads to a high return on tangible assets (ROTA), which is calculated by dividing profit by the tangible assets (such as machinery, buildings, and equipment). Basically, it measures how efficiently a company uses its assets to generate profits. As you may remember, this is a key metric Warren Buffett uses to evaluate companies. And Matt considers companies with a ROTA over 25 percent to be very successful. Diploma's ROTA is 32.6 percent. To put that into perspective, Microsoft, which doesn't have expensive factories and is a software business, has a ROTA of 37 percent.

5 to 20: Diploma then takes its profits and converts 90 percent of it into cash that it can use to fund acquisitions. The companies Diploma acquires work with each other to share warehouses, expand into new territories, and even cross sell products. This ability to bring companies into the corporate tent and give them the relationships and partnerships to expand is what allows Diploma to acquire a company at a multiple of five times their EBITDA—and then immediately have it valued by Wall Street at twenty times EBITDA, once it's a part of the group.

Since 2019, it has made thirty acquisitions—most were bolted onto existing companies. That's a level of M&A targeting, execution, and integration that is rarely seen within a public company. In most of the cases, Diploma was the only potential buyer. That's because it nurtured relationships with these private companies, often for years or decades, and made quick and easy

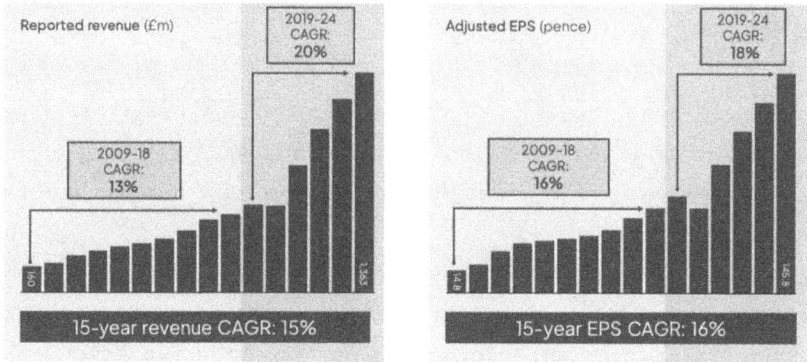

Reported revenue (£m)
2019-24 CAGR: 20%
2009-18 CAGR: 13%
15-year revenue CAGR: 15%

Adjusted EPS (pence)
2019-24 CAGR: 18%
2009-18 CAGR: 16%
15-year EPS CAGR: 16%

7.2 Fifteen-year revenue and EPS CAGRs for Diploma.

offers as soon as they were ready to sell. And the sellers also knew Diploma had value-add technical expertise and distribution acumen that other potential suitors couldn't match.

"Diploma has perfected a system and model to compound value," says Matt. "Not only is the revenue growing at a fast clip (at a 15 percent CAGR since 2009), but earnings per share is also growing by double digits (at a 16 percent CAGR) too." See figure 7.2, which features its 2024 year-end earnings numbers.[3]

To underline this company's ability to be a long-term compounding machine, Matt urged me to read another one of his favorite beach reads: Hamilton Helmer's book, *7 Powers: The Foundations of Business Strategy*. Helmer is the chief investment officer of Strategy Capital; grew up professionally at Bain & Company; taught business strategy at Stanford; and advises companies including Adobe, Spotify, and Netflix. In fact, Netflix's Reed Hastings wrote the foreword to his book. Anyway, Helmer believes that if a company doesn't have one of the seven powers outlined in his book (for example, scale economics or high switching costs, etc.) it lacks a viable strategy and is, essentially, vulnerable to competition.

Matt believes Diploma also has one of the rarest of Helmer's *7 powers*: process power. Helmer used Toyota as his example of a company with process power, highlighting its exacting production process and the high quality of cars that rolled off its assembly lines. It helped Toyota take shares from General Motors over the decades, and GM could never duplicate the same process. Matt believes

Diploma has perfected an M&A process that compounds value unlike any other company in its space. So, what's the risk?

Are there enough companies for Diploma to buy? Yes, Matt points to the company's pipeline of two thousand companies, with fifty near term active opportunities.

Do they have a massive debt load? No, their debt to earnings ratio is relatively low.

Does Amazon sell seals? Yes, a couple hundred of them. Diploma has close to one hundred thousand. "Amazon has looked at going into industrial and never went into it," Matt says, adding, "It doesn't want to deal with bespoke solutions. It wants to sell the exact same copies of *Grapes of Wrath* year after year!"

So, what is the risk? One word: culture.

When Bruce Thompson retired, the company hired a CEO that only lasted four months; this was due to a cultural mismatch. When you have a company that prides itself on compounding value by bringing in more companies in a decentralized structure, preserving culture becomes critical. The company quickly realized it had made a mistake and said another change at the top was "in the best interest of the company and its shareholders."[4]

A second successor CEO, Johnny Thomson, who hailed from a decentralized company, then came in January of 2019. According to Huggins, when asked about risk, Thomson said humbly, "I'm the guy most likely to mess things up."

After a recent investor meeting with the company, a three-to-four-hour ordeal, Thomson took questions from analysts. Matt, who dialed in from Kansas City, decided to test Thomson's commitment to the already aggressive growth plan for the company. In these kinds of situations, Matt doesn't ask for facts or figures—that he can get from documents or the investor relations team. Instead, he uses the opportunity to get a better feel for the CEO. It's something he learned at Janus when the company brought in an FBI detective to give the team advice on how to ask questions. "Never ask basic confirmatory questions," the FBI consultant told Matt and his team. "Never ask someone, 'Do you love your wife?' Of course they will say yes. Instead ask them a disconfirming question, 'You don't really love her, do you? And see if they push back.'" Here was Matt's question, which the moderator directed to the CEO and read out loud in front of everyone in the room: "And then one [question] on organic growth: you talk about the huge opportunity. Seems you have the right team. Seems you have lots of capital available. So, what stops you from being more aggressive about organic growth?"[5]

After hours of watching Diploma leadership present a very aggressive plan, the moderator was dumbfounded by the question—that anyone could ask for even more growth. Her eyes went big and bright with disbelief by the audacity of the question as she tried to control her nervous laughter and waited for Thomson to answer.

After a pause and a big smile, Thomson said, "Who asked that question?!?" The room of analysts laughed. Instead of trying to kowtow to Matt and say there was still some opportunity to be even more aggressive, Johnny said, "I think the answer to that is don't be greedy." Again, more laughter in the room.

"It's not about 1, 2, or 3 years, but 10, 20, or 30 years. We are doubling our size in 3 or 4 years. And that's already very significant. So, I'm comfortable at this pace, and we're building an organization around it to sustain it," Thomson said. "That's what's great about this: it's incremental, sustainable compounding for the long term, not just tomorrow."

Matt was impressed that Thomson didn't cave to the question and protected the team's approach to deliberate growth.

The Diploma team has clearly embraced Johnny. The body hasn't rejected the organ, acquisitions have continued, and the numbers have continued to climb and compound (figure 7.3). So has the stock.

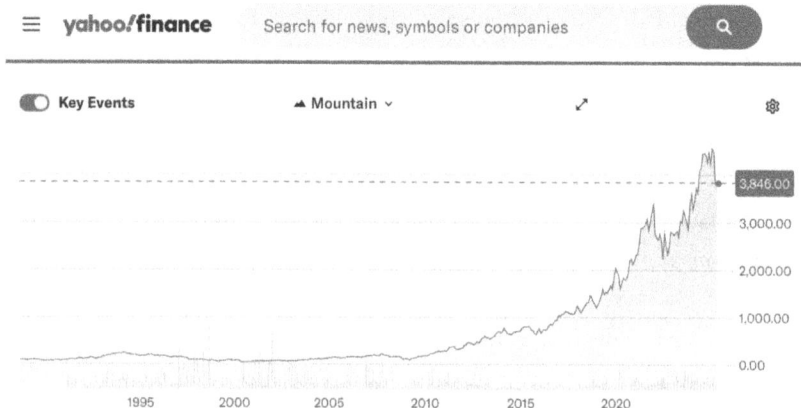

7.3 Diploma stock chart.

Source: Yahoo Finance.

AT THE TABLE

Matt shared his excitement over Diploma with his family over dinner one night. The girls didn't know he was contemplating putting it into a coffee can for them, but they were used to him talking about good companies at the dinner table. Here's what they asked him (with the first question being innocent and somewhat humorous):

PIERCE: First question—is this an education or training company?

Matt smiled and immediately explained that Diploma was a nearly one-hundred-year-old value-add distributor. The initial response from them was a collective yawn of boredom. They then asked their dad how can a company add value when it is selling seals and wire? After Matt walked them through the story in more detail, they were still trepidatious, largely because it didn't sound too exciting. When he explained how all of Diploma's customers require the products it distributes—using the example of the $1 seal that a $1 million Caterpillar vehicle needs and cannot run without—they started to understand. As Matt said to me, "Selling boring is, well, boring." But when he discussed how Diploma's systematic approach to growth would compound its cash flow over time and what that meant to the stock price . . . the girls seemed to get a bit more excited.

PIERCE: The businesses themselves seem pretty boring, but I really like the way they can continually reinvest the money to keep growing its company. I didn't fully appreciate how the seals, controls, and life sciences fit together until you mentioned the capital to compound component.

PEYTON: Diploma's strategy seems as if it is like watching paint dry, but the company keeps getting bigger and more valuable every year. To know that it was founded almost one hundred years ago tells me that it is a business built to last, and they know what they are doing.

The company's long history was the perfect segue for Matt to talk about its culture and the quick decision to replace the first successor CEO. The questions continued.

MORGAN: If culture is so important, how did you determine Diploma has a great culture? And how did you get comfortable that Diploma can maintain it for a long period of time?

MATT: Assessing managerial quality and culture is probably the most difficult part of investing because you are evaluating human beings and, harder still, you are judging people's decisions across time and through their interaction in an ever-changing world. It is definitely more art than science, but it is a skill you gain the more you engage with individuals and teams. For Diploma, its annual report not only spends an inordinate amount of time discussing culture and the team, but it sends out annual surveys to all of its employees to engage their satisfaction/frustration. Diploma has apprenticeships and other programs to develop its future leaders with continuous communication and feedback to/from its leaders. However, for me, when the Diploma Board fired the new CEO after only a few months, that was the clearest indicator of the company's commitment to protecting its cherished culture and identity.

PEYTON: You said Diploma's competitive advantage was the process it uses for M&A; why can't other companies simply copy this and compete more effectively with Diploma?

MATT: One of the reasons Helmer's "Process Power" is so difficult to copy is that it takes decades for a company to perfect a way of doing something that differentiates it from others. And that perfection is very specific to that company. Another company would have to create and perfect its own process that would be ideal for its own company and its situation. In fact, many of these "Process Power" companies can pass along their entire handbook to their competitor with no fear that they will be undermined. It is just too difficult to replicate—you must win the hearts and minds of your employees that truly believe in the new process. That is why it takes decades to get the right people in place doing the right things. The risk is that the company (in this case, Diploma) screws it up, not that a competitor takes over.

With his homework done and his daughters educated about the opportunity, Matt had to check the box on one more item: valuation. As he always reiterates to me: Valuation is the final arbiter on a purchase. Although it may be a great company, you cannot significantly overpay as it will no longer be a great investment. But with 100-baggers that you want to own for thirty-plus years, as he saw in his original study, the long-term operating performance and return of the business is dramatically more important than near-term valuation.

He also reminded himself of what Charlie Munger had said: "Over the long term, it's hard for a stock to earn a much better return than the business which underlies it earns."

Matt felt the valuation was justifiable and certainly felt he was getting into one of those better businesses. He was now ready to pull the trigger . . . and the bullet was more like the size of an artillery shell. He decided to put a little over $250,000 into the stock . . . with the belief that it can grow a hundred times . . . and someday be worth $25 million.

THE BEGINNING OF THE END (OF THE CHAPTER) AND THE END OF THE BEGINNING (MINE)

This would ordinarily be a good place to end a chapter, but not today. The size of both the investment and the potential eventual valuation hit me hard. Up until this point, everything seemed theoretically plausible. But now it was becoming very real . . . very fast.

I had read every book Matt suggested: From *Seven Powers* to *100 to 1 in the Stock Market*, from the *Billion Dollar Mistake* to the *Psychology of Money*, from *the E-Myth Revisited* to *Where the Money Is*, even business classics from *Good to Great* to *Rich Dad Poor Dad*, and so many more.

I had listened to and watched a whole new world of smart people reporting and covering the investment space one podcast, one YouTube video at a time—all sharing content on the inner workings of successful companies, their business models, and their founders—content too niche even for cable news. Together shows like Stig Brodersen's *We Study Billionaires*, William Green's *Richer, Wiser, Happier*, Patrick O'Shaughnessy's *Invest Like the Best*, Ben Gilbert and David Rosenthal's *Acquired*, Matt Reustle's *Business Breakdowns*, and David Senra's *Founders* were erecting a towering virtual library of business, entrepreneurial, and investment history—each and every week. And they had inducted the late Charlie Munger and Warren Buffett into their virtual Mount Rushmore of investing greats, right next to Benjamin Graham.

All of it—the ideas from the timeless books and the investors celebrated by the next generation of thoughtful analysts—seemed to support or ladder up into Matt's overall long-term investing approach. There was also my own experience; as a media executive and an investor, I shared a similar sensibility with Matt for the kinds of companies that could endure for decades to come. Even when I was overseeing Hearst Entertainment (with its stakes in ESPN and A&E Networks), I started to diversify by investing in entertainment B2B businesses such as Kobalt Music, which provided a digital platform for artists to collect payments every time their songs played on radios or streaming platforms such as Spotify all over the world. So I asked myself: Should I invest alongside him?

As someone who grew up in Queens, New York, the oldest son of working-class immigrant parents who didn't invest in stocks because they thought it was tantamount to "gambling" and, more important, didn't even have the disposable cash to invest in the first place, I limited my investments one generation later to mostly index funds and Treasury bills because they seemed safest.

I didn't day trade, and as much as I loved the populist movement behind the retail investors that pushed up the price of Game Stop a few years ago when large hedge funds were shorting the company the other way, I was not going to engage in momentum plays, no matter how noble the cause.

I wanted to invest in a way that I could pass on to my own children—both in terms of education as well as, hopefully, a small safety net someday. I wanted to teach them what I wished I had learned at their age.

So, as someone the same age as Matt, I decided I, too, would join Kirby's call to experiment with coffee can investing. I, too, would invest in Diploma. Not at the same level as Matt—most journalists make far less than portfolio managers! But the compounding impact would be the same; the potential to multiply my investments one hundred times would be the same. Together, along with our wives, we could be the first of the next generation of coffee can moms and dads trying to pass on the ultimate lottery ticket to our children. And what would be more of a tribute to today's populist movement than to share Matt's recommendations for companies that have promising long-term futures with everyone.

CHAPTER 8

THE NEW MAGICIANS

n 2003, investors were still recovering from the boom and bust of the dot com bubble. Pets.com, eToys, and grocery business Webvan had gone bankrupt or had been liquidated. Time Warner removed AOL from its name after combining companies in one of the biggest media mergers in history. But it wasn't all over. There were many who still believed that the internet was just getting started. In fact, Tom Anderson and Chris DeWolfe accelerated social media when they started Myspace, and Reid Hoffman launched LinkedIn that very year. Another one of those true believers was Martin Migoya (figure 8.1), who was sitting in a bar with his three friends—Guibert Englebienne, Martin Umaran, and Nestor Nocetti—more than six thousand four hundred miles south of Silicon Valley in Buenos Aires, Argentina. "Buenos Aires" in Spanish means "good air" or "fair winds." The four friends felt that every company, despite the recent bust in the market, would need to eventually adapt to the prevailing winds of the internet. They were inspired by the rise of the large IT and digital consulting companies in India (such as Infosys and Wipro) and wondered if they could do the same thing from Latin America, tapping into the engineering and design talent in a population of more than 600 million people. They left the bar committing to put in $5,000 to start a company that would help other companies around the world embrace digital transformation. Englebienne, who would go on to be the chief technology officer (CTO) of their company, wrote a program to identify names for their company that were also available as domain names.[1] They liked tech company names that ended in "nt" and wanted something that matched the size of their ambitions. They settled on "Globant." But there was still one small problem: they needed a client.

8.1 Globant CEO Martin Migoya.

In the great tradition of consultants looking for work, they boarded a plane to pitch their capabilities. They planned a sales trip to the United States and the UK. "It was a very interesting trip. It started in Virginia. Then we came to New York, and then we flew from New York into London," recalled Migoya in an interview with Inside the ICE House.

I said to my wife, listen, Caro, I will be on this trip because we want to sell, we want to start a company. And she said, Martin, I trust you. Just go.

When I came back, she asked me, hey, Martin, how things went? I said, extremely bad.

Why?

Because we didn't sell anything. We were not able to convince anybody. But it was very funny, but that was on Monday.

And then on a Thursday, the phone rang. And I picked up. And it was one of the guys that we visited in London.

He said, Martin, can you come here to London on Monday?

I said, are you sure? I don't have money to go to London on Monday. But are you sure?

No, you need to come, because there's a guy that is the CTO of Lastminute.com that wants to meet you, that has an opportunity for you.

So, we flew there. It was extremely terrible, because when we arrived there, all our luggage was lost, so we came to the meeting without new clothes. And suddenly we started to talk with Chip, that was the CTO, and after 15 minutes of pitch, he said, enough, guys, I believe you.[2]

At the time, Lastminute.com was one of the largest travel websites in Europe, generating one billion pounds of revenue a year, and Migoya said that the company needed help making sure the site was secure and stable. Once that was done, they wanted to raise the bar and do something amazing: allow customers to book flights, cars, and hotels all together for one price. Migoya assured the CTO he could do it and raced back to Argentina to put together a team. He hired a small group of designers and engineers with European passports and moved them into a five-room house in London to complete the job.

One client led to two, two led to four, and so on. And each month the company was profitable. They opened offices in Argentina, and in 2005 MIT did a business case study on them called, "Globant, Leading the IT Revolution in Latin America."

In 2006, Migoya got a tip from a friend at Google that the Mountainview company was looking to outsource work for the first time but there was a long list of companies that would be vying for the opportunity. Up until this point, Google had built everything itself. Now it was interviewing companies from the outside. Migoya, with nothing more than his soft touch when it comes to developing relationships and the knowledge that his team represented the best of the best across Latin America, went to Google's campus to audition . . . for three months.

And suddenly one day after three months of analyzing and understanding team members, our people and understanding how Globant was, they told me, hey, Martin, you won.

I said, no, this must be a mistake here because we never talked about the price.

We will come to an agreement on a price, but you won, and we want to work with you.

Of course, we came to an agreement with the price in 15 seconds.[3]

According to *Forbes*, "Google hired it to help test the new Google Checkout payment system. The results so impressed Google that Globant has become one of Google's favorite partners."[4]

In fact, the Google logo on their brochure became the company's calling card. "Google was that company that had a great impact on our culture and on who we are today. Very soon, we started to work on many hundreds of projects inside Google, and we became the best-kept secret in Silicon Valley because many companies were saying, 'Oh, if these guys are working for Google, then work for me.' "[5]

GLOBANT'S RACE TO THE TOP

Word about the company and their approach spread quickly. They signed Formula One, home to the fastest regulated road-course racing cars in the world. Their cars are technical marvels, from their aerodynamics to electronics—and the epicenter of information for each team of race engineers monitoring the performance of a driver and his car at a Grand Prix event is the pit wall. Globant is working with Formula One to improve the pit wall system experience, which requires weaving together numerous camera angles, communications with the driver, and data feeds from the car (figure 8.2). It's also working to reimagine the sport's app as well as the guest experience at the tracks, which had nearly six million fans last year, according to *Sportico*, which covers the business of sports.[6]

Globant's overall sports business continues to put points on the board. It is working with football league La Liga in Spain to manage its technology to enhance the way fans watch games, as well as help trainers and coaches better manage their teams. It also signed a partnership with FIFA to supercharge its streaming platforms. And it helped Steve Ballmer, the former CEO of Microsoft, to build a next generation stadium experience for the LA Clippers—the $2 billion Intuit Dome. Migoya said Globant helped build the fan identity system that uses high speed facial recognition technology and apps to connect participating

8.2 Globant's pit wall system.

fans with their tickets and wallets. They can enter the stadium and check out from stores without dealing with ticket takers or cashiers.

You would expect high tech in a Steve Ballmer owned stadium, especially things designed to make the fan experience better. But you may not expect some of the tech designed to convert fans' energy into player performance. Ballmer told

60 Minutes, "We have sensors around the building that can tell down to the individual seat level how loud you are. Now, we're not listening to your conversation, but let's say, we say, okay, for this game the person who produces the most decibels the most consistently will get a free hamburger for the next game."[7] The idea is that the more noise the fans make, the more baskets the Clippers will score.

If you put away the basketball and fly from LA to Scotland Yard, home to London's Metropolitan Police, you will also see Globant's digital transformation fingerprints. Prior to their arrival, most contact between the public and the Metropolitan Police happened on the phone. But, according to Globant, of the 4.6 million calls received a year, only a quarter were crime related. In other words, officers were deployed when they weren't needed; the system was clearly overloaded. Globant provided a twenty-first-century solution.

"What we set out to do was to create a digital police station that was accessible to all Londoners," said Michael Lobenberg, Chief Superintendent, Head of Tasking & Resilience, Thames Valley Police.[8] What that meant was creating a site for citizens to report crimes online, digital neighborhood maps for citizens to monitor what's happening in their neighborhoods, and access to Metropolitan Police social media feeds so the police and citizens could communicate with each other.

After the implantation, Globant said the Metropolitan Police saw an increase of twenty-two million site visits in one year, a 61 percent increase. Two-thirds of all road traffic incidents were now reported online—a 500 percent increase, saving 7,200 hours of valuable police time. In addition, 1,500 officers in the department were trained in social media to be able to communicate with citizens, resolving approximately 14,500 inquiries. Overall, of the one hundred thousand crimes reported online, 90 percent did not require deployment.

"I've been a police officer for thirty-five years. I have never worked on any project that has had the same impact in terms of combining technology, innovation, and responding to the needs of the public," said Mark Simmons, who retired as Assistant Commissioner of the Metropolitan Police Service.[9]

WHERE THE MAGIC HAPPENS

Part of Globant's winning formula is that it is not a traditional IT services company that focuses just on engineering. Globant insists that designers and storytellers work together with engineers to offer solutions that simply remove the boundaries between departments and offer their clients' customers pure, unadulterated innovation. For Globant, it's about creating journeys and experiences for customers that surprise and delight . . . just like magic.

It reminds me of what Steve Jobs used to say about his hardware as well as the process of creativity behind the creation of them. When Steve Jobs introduced the iPhone, a device that combined a music player, a phone, and an internet browser into one package with a multitouch user interface made of a single piece of glass, he simply said, "it works like magic." In other words, it just works. You don't even need to know how it works. In fact, the less that you can see, the fewer the distractions, the more you simply enjoy the experience.

The process of getting there, the journey the team takes to make such amazing products, according to Steve Jobs, is also magic:

> There are certain things you can't make plastic do, or glass do, or factories do, or robots do, and as you get into all these things, designing a product is keeping 5,000 things in your brain, these concepts and fitting them all together and kind of continuing to push to fit them together in new and different ways to get what you want. And every day you discover something new that is a new problem or a new opportunity to fit these things together a little differently. And it's that process that is the magic.[10]

It's a lesson Steve Jobs learned during his childhood from an elderly gentleman in his neighborhood who one day let him play with his rock tumbler. A young Jobs put in some regular rough-edged rocks, along with some liquid and a grit powder, and let the machine tumble overnight:

> I came back the next day and we opened the can, and we took out these amazingly beautiful, polished rocks. The same common stones that had gone in through rubbing against each other like this, creating a little bit of friction, creating a little bit of noise, had come out these beautiful, polished rocks. And that's always been in my mind, my metaphor for a team working really hard on something they're passionate about is that it's through the team, through that group of incredibly talented people bumping up against each other, having arguments, having fights sometimes, making some noise, and working together, they polish each other, and they polish the ideas and what comes out are these really beautiful stones.[11]

Migoya, his cofounders, and their teams seem to be doing for their clients what Jobs and his working groups did for Apple—bringing disparate talents to work and butt heads together in an ongoing technical and creative process to deliver magic.

There may be no better example of the spells they help cast on their clients' customers—including Matt Ankrum and his three wonderful daughters—than its collaboration with the Walt Disney Company.

Matt and his wife have taken Peyton, Morgan, and Pierce to Disney World or for a Disney Cruise at least half a dozen times. For his girls, it's truly the happiest and most magical place on Earth. And Matt remembers their first magical moment—a visit to the "Bibbidi Bobbidi Boutique" at Magic Kingdom Park, where each girl was dressed up to look like their favorite princess (figure 8.3). It included shimmering makeup, nail polish, a signature gown with heirloom-quality fabric, crystal tiaras, face gems, sashes and cinch bags, and, of course, princess hairstyling.

"All the girls dressed up at the Bibbidi Bobbidi Boutique. Their hair was pulled so tight, I was surprised it didn't fall out. Then they got to meet their favorite princesses and take pictures with them. Even my father-in-law was infatuated with the princesses. It cost $400 per girl but it didn't matter to me. It was a fabulous experience for them and what Disney does. It empowers every one of its employees to do a magical moment. When we were walking out, the janitor walked up to my daughters, and said, 'Hey princesses, can I get your autograph?' It made my girls feel so special."

Every day and every trip was filled with these kinds of magical moments. Disney created the space and opportunities for these moments by making all the logistics along the way easy, Matt said. The Disney "MagicBand" was given to every member and allowed them to find their kids at any time, coordinate where to eat, navigate the park, and access rides right from their wrists. Today the MagicMobile service on an Apple watch or smartphone does the same thing for Matt and his family, as well as for the thousands of other people at the park at the same time. Matt wasn't surprised when he learned that Globant had helped Disney develop the technology to connect all the dots between the band and different aspects of the park. It's invisible; the technology just melts away.

Martin Migoya told Bloomberg Intelligence Tech Disruptors that Globant began working with Disney on the digital transformation of their theme parks in 2009.

8.3 Matt Ankrum's girls at the Bibbidi Bobbidi Boutique in Disney World in 2009.

We were the partner of choice for doing all their, not the Magic Band itself, but just all the technology around the Magic Band, the mobile apps and the web apps and everything connected to the parks. And really, we learned about connecting emotionally with those guests and how cast members can use that same technology to be able to connect with the consumers in a much better way.[12]

As Globant's relationship with Disney grew, Migoya says Globant started participating in in streaming initiatives such as Disney+ and ESPN+. As part of the Hearst team that invested in the launch of ESPN+, I had a deep understanding and appreciation for the complexity of the endeavor. Imagine the number of different form factors for the experience, from connected TVs to computers and tablets to phones. Imagine a media company building a personalized recommendation engine. Imagine how many different payment options have to be offered (from credit cards to PayPal to Apple Pay and so on). Then there's the complexity of pricing, and that's even before you start the most important piece—creating world class content.

Disney CEO Bob Iger did a one-on-one interview with Migoya at Globant's annual Converge conference about the necessity of reinvention in a world that is constantly changing. "You have to train an organization and develop a culture that is willing to perform well today but also considers what tomorrow will bring and how to perform well tomorrow." Iger added, "When you articulate it with great clarity, organizations tend to start believing it. I think you get people excited about the opportunities that exist. When you do that, you create momentum and a desire to not just be part of the present, but to be part of the future."[13]

Being a part of the future requires a constant investment into digital transformation. Gone are the days of doing a single digital project and calling it a day. Everything keeps changing. And most companies don't have internal teams to tackle each new digital breakthrough. That's why Disney, among other clients, according to Matt, has been steadily growing its relationship with Globant, increasing the amount it pays year after year more like a recurring revenue business than a one and done consulting business. In 2023, Matt said Disney paid the company $183 million, making it Migoya's single largest client. If that doesn't make your inner magician say "Alakazam," I don't what will!

THE HARD NUMBERS

Globant has grown revenue, now over $2 billion, at close to a 30 percent CAGR since 2014—the year it became the first Latin American IT company to be listed on the New York Stock Exchange (NYSE). It has more than nine hundred clients and a 15 percent margin. And because it has a low cap ex, it converts most of that margin into free cash flow. Here are Matt's three key numbers for understanding the Globant business.

KEY NUMBERS TO UNDERSTAND GLOB

>30K	100×100	>$700B

>30K: "When people ask me about Globant, I say, look, you know, Globant is like a Tesla. From the outside, it looks like a normal car. But then when you enter into the car, you start discovering that, oh, well, no, there's no motor. And the batteries are on the floor," says Migoya. "So, at Globant, we say the same. From the outside, we may look like any other company offering professional services out there. But on the inside, the things are totally different."[14]

When you look inside the organization chart at Globant, you will discover a unique studio and agile pod system that organizes its now more than thirty thousand employees across twenty-five countries, or "Globers" as they call themselves. There are thirty-nine studios, each of which specializes in an emerging digital trend such as the banner headlines from the tech press each year pronouncing the next big thing. Think artificial intelligence, blockchain, metaverse, spatial computing, big data, internet of things, mobile, UX and Design, and even gaming.

"In 2008–9, we launched our gaming studio, and that was supposed to help all the gaming companies out there. We started for Electronic Arts, but we didn't stop there. Started working for Ubisoft Activision. We're involved in very successful games like FIFA or Hogwarts lately. And we ended up having the largest, I would say, gaming 3D rendering studio in Latin America, and one of the largest in Americas," says Migoya.[15]

And sitting on top of the different studios are 1,200 pods, according to Globant's CEO.[16] These are groups of eight to twenty people coming from the different studios, and they own the relationship with each client. Globant uses AI to suggest the right available internal people to populate each pod, and they have complete autonomy to satisfy everything their client needs. Once together, each pod writes its own "constitution," laying out the goals of the group and what role each person plays within the pod, ultimately ensuring the delivery of software that helps their clients hit the key metrics they are trying to accomplish. It's an inverted pyramid in which management is at the bottom and the studios and pods are at the top.

"A culture that focuses on its people is paramount to the success of a consulting business," said Matt. "In most consulting firms, your assets walk out the door every day. Your employees, your brains, your experts may leave and never come back. What Globant has done is create profoundly powerful reasons for its people to stay. A Glober who is working in block chain can say they want to go work in the metaverse. Someone working for banking can say they want to go work in the entertainment sector. A person can say I would like to travel and work for a different client for a year. Globant will try to make it happen for you. A Glober can say they want to create a new product, and Globant may fund it for you so you can try to commercialize it. Their consultants want to keep learning and doing new things. And that keeps human capital assets inside the company." Once again, Matt said, this is another example of Hamilton Helmer's cornered resources.

Second, Matt noted, employees want to work on the coolest projects with the coolest companies. Working at Disney's theme park experience, working on Formula One's pit wall system, working in Scotland Yard to improve policing are all the kinds of projects that not only retain their best employees but attract new people from the frontiers of innovation as well. And that then makes talent-stocked Globant the digital consulting shop to beat.

The company also has an early warning radar system to detect dissatisfaction. It uses artificial intelligence to measure an employee's engagement with the company's social platforms.

"The system tells us when an employee is disengaging from the company because the amount of interactions they're having with the core platform are going down," Migoya said to *Fast Company*.[17] "Interactions tell you that a person is connected. An absence of interactions tells you that you need to brace for impact or do something about their career to reengage them."

Migoya explained that he uses the opportunity to engage an employee to see if they want to work elsewhere in the company, in a new role or geography. "Having the tools to detect their disengagement allows us to have those conversations," he says. "We can detect within twenty weeks when someone is thinking of leaving."

"Globant creates a virtuous circle by focusing on quality Globers and clients, cutting-edge interesting projects, and protecting an empowering culture," Matt confirmed.

He also calls out the company's "Be Kind" initiative. "It's the type of company people say, 'I want to work for.' It asks its employees to be kind to themselves, to the planet, to live their best lives, achieve wellness, and strong relationships with their peers—and gives them the time and resources to pursue these goals. By the end of 2025, they are planning to give up to 15,000 scholarships to kids who want to code. And employees give stars to each other on a peer-to-peer recognition platform for jobs well done and being positive influencers within the organization. Globant knows how to focus on its people assets. I've known too many companies' CEOs who come in and reduce salaries and fire people and then their stock goes up. That's fine if you believe people are replaceable. Globant makes its employees ask themselves, 'why would I want to work anywhere else?' "

100×100: When I was working at Yahoo!, we would have meetings outside of the normal annual budget process where we would brainstorm BHAGs. It stands for "Big Hairy Audacious Goals." How could we grow the business not by $10 million but by $100 million or $1 billion? It was designed to help us think bigger, invent new businesses, and set larger goals for ourselves and our departments. I was reminded of those sessions when Matt told me Globant had its own BHAG: to have one hundred clients spending $100 million each year. We already learned that Disney spent $183 million in 2023. Globant had sixteen clients spending more than $20 million each year, thirty-four clients spending more than $10 million a year, eighty clients spending $5 million a year, and three hundred eleven clients spending more than $1 million a year. Revenue from its top ten clients has grown at a 25 percent CAGR since 2014, and revenue from its top twenty clients has grown at a 24 percent CAGR. Globant's BHAG is to aim for more than one hundred clients each generating more than $100 million a year. Matt says it is a good sign because it actually replaced and revised up their previous internal BHAG of fifty clients generating $50 million a year. If you think this is pie in the sky thinking, stay tuned—the market for digital business services spending is astronomical.

$700B: According to Gartner, the market is growing at a 10 to 11 percent CAGR and will be more than $700 billion by 2027.[18] In its CEO survey, Gartner found that inflation would not stall digital transformation, especially when customer experience is a focus: 85 percent of CEOs reported increased investments in digital capabilities, and 77 percent are increasing investments in IT. By the end of 2027, approximately 75 percent of organizations will be using service providers to scale digital business innovation efforts, up from 60 percent in 2022.[19]

For Matt, it's a fait accompli. "Globant's customers don't have a choice. If they don't move, they are going to die. They have to make the change and become digitally focused. They are either going to be on the train or the train is going to run them over. And how do they make the change? They don't have the skills internally. So, who do they go with? The last thing they do if they are looking to do big transformational things is to go to with a second-tier firm. They go to Globant, the pure play that all the cool companies are working with."

He explained that Globant's ability to create software that appeals and connects with millions of consumers positions it well to compete effectively. And there's room for growth for everyone in the space. Matt noted that the top five players, including Accenture with more than $64 billion in revenue, all combined only have a 20 percent share of a huge $700 billion market.

"In a $700 billion market that grows even at 5 percent a year, or half of what Gartner expects, means that there is an additional $35 billion of new revenue each year to be had. The Big Hairy Audacious Goal of aiming for one hundred clients generating $100 million each seems even more doable in that context." And also to help get there, Globant, currently debt free, is using its high free cash flow conversion to acquire strategic tuck-in companies, not for revenue but for additional capabilities and geographic presence. In 2023, it bought a majority stake in creative agency GUT after Cannes Lion as well as *Adweek* named it the agency of the year. Matt says it has already acquired a company called WaaSabi for its wallet-as-a-Service solution that can facilitate microtransactions on just about any platform and has started to add small AI companies to make code easier to write or append as well as do quality assurance testing (which can reduce engineering costs by 20 percent). And according to *LatinFinance*, "the company said it will invest $1 billion through 2028 to boost its reach in Latin America, with a focus on artificial intelligence and other emerging technologies."[20]

"The market is massive and getting to $20 billion+ in revenue, or up tenfold, for Globant is quite reasonable over the next fifteen to twenty years," said Matt, adding, "That's a 12–15 percent CAGR."

Part of Matt's confidence also came from his original 100-bagger study. Only one consulting company made the list: Cognizant (Ticker symbol CTSH), which provides technology, automation, and process consulting and services and generates close to $20 billion a year in revenue. "What differentiated the company early on was its ability to arbitrage its Indian consultants and developers' lower wages relative to US consulting firms. It was a huge competitive advantage for them. As they matured, the wage differential has shrunk (though still material), its quality reputation and brand has enabled Cognizant to continue to grow and thrive in the massive technology transformation sector (just like Globant). But Globant competes on the high-end, whereas Cognizant typically focuses on the lower/middle market opportunities." In Matt's original study, Cognizant was a 289-bagger!

AT THE TABLE

One fall weekend, Matt shared his excitement for Globant with his daughters. He knew they would be surprised by their involvement with Disney and were responsible for some of the magic behind the magic. Pierce, the youngest, pounced immediately.

> PIERCE: Oh, I loved the wrist bands at Disney World, I had no idea
> Globant helped connect it to the rest of the park. Can we invest in them?

Morgan, who had been battling a cold, came alive and quickly climbed on board too.

> MORGAN: Globant's collaboration with Disney made our trip smooth,
> seamless, and truly immersive. Everything just worked; it was an
> unforgettable experience.

Peyton, who was finishing up her psychology homework, had an even more nuanced reaction.

> PEYTON: I thought it was very interesting how Globant stands out from
> their competition on an emotional level—they make their products
> more desired and feel special. I also was surprised about the diversity of
> the companies Globant engages in from the Gap to airlines to Disney.
> One can also appreciate their commitment to sustainability, creating
> scholarships and having an inclusive team, and it feels good to invest in a
> company that is doing good.

They all ended up buying shares for their personal accounts, but they didn't know their dad had also bought the stock for the coffee can. That would be a bigger surprise for them down the road.

MIGOYA'S VISION

Meanwhile, Martin Migoya continues to invest in capabilities for his company. He is in the business of understanding the next new thing . . . and staying one step ahead. He is very much a dreamer and a philosopher, trying to make sense of artificial intelligence for the corporate world.

"Anything that is happening today was impossible to explain seven months ago, right?" said Migoya in a streamed conversation in Buenos Aires meant for Globant employees with Thomas Dohmke, CEO of Github, the Microsoft owned platform for developers to create, store, and share their code.

Dohmke said he could imagine a future where he could speak German and Migoya could speak Spanish, and their respective Air Pods would do real time translations like a universal translator (Apple's latest AirPods attempt to do just that). He also said someone with vision impairment could use AI to describe their environment or what is on a screen. "It's a bit like Geordi La Forge on *Star Trek Next Generation*, right?"[21]

Migoya, who's already using AI to assign team members to pods, detect when a team member may be getting less engaged, or make coding faster and easier, believes that humans will need to get better at giving context to artificial intelligence engines in order to get the right answers. And he predicts the next big chapter for AI will be in transactions.

"I think a big use of AI, for me, you know, okay, chatting is great. Suggesting creating stuff is great. Now, transacting is much better. And I think transactions are the next things that are coming into the AI space." He added, "Google has a team of about 166 engineers in a project called Maggie, and in that project, what they are doing is they are trying to transact from the text. I need a ticket for Monday to Madrid. Boom. Here's a ticket. I mean, nothing, no questions asked in the middle, hopefully."

The only constant these days is the accelerating speed of change. And the best products and experiences we enjoy require little understanding of how it all came together. As science fiction writer Arthur C. Clarke once said, "Magic is just science we don't understand yet."

CHAPTER 9

DEATH AND TAXES

I n 1789 Benjamin Franklin wrote, "Nothing is certain except death and taxes." More than 235 years later that statement still rings true for Matt Ankrum, especially when it comes to two new stocks he recently added to his coffee can.

THE FIRST CERTAINTY

Let's start with death. I know, I know—not a particularly inviting proposition. No one wants to be a death profiteer. But Abacus Life (Ticker symbol ABL) is actually helping people cash in their life insurance policies for far more than what insurance companies offer. Let's start with a few stats that will amaze you.

The value of all the life insurance policies in the US is $13 trillion. That is two and half times larger than the US residential real estate market. It is, quite simply, a HUGE industry.

And according to Jay Jackson, CEO of Abacus Life, insurance companies only pay claims for 10 percent of all those policies (figure 9.1). In other words, 90 percent of life insurance policies, he says, don't pay claims.

"What happens is people treat life insurance like debt, meaning that it's an expense to their bottom line. So let's just take somebody who is now 75-years old, after paying into their life insurance policy for 20 years. They don't look at that like a mortgage payment, which is how they should. Instead, they look at that and they say, 'Okay, well, that's the insurance I never wanted or had to use, thank God,' when in reality that has been accreting value the entire time." said Jackson in an interview with Eric Chemi at Wealthion. "And so what do they typically do

9.1 Jay Jackson, CEO of Abacus Life.
Source: Nasdaq, Inc./Vanja Savic.

when they're 75? Their kids are in their 50s. And they say to themselves, I don't need a million dollars, or 2 million or half a million dollars of life insurance coverage, I'm just going to stop paying on it."[1]

When a person says they are going to stop paying, the insurance company simply gives them the cash value of the policy at the time they cancel. But Abacus Life believes policyholders should be getting a lot more money. And it is willing to buy their policies from them . . . for a premium.

What most people don't realize is that they own their policies; the Supreme Court made that clear all the way back in 1911, during the case *Grigsby v. Russell*. Dr. Grigsby was treating a patient named John C. Burchard, who needed a surgery he couldn't afford. Burchard offered to sell his insurance policy to Dr. Grigsby for $100 and an agreement to pay the remaining premiums. Dr. Grigsby agreed. But when Burchard later passed away and Dr. Grigsby tried to collect the benefit, an executor of Burchard's estate, R. L. Russell, tried to block it. The case went all the way to the Supreme Court. Justice Oliver Wendell Holmes Jr. noted that life insurance possesses all the ordinary characteristics of property, and therefore represented an asset that a policy owner could transfer.[2]

The practice of selling insurance policies, however, didn't start to gain steam until the 1980s during the AIDS epidemic. Young people in good health were suddenly facing death sentences, and the experimental medication was prohibitively expensive. Many sold their insurance policies to gain access to the money needed for treatment. The secondary market for insurance, also known as life settlements, started to take root. Although the industry has had a dodgy reputation, today it is a highly regulated field, and Abacus has a license to operate in forty-nine states. In 2023, after almost two decades as a private company, it became the first one in the space to become a publicly traded company.

THE HARD NUMBERS

As a human being, Matt sees great altruistic value in the payments Abacus offers its customers. As an investor, he sees strong potential for the Orlando, Florida, based company to compound cash flow for decades to come. And, as usual, he boils it down to three key numbers.

KEY NUMBERS TO UNDERSTAND ABACUS LIFE

2%	$8_x = 15 + \%$	1 TO 5

Let's start with 2%: $233 billion of life insurance policies lapse every year, and the annual life settlement industry only acquires about $4 billion worth of policies annually. In other words, there is only a 2 percent market penetration, and the opportunity is enormous. It's why you've probably seen or heard Jay Jackson on commercials on cable news channels or on the radio trying to educate viewers on their choices.

$8_x = 15 + \%$: To understand this equation, Matt walked me through the following example. Let's say you have a life insurance policy that pays out $1.5 million upon your death, and so far you have been paying into it for twenty years. For whatever reason you want to stop paying, and the life insurance company says okay, we will give you, for example, $50,000. But if you call Abacus Life, they will pay out, on average, eight times that amount or $400,000—more than the insurance company and less than the ultimate death benefit. Abacus, after gaining permission from your beneficiaries, takes ownership of the policy, pays an annual $25,000 premium, and you pass away seven years later. In total, Abacus has paid out $575,000 (400,000+175,000) and then collected $1.5 million. The $925,000 they made against an initial investment of $400,000 + $175,000 over a seven-year waiting period results is a 15+ percent return on investment. If a person lives longer than seven years, the return is lower. If the person lives less than seven years, the return is higher.

If this sounds like morbid math, Matt reminded me that "this is a win-win-win scenario: the policyholder gets $400,000 instead of $50,000. Abacus generates an average of 15+ percent returns on its investments, and the insurance companies get screwed! But then again, it's the contract they wrote, and they've made *beautiful money* for so long while working in *beautiful buildings* because they're used to having 90 percent of their policies lapse. The more Abacus Life becomes known, the less these policies will lapse."

1 to 5: You may be wondering how Abacus Life can know so much about how long a person is going to live. After all, to average 15+ percent returns after paying a policyholder eight times more than the insurance company, it must know something about, well, mortality. And that's where biology meets big data. Abacus Life has a proprietary pricing algorithm that accesses its comprehensive data over twenty years to help it determine what it is willing to pay for a policy. It is basically taking what individuals share about themselves and compares it to a distribution curve of longevity for individuals that have similar traits. Jackson says his company looks at obvious things such as age and gender but also some aspects of genetics (certain phenotypes indicate a person could have a 50 percent higher probability of living past ninety). The biggest factors include your body mass index (how much weight you are carrying above your muscle mass at certain ages is super important), whether you have diabetes or kidney or cardiovascular disease, and then cross references how that has affected a person's lifespan historically. They even factor in a person's social community, such as whether a person lives close to their relatives.

Jackson says "we've got a 20-year history of those inputs of really tracking different types of mortality experiences related to different types of impairments, right, related to different types of genetics, and family history. We then aggregate all that data along with utilizing third party lifespan firms that have medical actuaries on staff and their own sets of data, and then, additionally, that will seek a physician review as well. But then you now overlay the technology on top of that."[3]

That technological algorithm essentially scores each person, each policy, on a scale of 1 to 5. That score helps them to price policies to ensure the optimal return for each transaction—one that offers fair prices to policyholders and still delivers strong returns on its investment (table 9.1).

Beyond the business ramifications, the data also yields some rather startling insights about longevity. Some simply reinforce the finite nature of life, even if breakthrough medical advancements happen over time.

"Let's just start with cancer," Jackson says. "If you cure cancer, do you know how long lifespan is increased? Total for the population? How much? 3.2 years? That's it. That's it. If you cure every disease known to humankind, you know how much the lifespan increases? 5.6 years on average."[4]

And then there was an insight for someone like me—a 6 ft. 1 in. tall male—that just plain sucks. "There's never been a centenarian over six feet tall," Jackson said.[5] There goes my hope of receiving a one-hundredth birthday greeting in 2070 from an AI-generated Willard Scott on Peacock's streaming *Today* show.

But some insights Jackson shared gave me ideas for helping my seventy-seven-year-old mother live as long as possible.

"If you want to give someone a gift, who's over 75, you can give them significant extension in lifespan by doing one thing. Send them a subscription to learn a second language. Why? Think about what that does? One, it activates their neurological, right? Two, what else does it do? Build communication. Three, what else? Community, travel, movement, engagement. And fourth, purpose. I think that the mental aspects and neurological aspects of who we are, are going to really matter on a go forward basis."[6]

All of these insights from the company's data, and the 1 to 5 scoring, is helping position Abacus at the center of the secondary insurance marketplace. In addition to customers coming to them directly, life insurance brokers and agents as well as financial advisors reach out to them on behalf of their clients. Famed firms such as KKR, Apollo, and Berkshire Hathaway have entrusted Abacus to buy policies for their portfolios leveraging the Abacus platform.

The biggest critical risk to Abacus, according to Matt, is the lack of access to cost-efficient capital to keep their flywheel moving at scale. To help mitigate that risk, the company announced a public offering of stock that raised more than $90 million that they will use to purchase more life insurance policies. The second risk is irrational pricing by other existing players or new entrants. Matt explained that the company believes that is a potential risk but thinks its

TABLE 9.1 Abacus Life risk rating heat map.

Purchase Price	Policy Type	Carrier Rating	Lead Source	Policy Face Value	Expected IRR	Life Expectancy (LE)	LE Extension Ratio	Age	Age on LE Date	Age on B/E date	Surv Prob on B/E Date	Risk Grade
$ 152,500.00	GUL	A+	Broker	$ 500,000	15.60%	65	196%	72	80	90	0%	1
$ 150,180.00	UL	A	Agent	$ 250,000	15.50%	25	614%	67	73	86	0%	2
$ 150,180.00	UL	A	Agent	$ 250,000	15.50%	25	614%	67	73	86	0%	2
$ 556,705.00	UL	A+	Insured	$ 1,000,000	15.50%	31	903%	49	52	75	0%	3
$ 168,945.00	GUL	NR	Insured	$ 750,000	15.40%	91	275%	60	68	89	0%	1
$ 23,488.00	GUL	A	Broker	$ 100,000	15.40%	88	113%	69	76	84	1%	4
$ 325,000.00	UL	A-	Insured	$ 500,000	15.30%	26	527%	97	99	110	0%	1
$ 223,434.00	GUL	A+	Insured	$ 5,300,000	15.30%	133	92%	72	83	93	1%	2
$ 115,502.00	UL	A	Insured	$ 550,000	15.30%	48	125%	86	90	95	2%	2
$ 108,111.00	GUL	A	Agent	$ 400,000	15.20%	53	527%	90	97	121	0%	1
$ 47,079.00	UL	A	Agent	$ 400,000	15.20%	103	21%	87	98	100	34%	4
$ 22,976.00	UL	NR	Agent	$ 189,964	15.20%	75	66%	84	90	94	10%	5
$ 37,405.00	GUL	A+	Agent	$ 1,000,000	15.20%	157	135%	68	81	99	0%	1
$ 165,000.00	GUL	A	Broker	$ 500,000	15.20%	26	107%	90	92	94	6%	4
$ 181,527.00	Term	A+	Insured	$ 250,000	15.10%	12	354%	62	63	67	0%	5
$ 158,360.00	UL	NR	Agent	$ 1,000,000	15.10%	132	170%	69	81	100	0%	1
$ 112,500.00	GUL	A+	Agent	$ 300,000	15.10%	58	218%	82	87	98	0%	1
$ 37,816.00	UL	A++	Insured	$ 100,000	15.10%	40	98%	69	72	75	10%	5

decades-old database and smart algorithms give it the ability to offer the best payment options . . . and given the heavy regulations involved, it would take three years for a new entrant to even enter the market. Matt acknowledged that the most challenging aspect of this is projecting forward estimates due to Abacus's nascent time as a public company and no representative comparison. But, he stated, "They control their destiny. Like previous 100-baggers, they have a huge addressable market. And in the end they know their cost of capital, they know the science of longevity, so it's just a matter of adjusting pricing to maintain 15+ percent growth and keeping focused on the opportunity at hand. And it's a matter of time before the Street begins to catch on to Abacus's model."

AT THE TABLE

Meanwhile, at home, Matt had a chance to debrief his girls on the company. I was curious how they would react because they are just starting their adult lives. Death is just about the last thing on their minds.

PIERCE: It is a bit creepy, but who thought they could create such a great business on death? I wonder if Abacus will put a lot of pressure on insurers because they will have to pay Abacus on the full value of the policies when it comes due.

PEYTON: It really feels like data is the lifeblood of a company's ability to create an advantage—look at Abacus and how they use their proprietary data to price policies better and beat out their competitors.

MORGAN: As Abacus professionalizes the life settlements business, I would think that would mean they will attract more people interested in selling their policies and make a lot more money. Also, if Abacus can also get more institutions to lend them money at lower rates . . . that would be huge for their profit margins.

For Matt, the fifty-five-year-old investor, Abacus has all the ingredients to be the kind of company that becomes a future 100-bagger in three decades—or just about the same time he decides to sell his own insurance policy . . . to Abacus Life. He bought the stock for his girls' coffee can and moved on to an opportunity in the other certainty in life: taxes.

THE SECOND CERTAINTY

That's right, taxes. As Matt likes to say, "You hate to pay them, but now you can make money from them." Matt is referring to a company called Vertex (Ticker symbol: VERX), which sits at the corner of tax and technology in King of Prussia, Pennsylvania. And its CEO, David DeStefano, likes to say at industry conferences that even the simplest products require complex tax calculations (figure 9.2).

"I saw many of you in line this morning buying a cup of coffee: $3 cup of coffee. 27 cents of sales tax. Simple product, actually a very complex tax calculation. What size was the cup? How much extra ingredients did you put in? Did you put hazelnut in? Where was it sourced from? How was it served to you? All of those things impact the calculation. Now imagine you are the company delivering that, and you've got a thousand locations and there are different rules and rates applied for every transaction. It's now become a complex problem," says DeStefano. And that's just half the equation.

> The second thing we do is take that tax calculation once it's been determined and make sure it gets remitted to the government effectively. Every local jurisdiction—whether it be a county, a city, a state or a country—has different forms, formats and requirements for how that tax has to be remitted.

9.2 David DeStefano, CEO of Vertex.

A very complex problem. Fundamentally, what Vertex does, is we help ensure their end customer's experience works for them, meaning you got the great cup of coffee, and you didn't pay $3.87 because they got the tax wrong.[7]

Vertex makes B2B software that companies embed into their enterprise resource planning (ERP) systems, like SAP. These systems are large business management programs that offer finance module tools for accounting (such as accounts receivable and payable), general ledger, expense management, reporting and analysis, etc. Vertex provides a solution for calculating indirect taxes across the world (not what a person or company pays directly to the government). These are the taxes a company collects when a customer buys something and then passes on to the government. It includes everything from sales, service, and VAT taxes to hotel, airport, or activity-based taxes, as well as customs and excise duties. Which includes things like sin taxes—as Matt reminded me, "Every time you buy a Coke in Philadelphia, you have to pay a sugar tax." In case you're wondering, it's 1.5 cents per ounce of sweetened beverage distributed.[8]

THE HARD NUMBERS

But before you get angry and dump your *sweet tea* into the harbor, Matt has found a way to get *sweet revenge*. He thinks Vertex has a long, profitable road ahead—and here are his three key numbers to understand the business.

KEY NUMBERS TO UNDERSTAND VERTEX

900 MILLION+	111%	10%

900 Million+: Vertex has been in business for forty years, much of it as a private company under the management of the late Ray Westphal and his family; today it is a public company. They employ 100+ tax subject matter experts who follow and track over 900 million data-driven rules and regulations in more than nineteen thousand jurisdictions to ensure Vertex's database is in full compliance with every tax in every part of the world. The cumulative amount of these tax rules is significant and growing: the company estimates $4.4 trillion of indirect taxes are levied around the world annually. Matt said this "comprehensive content database that is deeply integrated into ERP systems like SAP and Oracle results in tremendous switching cost power." In other words, once you fully embed it into your overall business, your business management software, and start using the system to make real-time calculations across the world, you are unlikely to cancel or switch to another provider. It's now part of your process and something you are counting on to make the right tax determination. The other benefit for customers, according to Matt, is that they are seeing improved audit performance. A missed application can cost a company millions of dollars in back taxes, fees, and penalties, years after the mistake, which the company cannot recoup. Companies need to know all the current rules and apply them in real time.

111%: That switching power Matt referred to is not theoretical—you can see it in their year over year revenue results. When you look at Vertex's growth, 25 percent of it comes from new customers, 25 percent from typical 4 percent price increases, and 50 percent from what they charge for higher tier products as well as brand new ones. All of that contributes to a net revenue retention rate of 111 percent. I'm not one to get naturally giddy due to any one financial metric, but this is one that really speaks to the beauty of digital subscription businesses. Forget about streaming channels that you can switch on and off when the series you are watching is over or after the NFL season ends. This is a B2B digital subscription product that certain businesses always need, because it is essential to calculate taxes in real time all over the world. Of course, some customers leave (less than 2 percent churn), but others take their place; 111 percent net revenue retention means you are retaining 100 percent of the revenue and actually growing another 11 percent. It is a steady stair step of revenue growth, predictable as a Swiss watch: not something you have to start from scratch with each new year. "For example, Nike is a great company, but every year they have to sell all those shoes again just to get back to where they were last year," Matt said. For Vertex, the ongoing revenue growth didn't miss a beat during the last major recession or even COVID (figure 9.3).

10%: The company currently has more than four thousand customers, including 63 percent of the Fortune 500. They range from financial and business services to communication, transport, and manufacturing companies as well as marketplaces, retailers, and wholesale traders. Even Shopify has added Vertex to their tax platform to help its retailers improve their tax calculations and streamline global tax compliance. One very telling statistic is that three out of the top

Annual Revenue ($ in millions)

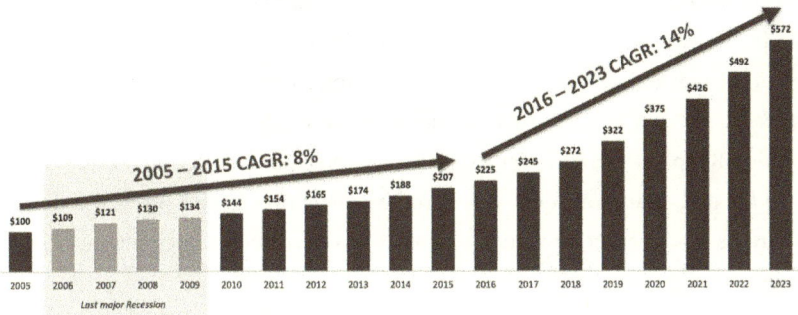

9.3 Vertex revenue growth over the long haul.

four tax/accounting firms use Vertex for their own internal systems. Despite their success, Vertex still has a very small percentage of the total addressable market (TAM). The company estimates that the total TAM, across enterprise, mid-market, and small and medium-sized businesses, is $22 billion ($7 billion in the US and $15 billion across the rest of the world).[9] And so far, Vertex believes that only 10 percent of that total has adopted automated software to handle these kinds of complex tax calculations and remittance. As companies globalize organically or through M&A, evolve their supply chains, sell more products online across borders, leverage more data, move their systems into the cloud, and require real-time reporting, the less they can count on manual processes and in-house systems to manage this complexity. Matt noted, "There really is no choice. Companies need to have an automated, highly compliant solution that becomes an integral part of their processes and systems." In other words, Vertex has a massive pond to fish in for years to come.

RISK AND REWARD

In terms of risk, Matt feels the company needs to focus on growing its 60 percent gross margin after years of building its team of tax experts and investing in its platform and products. He also believes it will have to create a formal M&A process and integration team. "Eventually, Vertex will have to put excess free cash flow to work via acquisitions to deliver future returns, and the company has to avoid large, misguided acquisitions."

Vertex has limited competition: two private equity owned businesses in Sovos (big in the EU) and Avalara (which focuses on the small and medium business end of the market), as well as the tax automation software division within Thomson Reuters. Matt believes there could be consolidation at some point or one of the big ERP players could eventually decide to acquire Vertex.

In the end, Matt considers Vertex to be a key player in this space and decided to buy its stock, eager to watch how they navigate their dance partners in the future.

While his two oldest daughters were at college, Matt explained Vertex to his youngest, Pierce. He wasn't sure if she was paying attention, but the next day, after watching the national news report on the tariffs the Trump administration might impose on other countries, she asked her dad, "How do companies keep up with all the different tariffs and how do they calculate them? Is this what Vertex does? If so, that could be really important over the next few years." Smart girl!

Death and taxes, as the American statesman Ben Franklin once said, are inevitable. And Matt believes he can count on and profit from those eventualities for his coffee can, both with a B2C company such as Abacus Life as well as a B2B company such as Vertex. "Both Abacus Life and Vertex are leaders in huge, growing, and *unfortunately* necessary industries," says Matt. Perhaps there's a reason Benjamin Franklin is not only honored on postage stamps and in the names of warships, towns, schools, and corporations but is also featured as the face of the $100 bill.

CHAPTER 10

NICHES MAKE RICHES

High atop the eucalyptus trees in Brisbane, Australia's Lone Pine Sanctuary, adorable koala bears with large round heads, fluffy ears, and big black noses sleep on average eighteen hours a day, waking up just long enough to eat a pound of leaves. It's a sleepy spot, but less than a twenty-minute drive away from downtown Brisbane, where a small army of engineers in a Silicon Valley–styled office at the headquarters of TechnologyOne (Ticker symbol: TNE) are in overdrive, enjoying their success in the battle for market share in the enterprise resource planning (ERP) software business that companies use to manage their entire operations. Even taking a small sliver of the market is worth hundreds of millions of dollars in revenue, and they are going after and building software products customized for the kinds of small organizations most of the big players, like sleeping koalas, seem to ignore—governments and educational institutions.

In chapter 9, we learned about a company called Vertex that was a tax module embedded within an ERP. Now let's go the other way around and look at the ERP market itself. For the team at TechnologyOne, it's a classic David and Goliath story. They are in the ring with heavyweights such as Oracle (which generates $50 billion in revenue), SAP ($33 billion), and Salesforce ($31 billion). Think Rocky 4 (versus Drago). But it doesn't seem to stop them from thinking they can build a successful company in the space, even with a fraction of the revenue, now at $350 million annually.

Edward Chung, the forty-four-year-old CEO of TechnologyOne who is at his desk by 7 A.M. and has five cups of coffee by 11 A.M. (figure 10.1), says, "There's companies in the world like . . . they're called SAP and Oracle, and they're massive, they're worth 200, 300 billion dollars and they've got hundreds of thousands

10.1 Edward Chung, CEO of TechnologyOne.

of developers. And we do the same if not more and better out of Brisbane with 400–500 developers. It's insane."[1]

The company today, according to Chung—the son of Chinese immigrants from Papua New Guinea—has 1,300 people on staff. They are spread across Brisbane and the other capital cities of Australia, as well as Auckland and Wellington in New Zealand, two offices in the United Kingdom, and in Indonesia, and Malaysia. Their pitch to potential clients is, "Your best tech partner is not global, but local," and they believe they know governments, city councils, and universities better than the big multinational ERP companies.

"Our customers are mainly in local government and universities," Chung says. The company works with 60 percent of higher education in Australia and New Zealand, and 73 percent of residents in both countries live in a council powered by TechnologyOne.

> If you live in Australia, you register your dog through our software, get parking fines through it. If you have a small business and [are] applying for a café license, it's probably coming from our software. If you are going to build

a pool and put an application in, it's through our software. If you went to university in Australia like I did, you probably applied through our software, paid your fees. A lot of people don't know about TechOne. In short, that's what we do—enterprise software that is mission critical and runs big organizations like councils and universities.[2]

NEWCASTLE

Consider the city of Newcastle, a tourist destination outside of Sydney. The city is responsible for maintaining six main beaches, 79 kilometers of creeks, eighty-eight bushland parcels, more than 98,000 street and park trees, 850 kilometers of roads, 974 kilometers of pathways, 147 sporting grounds, 116 playgrounds, and seven ocean baths and aquatic centers. With twelve hundred employees and more than ten office locations, the city of Newcastle's payroll team was spending countless hours manually handling and processing paper time sheets.

"Staff would have to manually fill out time sheets, scan them in and then email them to payroll to input. We even had people who had to drive around and collect time sheets from our various office locations and drive them to the payroll office so they could be inputted," David Clarke, Newcastle's CFO, told TechnologyOne.[3]

After moving to TechnologyOne's ERP platform, the whole process was digitized. Clarke says it eliminated 80 percent of manual repetitive data entry work, saved twelve tons of paper with automated accounts payable and 6.5 trees moving to electronic time sheets.[4]

Those are just some of the features of the platform. The company, founded in 1987 by Adrian Di Marco as one of Australia's first tech start-ups, now provides governments and universities with a series of dashboards to view and control their financial performance, HR employee breakdowns and org charts, budgets, supply chains, schedules, automated approval processes, and so much more. It offers end-to-end management of operations from any device and connectivity to its users, from students, to residents paying for services, to employees accessing pay and leave details.

This Australian moxie and local entrepreneurism are attractive to Matt because he is a believer in the old saying, "Riches are in Niches." In smaller markets there are few competitors, and the heavyweights are not focused on products for this segment. Over time the company has expanded from universities and local and national government and is slowly making inroads in other local niche verticals, including health care, financial services, and infrastructure businesses. And here are Matt's three key numbers for understanding TechnologyOne's business.

THE HARD NUMBERS

KEY NUMBERS TO UNDERSTAND TECHNOLOGYONE

1	115+%	2×

1: TechnologyOne is one company built on one codebase. Matt referred to this as the power of one: "SAP and Salesforce have all this customized stuff, things that are on premise, some in the cloud, all these different instances of the codebase. At TechnologyOne everyone is on one codebase. It is an easy way to run a company. For example, Tesla is a software company that just happens to build automobiles. If something doesn't work, they upload a software fix, and everyone gets it at the same time. If something doesn't work at SAP, it must upgrade every single version that they have. TechnologyOne doesn't have that complexity; they don't have to have coders building version 2.0 and other teams working on version 18.3. That simplicity translates into 31 percent going to 35 percent and higher operating margins. Operating margins at Oracle are 27 percent, at SAP 26 percent, and at Salesforce 22 percent. It also means that TechnologyOne can afford to spend more money as a percentage of revenue on research and development (R&D). It is currently spending 25 percent of revenue on R&D, whereas Oracle spends 17 percent, SAP 18 percent, and Salesforce 13 percent. That R&D spend allows them to build more easy-to-use modules on their platform, and they can afford to spend this much because the rest of the business is so efficient."

Matt, who dials into their investor calls religiously, loved when TechnologyOne's management said they were making investments today that will result in outsized revenues years from now. It reminded him of Jeff Bezos once saying he was realizing profits made from investments made five years ago. David, meet Goliath.

115+%: In chapter 9 we learned that Vertex had an astounding 111 percent net recurring revenue (NRR) number. Each year all their revenue reappears and grows by 11 percent before any additional plans for growth. Well, TechnologyOne is also a subscription business (commonly known as SaaS or Software as a Service) and set an NRR goal for itself of 115 percent. In 2023, it had a very low churn rate of 1.6 percent, and coupled with new customers and price increases it hit an all-time high NRR of 119 percent.

And it has introduced a new plan to onboard new customers even faster. Matt likes it because he still has nightmares from when he tried to install an ERP system at one of his small business ventures. "We implemented Salesforce," Matt recalled. "It took us six months to do it, and it was so complicated, and we had to get it done, and in the end we said, 'This just sucks.' We spent $250K on the software and consultants to implement and customize it, and integrate our data, and in the end, we had to figure how to get out of the contract. It was so bad. The problem is these big, generic companies tell you that they will do 100 percent of anything you want and then outsource the work to consulting firms like the Accenture's of the world. Most people don't know what they want. Imagine government employees trying to figure this out."

Along with the complexity of integration, the cost of implementation is the largest friction point for each new sale. TechnologyOne introduced something called SaaS+ to make the cost of onboarding even easier. "Let's say you want an ERP, and it will cost you $200,000 a year for five years, or a $1 million contract. But to implement it, I will charge you $200K upfront to implement it. That first year you must pay $400,000. That's hard for a company to approve. What Technology One does is it says, 'Don't worry about that extra $200,000 the first year, just pay us $50,000 a year moving forward.' So, while TechnologyOne loses money on the installation piece the first year, they end up making more money over time."

Plus, TechnologyOne makes the process easy. They don't use implementation consulting partners or value-added resellers. They take complete responsibility for building, implementing, and supporting their enterprise platform for every customer.

2X: The 115+ percent net recurring revenue means that TechnologyOne will 2X or double their revenue every five years. Remember the curves you saw for 100-baggers? Well, this is the same kind of exponential growth. Matt believes the company will also grow its margins as the company gets scale and will likely grow even faster: "This is one of the great flywheels. TechnologyOne provides a product that is essential to their customers—companies manage all their data and overall business all from one platform. ERP systems have massive switching costs. What TNE came out and did was to focus on a few verticals and became so valuable to them. And on day one they get them up and running without having to customize 85 percent of what they need on a day-to-day basis. They have it all in one experience, and they do full implementation. The company is not going to say we're going to have somebody else come in and do this for us. TechnologyOne spends a large percentage of their revenue on R&D on what the different verticals need and keeps opening white space by building new modules that bring more value to their clients. They then pick up new logos—new customers—in those verticals and they offer SaaS+ to remove the barriers of upfront costs but becomes a stream of future revenue for TechnologyOne."

Matt believed he found a new candidate for the coffee can, but on the surface of it the price of the stock seemed expensive. It was trading at a fifty times its price to earnings (PE) ratio. In comparison, at that time the S&P was trading at a twenty-five times PE ratio (table 10.1).

"Valuation is an art as opposed to a science," Matt said. "Some people do a valuation analysis down to three decimal points. What investors like to do is price things on a relative basis. If I am paying fifty times PE but in five years the business doubles, I am paying a twenty-five multiple, and if it doubles again in another five years, I'm paying a 12.5 multiple. With the S&P, I'm paying a twenty-five times PE multiple, but it is only growing 7.5 percent, so in five years, I'm paying a 17.8 multiple, and then in another five years, I'm paying 12.7 times. In other words, we get to roughly the same multiple. What looks expensive today looks relatively cheap in five years when you have the compounding value of growth. And our confidence level on their future is high based on how they are investing their R&D dollars."

Comfortable with the PE ratio over time, Matt turned to the only thing that really matters: cash flow.

TechnologyOne converts earnings into free cash flow at a gravity defying rate of 125 percent. How could they possibly generate more cash than earnings? First, it has noncash capital expense charges (such as things they have already paid for in the past and are still showing up as depreciation expenses). Second,

TABLE 10.1 Technology One versus S&P, PE ratios, and free cash flow yields.

Assumptions		
Free Cash Flow/Net Income Conversion	125.00%	50.00%
Growth	14.90%	7.00%
	TNE.AX	**S&P 500**
Current		
PE	50.0x	25.0x
FCF Yield	2.50%	2.00%
In 5 years		
PE	25.0x	17.8x
FCF Yield	5.00%	2.80%
In 10 years		
PE	12.5x	12.7x
FCF Yield	10.00%	3.90%

they collect most of their fees from customers up front, but their expenses (like employee salaries) are layered in monthly throughout the rest of the year. That creates a positive float on working capital and contributes to free cash flow conversion rates of higher than 100 percent.

"We are not buying just a piece of paper but buying a piece of a great business," Matt said. "We want the cash flow that is generated from that business. Investors want a piece of that cash flow. This is a very good business that beautifully converts its earnings into free cash flow."

In the table Matt provided, PE ratios decline over time, but TechnologyOne's free cash flow yield (free cash flow/equity value) grows over time—and at a rate even faster than the S&P's. After ten years, TechnologyOne's cash flow yield of 10 percent is more than double the cash flow yield of 3.9 percent for the S&P 500.

"This demonstrates the tremendous cash flow capability of TechnologyOne and the compounding effect of its growth rate," said Matt. "To me, in the long term, it will be dramatically cheaper than the S&P 500, yet I will be owning a much better asset. TechnologyOne is a buy for me!"

AT THE TABLE

Matt's daughters rarely see their father so enthused about a company and were eager to hear all about it. One of them even offered to do a site visit to Australia!

> PIERCE: TechnologyOne really has a cool business, but the crazy part is that no one has heard of them and yet they keep growing and making the stock go up. I really like that the company is offering its product to customers (the government particularly) that are not going away, and every government could really use some help. And since TechnologyOne is in Australia, I wonder if I could go visit them when I study abroad during college someday?
>
> PEYTON: TechnologyOne seems to keep growing and growing, and they believe they can continue to double every five years. That is incredible! One day TechnologyOne's growth may slow, but if they keep spending on R&D and coming up with new products, it feels like they have a long tail wind that they are creating for themselves.
>
> MORGAN: I love that TechnologyOne has such a consistent, steady business and really low churn rate—this should mean they can really sell more stuff to their customers and there isn't so much pressure to get new customers all the time. I don't know if I really understand what net recurring revenue (NRR) is, but since it is so high, I like that it means they can grow from their existing customers and still hit their growth targets.

Without telling his daughters, Matt bought TNE stock and summed up his thesis by saying: "TechnologyOne is about the power of one: one experience, one code-base, one amazing scaled-model, one serious compounder."

Like eastern Australia's other famous animal, the laughing kookaburra, a kingfisher bird that laughs to mark its territory, Matt hopes he too will be laughing all the way to the bank as TechnologyOne zeroes in on one niche after another.

CHAPTER 11

NICE GUYS FINISH FIRST

When you write about someone and their family for a long time, your families become interconnected too. It's bound to happen. And in this case, the gravitational pull was a combination of endless curiosity . . . a willingness to teach . . . and a shared devotion to empowering the next generation.

THE KHEMLANIS

My twins, Ian and Samantha Khemlani, grew up at a dinner table where they were constantly regaled with stories of great reporting adventures that both my wife and I have had over our careers. They knew their mom, Heather, had traveled the country: covering stories from Columbine to the D.C. Sniper in Washington, reporting live during torrential hurricanes in the Caribbean, or filing updates during the Martha Stewart trial. They knew I had spent my formative years roaming the former Soviet Union interviewing soldiers and scientists in closed and secret nuclear facilities, following Haitian refugees by boat as they made perilous trips to Miami, tagging along with the young commandos who took down the Medellin and Cali cartels, or avoiding Serbian snipers in the Holiday Inn in Sarajevo. We always encouraged our children to get out into the world, to try to make sense of it all and to make an impact, meet exciting people from every stripe of life in the middle of important journeys, and in the process discover something new about themselves. Family vacations sometimes feel like Indiana Jones–style adventures from the ancient temples of Angkor Wat in Cambodia to the heart of Havana in Cuba, from Mayan structures and shamans

11.1 Samantha Khemlani, 2024.

in Central America to former fighter pilots in Vietnam. It comes as no surprise to us then that our daughter Samantha, who is studying at Rice University in Houston and is interested in psychology (because of the devastating impact of COVID and social media on her generation), is determined to go to Ulaanbaatar in Mongolia (figure 11.1). Why? Because it spends less per capita on mental health than any other country in the world, and her goal—at least today—is to help build out the nascent mental health infrastructure across Southeast Asia.

It also came as no surprise that our son Ian, who is also studying at Rice University because of his interest in business, energy, and technology, found himself two summers ago slipping on squeaky rubber waders and carefully sloshing his way into one of Denmark's bays past undulating, neon pink jellyfish (figure 11.2). It was there that start-up Danish founder Simon Weber revealed to him how he planned to use the seaweed floating around them to save the planet while building a multi-million-dollar company.

Weber handed Ian a fistful of spaghetti-like seaweed that produces 70 percent more oxygen than land plants and absorbs carbon more effectively than trees.

11.2 Ian Khemlani in Denmark, 2023.

With government permission, he was growing it in the public bay on underwater ropes that had been covered with fertilized spores. He chose this species after much testing in his basement laboratory for two reasons. First, it thrives in warm water—a plus as ocean temperatures continue to rise. Second, the seaweed has a delicious crunchy bite and a slightly salty taste. Weber had begun selling it to Danish restaurants—from world famous three Michelin star dining establishments to smaller, lesser-known eateries across Copenhagen—to incorporate it into their locally sourced dishes.

Ian was enthralled by the new market Weber had created from scratch. It was good for the environment and good for the bottom line. This experience inspired a belief in Ian that solving global challenges requires deep rooted curiosities, out of the box thinking, cross-disciplinary knowledge, and good old-fashioned entrepreneurship.

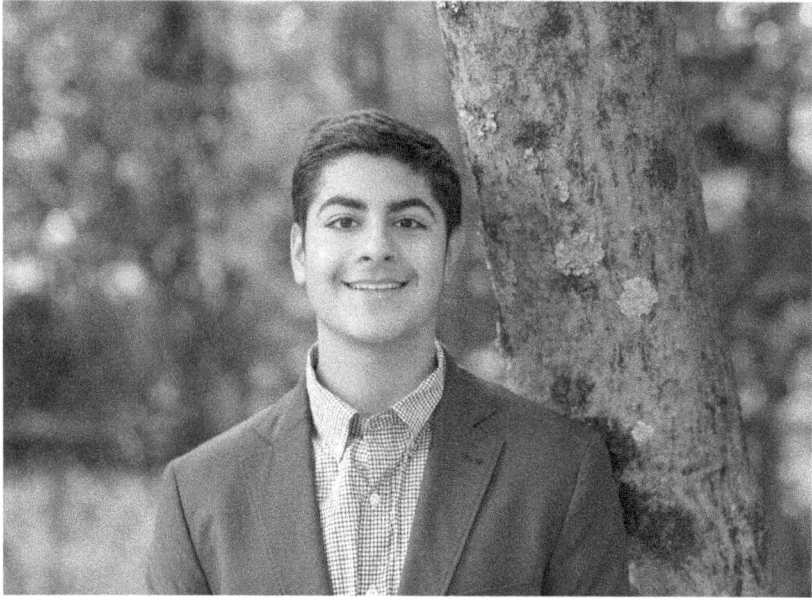

11.3 Ian Khemlani, 2024.

He liked studying arcane commodities and their importance in the global supply chains of computer chips and electric car batteries. He was fascinated by the world changing potential of artificial intelligence and the massive amounts of energy required to power all the servers behind it (figure 11.3). He liked how the world of investing allowed him to think about all of these subjects at the same time. His confidence levels in pursuing a career in finance grew leaps and bounds after he and his team won his high school investment club's simulated stock market competition, where he turned $10,000 into $52,000 over a few months. And he was completely fascinated by all the zoom calls I was suddenly having with a mysterious investor in Kansas City. When I told him what I was doing, he said, "Dad, can I call Mr. Ankrum to see if I could do a summer internship with him?"

A MEETING OF THE MINDS

Matt, ever open to the idea of explaining the right way to invest to young people, immediately agreed to spend Saturday mornings with Ian. I was thrilled. I wish

I had learned the investing principles I now know when I was Ian's age. It's like taking a golf lesson in your fifties, after decades of doing everything the wrong way. If Ian could develop the right mindset now, it would save him years of agony as an investor.

Matt decided to enlist Ian as a research assistant for one of the stocks he was considering adding to the coffee can portfolio. He wouldn't tell me what it was, but he said he thought it would be a good match for Ian's interests. Given his penchant for global travel, Ian was being asked to help research a company that was based more than five thousand miles away from New York in Israel. It also was deploying cutting edge artificial intelligence to turbo charge its business—something that revved up Ian's intellectual engines. And if Matt decided to pick the stock, he wanted Ian to present the opportunity to me and my wife Heather in a formal, but family only, presentation.

To start, Matt taught Ian the basics: how to use Excel spreadsheets, how to pull and read dozens of financial documents, how to pull data from the documents and then put them into highly involved financial models. At first Ian learned simple things such as when a number has brackets around it, it means it is a negative value. After a few weeks he was suddenly confidently talking about discounted cash flow models. It was as if my son had suddenly become a Goldman Sachs analyst. Ian has always had an incredible drive to teach himself things. When we told him he couldn't play on the football team because of the real risk of concussions and CTE, he quietly took lessons on how to make field goals and made the team as a kicker (where the odds of being tackled is greatly reduced) (figure 11.4). And then he and his team went on to win the New York State championship inside "The Dome" in Syracuse! (figure 11.5).

By the end of the summer, Ian sent Heather and I an invitation to receive a presentation. He, with Matt as a backstop, would present Matt's latest addition to the coffee can. The company was called NICE (Ticker symbol: NICE), and it is the world's leading customer experience AI platform. Get your popcorn now!

NICE, NICE

Ian and Matt started their presentation as if it was a segment on Mark Burnett's *Shark Tank* show—describing a problem we've all suffered through: poor customer support. "We've all called a company, waited on hold for a long time,

11.4 Ian Khemlani kicking the football, 2023.

11.5 Ian Khemlani receiving a medal after his high school team won a New York State championship, 2023.

and then bounced around from agent to agent, as we go in circles trying to get answers to relatively simple questions," said Ian. I could certainly relate. The mind-numbing exercise can make even the most patient of us feel like we need to sign up for an anger management class.

Well, NICE sells businesses customer support solutions: from locally hosted software for their call centers to cloud solutions that automate everything, from tools for human agents to chatbots that appear on company websites. The AI-powered cloud software listens to our calls, records everything, gathers all our previous interactions with the company across every social or commu- nication channel, and puts it all, including our contact information, on one screen for the agent to see. And then, in real time, it looks to understand our sentiment, what topics we want to address, and suggests a series of dialogue modules to the human agent or links to digital solutions that a chatbot can offer a customer to help solve his or her problem. It can even alert customer support managers in real time to heated conversations. The AI software can also make recommendations to management to build digital products to imme- diately increase customer satisfaction scores. At a bank, for example, that would include digital solutions to reset a person's password, unlock an account, check their balance, or transfer funds.

The CEO of NICE, Barak Eilam, who grew up in a suburb of Tel Aviv, went to a tech high school but barely finished (figure 11.6). "I wasn't a very good student. I mean, I was a good student. But I was somewhat, kind of, let's call it lazy."[1] After graduation, he started his compulsory military service. Because he went to a tech high school, the Israeli army assigned him to what was then the top-secret technology unit of Israeli military intelligence. The military's officer-training programs quickly turned him into a leader. He left when some of the reservists he commanded recruited him into a supervisory role at their company that recorded call-center interactions for quality control. They called it Neptune Intelligence Computer Engineering (or NICE), and it was founded in 1986. While working there, Eilam earned an electrical engineering degree at Tel Aviv University. Over the years he worked in the various departments, from engineering to sales, and eventually rose to CEO in 2014. Once in charge he decided the company had become unfocused and decided that it had to grow smaller in order to grow. He sold off surveillance software businesses in the defense and security areas and doubled down on enterprise cloud software two

11.6 Barak Eilam, former CEO of NICE.
Source: NICE.

years later by buying inContact, a US company specializing in contact center solutions for almost $1 billion. Today NICE is expanding from customer experience into financial crime and compliance, as well as the digital transformation of policing. It generates more than 80 percent of its revenue in the US and has a market cap of more than $10 billion.

After explaining what NICE does and its origin story, Ian told Heather (figure 11.7) and me that the company converts an amazing 20 percent of revenue into free cash flow and invests heavily—around $300 million—into R&D.

11.7 Heather Cabot Khemlani, 2024.

Heather asked, "Does that level of investment help the company create a moat?"

Ian responded, "Yes, that's a very high hurdle for its competitors to overcome."

"The company generates the capital to create their own destiny, to truly distance themselves from the competition," Matt added, explaining that the company can proactively acquire strategic assets, invest in its own platform, and invest to build critical global partnerships or execute share buybacks.

Trained in the art of Matt's signature presentation style, Ian then launched into the three key numbers that explain NICE's business.

THE HARD NUMBERS

KEY NUMBERS TO UNDERSTAND NICE

80–90	88%	2T/Bs

80–90: Since 2019, NICE has grown revenue from $1.58 billion to $2.38 billion, and its operating income has grown from $434 million to $704 million (a 13 percent CAGR). It's a 75 percent gross margin business, with 30 percent operating margins, a ROTA rate above 20 percent, and a $30.7 billion total addressable market (TAM). The runway for further growth is enormous—and much of it is likely to come from its existing customers as opposed to just adding more logos to their brochures. Today NICE's customer support solution has more than twenty-five thousand customers, and it's a who's who of corporate America, including ten of the top ten health insurance companies, five of the top five Telco companies, nine of the top ten global financial service companies, and six of the Fortune top ten. But most of its clients, somewhere between 80 and 90 percent of them, are still using call centers and on-premise software hosted on its own servers. With locally hosted software, Barak Eilam explains, customers use it for a few years then come to NICE to buy an updated version. With the cloud solution, the software is updated on a weekly basis with new innovations. Also, customers can buy additional products or services immediately without having to bring in a system integration specialist to make sure all of the software works together.[2] It's very much like the ERP system built by TechnologyOne. As each client moves to AI powered cloud solutions for customer support instead of costly human teams around the world, it reduces costs by more than 20 percent—and NICE gets to charge 50 percent more for its cloud platform that operates real time across every digital communication channel a customer chooses to engage a brand. It's a win-win for NICE and its B2B customers (as well as its ultimate B2C customers). It's also a killer recipe for long-term growth for the Israeli company as more and more of its clients move into the cloud.

Ian then explained there was a whole other avenue for growth as well. He was thrilled to share that Matt had invited him to join his diligence call with NICE's investor relations team. Ian had never talked to a real IR team and had spent a weekend preparing questions. He was nervous, but his ears perked up during their call when he learned that less than 10 percent of NICE's customer support

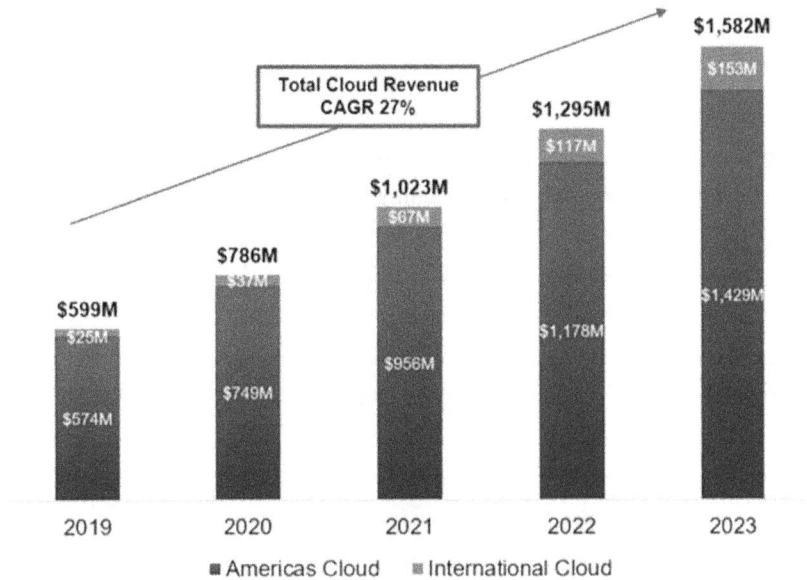

11.8 Global cloud revenue growth.
Source: NICE.

cloud revenue came from outside the United States. Although total cloud revenue was growing at a 27 percent CAGR, international is growing faster than the US, according to Matt, and can and should be a major contributor to NICE's future success (figure 11.8). The Asia Pacific region is a key part of their expansion efforts.

Overall, Matt believes the company is on a path to $5 billion in revenue and will be able to convert 20 to 25 percent of revenue to free cash flow. In other words, a cash generating machine!

88%: This one is simple and something we are starting to get used to in Matt's picks: 88 percent of NICE's revenue, or $2.2 billion, is recurring. First, Ian explained, the product is ranked the best industry solution by all the major analysts. Forrester Research named NICE the category leader, with the strongest offering and strategy. Gartner named it the top customer choice. Ventana ranked it first in value, and Aragon Research said it was a leader in conversational AI. Always hard for a business to contemplate switching to a competitor when these firms recommend NICE so highly. Plus, a company would have to incur the expense of retraining its customer support employees on a brand-new system if they did decide to switch. Second, they learned during their IR call that NICE revenue did not decrease during COVID because companies cannot afford the business risk of turning off customer support. In other words, there are incredibly high switching costs to canceling or moving to a competitor. Matt reminds us that "essential" products are one of his 4Es. But this is not just an ordinary SaaS business that is hard to untangle from day-to-day business operations. And that leads us to the third key number.

2T/Bs: NICE processes "2 trillion words" per day and has "billions" of recorded calls and digital communications that it is able to utilize to build a valuable AI service. Remember, the artificial intelligence the company uses to make predictions and supply dialogue content to human agents or digital solutions to chatbots are created by recognizing patterns across vast amounts of data. NICE has been collecting data across a range of industry verticals since the late 1980s and is using it to train hundreds of artificial intelligence models today. It has secured five hundred US and forty international patents.

When Matt and Ian were talking about this, I started to think about all the digital products I oversaw at Yahoo!, Hearst, and CBS News. All of them were predicated on a website as the main experience. When smartphones came out, we built apps. And all throughout, customer service was a back-office operation. At first it was on a lower floor at headquarters. Over the years they were moved to other lower cost cities and then eventually outsourced to other countries such as India. But while listening to the NICE presentation, I couldn't help but think companies like NICE were moving customer support to the front office. It is, after all, the first and last place a customer interacts with a company. The AI models were being fed every interaction we, as customers, have with a company. Not just our complaints, but they are being trained on every product we ever considered buying on a website. That information can be fed into a system that then directs the company how to market that product to us, improve the efficiency of its advertising, and even monetize future interactions. Massive amounts of information, personalized to each person, informing how a company interacts with each customer—all coming out of the customer support office. What once used to be a cost center is starting to be a company's knowledge center for how to grow revenue.

"For NICE, its customers are now starting to look at them to manage all the interactions, even if it comes from outside of the customer contact center," said Matt. "This is an opportunity to deepen its relationship with its client and drive incremental new revenue."

SHORT-TERMISM VS. LONG-TERMISM

While I was happily imagining the future of how companies interact with each of us, Matt was licking his chops about the stock's declining stock price: although there were short-term concerns, the long-term fundamentals still seemed strong. At the time of Matt's buy recommendation, the company was being punished for two reasons. First, after twenty-five years at the company, Eilam announced that he would be retiring but would stay on to help pick a new CEO as well as consult for them until end of 2025. Second, some Wall Street analysts were saying products like NICE would ultimately be replaced by generic AI solutions such as ChatGPT. Why would a company need to pay for specialized AI-powered customer support solutions if it could just embed ChatGPT on its website?

Barak Eilam answered those concerns in an interview with Yahoo! Finance:

> Many of them tried to use generic gen AI, and it just didn't work for that particular purpose. It's very different the way enterprises adopt AI versus the way individuals do that. So, the need is for a very specific, tailored made, highly tuned AI based on very specific data that we have . . . and we see that demand really happening as we speak.[3]

Basically, Eilam was saying that the AI being used to help the customer support team is training on the very specific data his company has collected for decades, across very specialized industry verticals, and all on one digitally native platform. Furthermore, he explained that the risk of getting something wrong was too big a gamble for clients:

> We see customers try to go down that path and then they come to us. If you think about how AI is being used in customer care, we would like to provide outstanding care. We don't want any issues of either privacy, hallucinations, wrong answers, biased answers. You need 100 percent accuracy. It needs to be fully secured. It needs to be able to augment people as well as provide an automated service. So, it is bit more complicated than just taking a generic AI and applying it to the enterprise.

Matt did some of his own diligence on this issue by talking to one of NICE's competitors. Many of its clients told that company that they wouldn't go to a full generic AI solution because "31 percent of all people will drop a brand if they have one bad experience with them. The first and last experience is usually a contact center. You think we will let generic AI determine how we talk to our customers?!"

Matt smiled and said, "That's why we get excited when great businesses go on sale. Has the growth changed? No. Has the quality changed? No. Investor perception is that analysts think AI will kill them. It's just noise versus truth. Our bet with NICE is AI won't actually kill it. That's why as a professional investor, when you do your homework and get good intel, this is the kind of situation you take advantage of."

Matt relishes that NICE is a contrarian stock pick, both because of the CEO departure as well as the threat from generic AI. But down cycles in stocks don't scare Matt. In his proprietary research about 100-baggers, he notes that over the decades *unicorn stocks drop 25–50 percent, on average, eight times.*

Matt told me he bought NICE for the coffee can, and Ian said he, too, made a purchase. He explained that he took the $400 scholarship he won for a history essay he wrote for the local historical society and bought NICE stock with it.

Ian then turned to Matt and said, "I learned how to use excel and how to value a company. I'm around a lot of kids who are used to day trading on their accounts. But I learned about long-term investing from you. I learned how to be an investor versus a trader. It's pretty irresponsible to trade on speculation or momentum or current events. I learned to understand and believe in what defines a high-quality company. Mr. Ankrum, you have been an incredible internship host, and every time I asked you a question, you made time to answer it. And even when I didn't understand something, you simplified things for me so I could understand it. It was very helpful. Thank you."

Matt then turned to Ian and said, "I enjoyed it, and it was great working with you. I hope that whatever you study in college, whether it is finance or political science, you learned how to obtain the right information and use it the right way. There is so much information out there. What's real and what's not real? You need to continue doing your own homework. That is what investing is all about."

After Heather and I both thanked Matt for providing an invaluable internship and continued mentorship to our son, we looked at Ian and said, "NICE job!"

A few weeks after the presentation, NICE announced they had found a replacement for Barak Eilam. It hired Scott Russell, the chief revenue officer and member of the executive committee of SAP, the German software giant, to

11.9 Scott Russell, new CEO of NICE.
Source: NICE.

be its new CEO (figure 11.9). Matt and Ian will be watching from afar to see if he can continue the company's incredible trajectory. They will be watching for any cracks in its competitive moat. They will track whether any key customers leave NICE to go to another platform. And they will monitor whether the new CEO continues to allocate capital to reinvest in the business to keep and attract new, larger customers. No one can predict the future, but if the company continues to be essential to its customers, Matt and Ian say they will continue to be proud shareholders.

CHAPTER 12

BOURBON AND OTHER STUNNING APPROACHES TO POLICING

In 1993, Rick Smith and his brother started a rather unusual company in their Tucson, Arizona, garage. Smith's goal was to productize a less lethal device than guns for law enforcement (figure 12.1). He hired Jack Cover, a NASA researcher, who had been developing something called a TASER. It was a loose acronym based on one of his favorite young adult science fiction books, *Tom Swift and His Electric Rifle.*

Recalling his early days in a public presentation in San Francisco in 2017, Smith said, "I turned to science fiction. Why is the state of the art in 1993 shooting people with lead balls? You would think we would have come further. Captain Kirk never whips out a Glock and blows a hole in a Klingon? That would look bizarre," said Smith.[1]

He looked at typical police belts that had spots for a gun, a baton, and chemical sprays, but nothing involving technology. So he began a long, and at times controversial, journey to develop a less lethal device to replace the gun. Mind you, the company currently uses the term "less lethal," not "nonlethal." According to Reuters, since 2000 more than one thousand cases have been recorded of people dying in the US after being shocked by police with a Taser (often in combination with other forms of force).[2]

Smith addressed the negative media coverage in his 2017 San Francisco presentation. "Over the past 20 years since we introduced this, these devices were used in 180,000 situations where police officers were legally justified to use lethal force. So, we have 180,000 cases where officers did not have a choice," he said with a slide behind him that read "180,000 lives saved from potential death or serious injury." He went on to say, "But I would guess what you've heard about these technologies wasn't about the lives saved. Unfortunately, as we have talked

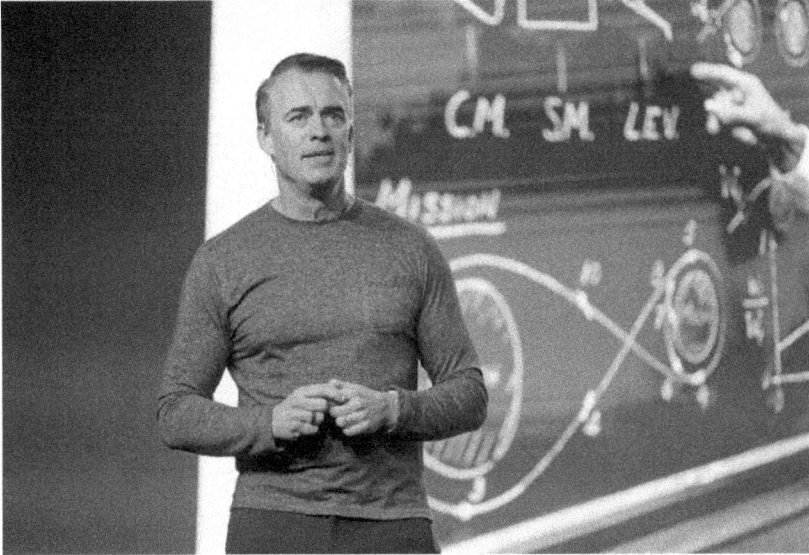

12.1 Axon Founder and CEO, Rick Smith.

about at this conference, the media focuses our reptilian brains on negative news, and so far [it's] more likely you've seen things like this (with a slide behind him of pictures of people calling for police reform and a banner saying 'NO TASERS') because there are still cases where people are hurt or even killed when these technologies are used although it is dramatically less than conventional technologies."[3]

THE NEW TASER AND BODY CAMERAS

Last year the company, now renamed Axon to reflect it's growing offerings, introduced its latest iteration, the TASER 10 energy weapon. It was the first key innovation from the company since it announced a "moonshot goal to cut gun-related deaths between police and the public by 50 percent in the next decade."

It's a bright yellow, water-proof handgun-shaped device, with a cartridge that holds ten barbed probes, compared to four previously. It can be shot from a maximum range of 45 feet, almost double the previous range. It has new de-escalation features, including a 1,000-lumen pulsing light, loud audible alerts, and laser

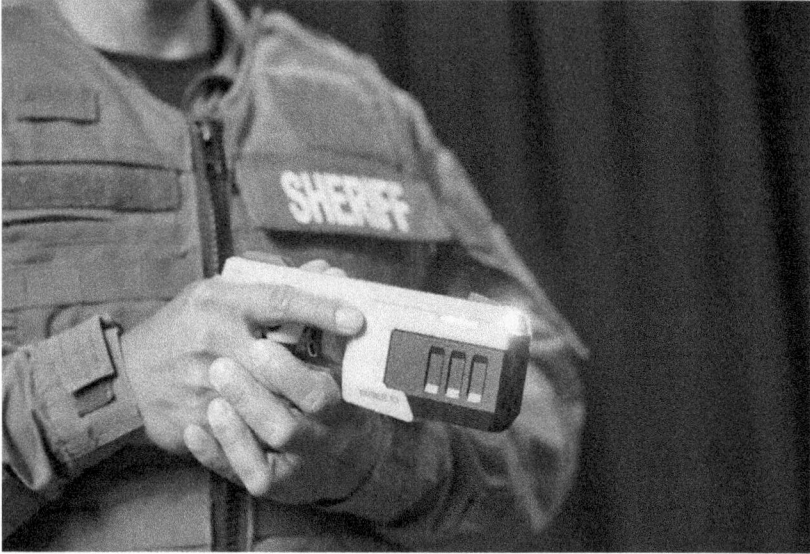

12.2 The TASER 10 energy weapon.

painting to warn a subject to comply before having to deploy probes (figure 12.2). When pulled out of the holster, the TASER activates the police officer's body cam. Once the trigger is pulled, the probe shoots out of the cartridge at 205 feet per second while connected to a wire. The officer then shoots a second probe at the target to complete the electric circuit, and 1,000 volts of pulsed electrical current (which previously was 50,000 volts) channels into the target's body. It is designed to disrupt the voluntary control of muscles, causing "neuromuscular incapacitation" and a temporary opportunity for a police officer to restrain a target with a lower chance of physical harm.

The new TASER has come a long way from previous versions. Initially, police officers used it as they would pepper spray. The increased distance and number of cartridges increases not only its capability but also increases the likelihood it could be used as a gun replacement.

The San Diego Police Department was one of the first units to announce it would be upgrading to the latest version, which comes with virtual reality training. "Our officers deserve the best equipment to enable them to protect this City," Police Chief David Nisleit said to the local FOX affiliate. "The TASER 10 design is a game-changer and will make the TASER more effective when used in situations that warrant less-lethal force. I'm grateful to our City Council for signing off on this much-needed upgrade for our officers." "Starting in the fall of 2024," the television station noted, "1,860 SDPD officers will be using the TASER 10, part of a five-year agreement between SDPD and Axon, which will cost around $1.95 million for the purchase and training in the first year of the agreement."[4]

TASER 10 is just one part of Axon's overall business. And that's what attracted Matt Ankrum to the company. He says Axon, now headquartered in Scottsdale, Arizona, likes to say it's "building the public safety operating system of the future." "The TASER is the first lock-in into the ecosystem Axon is building," Matt adds.

The company expanded outside of the core TASER product in 2005 when it created its first accessory, the TASER cam, which mounted on the grip and activated automatically when the safety is released and the device is armed. Three years later, it created its first body camera called the Axon Pro. The footage was uploaded and stored on a website called Evidence.com.

The Rialto, California, police department, according to the *New York Times*, used the grip mounted cameras, and when police chief William Farrar told his team he wanted to start using the body camera, "it wasn't the easiest sell," especially with some older officers who initially were "questioning why 'big brother' should see everything they do." He told the *Times* that he reminded his officers that civilians could use cell phones to record interactions, "so instead of relying on somebody else's partial picture of what occurred, why not have your own? In this way, you have the real one."

The department then participated in a research study with a visiting fellow at the University of Cambridge. According to the *Times*, "Even with only half of the 54 uniformed patrol officers wearing cameras at any given time, the department over all had an 88 percent decline in the number of complaints filed against officers, compared with the 12 months before the study, to 3 from 24. Rialto's police officers also used force nearly 60 percent less often—in 25 instances, compared with 61. When force was used, it was twice as likely to have been applied by the officers who weren't wearing cameras during that shift, the study found."

Farrar went on to say there were examples of cases where citizens arrived at a Rialto police station to file a complaint, and the supervisor was able to retrieve and play the video of what had happened. "The individuals left the station with basically no other things to say and have never come back," he said to the *Times*.[5]

12.3 Axon Body 4 camera worn by a police officer.

Today the Axon Body 4 camera has a full-shift battery even when being used for real-time services, a 160-degree field of view, and can feed the video to headquarters as well as to other officers approaching the scene (figure 12.3). The cameras Axon makes also extend into the police vehicle. The Fleet 3 camera can automatically detect and read license plates on cars moving up to 140 miles per hour. And, yes, Axon has also put eyes in the sky . . . and on the ground. Axon Air provides the hardware, software, and professional services to ensure department drone programs are successful. Manual and remote piloting offers first responders the ability to understand a situation before arriving on a scene. And once there, they can also deploy uncrewed ground vehicles with cameras in places the drones can't get to (figure 12.4). All the live streams are shared on Axon Respond, which facilitates two-way communications with supervisors, and then is saved on Axon Evidence in the cloud.

In February of 2024, Axon acquired Fusus, a real-time crime center in the cloud that allows police to seek permission and then gain access to video feeds from schools and local businesses in their district, expanding the overall data set of information coming into police headquarters during live situations.

12.4 Sky-Hero by Axon and Tactical Robotic Recon System provide uncrewed ground and aerial vehicles and cameras to improve surveillance.

GROWTH ACROSS THE BOARD

What started as a TASER company has evolved into a multidevice, multivideo, and multisoftware company, and now they are leveraging generative artificial intelligence with their offerings. All the video, photos, and text that have been uploaded to Axon Evidence are then transferred to Axon Records. Artificial intelligence automatically redacts any unnecessary personal information (blurring out innocent faces or license plates, etc.) and transcribes all the videos from the body cams and then prepopulates digital reports on misdemeanor cases within seconds for officers to read and then approve. The company calls it Draft One. Paper forms are no longer necessary (Axon says police officers spend on average three hours per day writing reports), long-term case files are easily accessible, and officers can spend more time in the communities they serve. And all of those reports as well as evidence are made available to prosecutors and defense attorneys through yet another product: Axon Justice. It's a stunning technological ecosystem that Tom Swift and his Electric Rifle could never have imagined.

During the earnings call at the end of the second quarter of 2024, Smith talked about how he was helping police departments amass large amounts of data that they can then use to drive productivity . . . and value for Axon. "Well, in April, we launched Draft One, a powerful new AI service that writes the first draft of a police report extracted directly from Axon body camera recordings. Our customers' response to Draft One is better than anything I've seen, better than we could have imagined. They want to put more data into the cloud with Axon. They want to better access that data, and they trust us to protect their data. And they can see that we can help them do their jobs better, put their data to use."

He added, "We run the largest sensor ecosystem by far, including TASERs, body cameras, in-car cameras, drones, robotics, and third-party cameras and sensors through Fusus. This vast network generates the data needed to drive the future of AI."

"By combining top-tier AI models with our sensor and software ecosystem, we can deliver exceptional workflows, all within a secured GovCloud environment. Our AI products not only offer tremendous growth opportunities for us but also immense value to our customers. Solutions like Draft One, automated license plate reading, transcription, video redaction, these services quickly pay for themselves."[6]

It's important to note that Rick Smith said Axon doesn't own the data, the police departments do.

THE HARD NUMBERS

Matt believes Axon is a "net positive to society," adding: "Tasers protect the lives of officers and targets, cameras record evidence for all the situations, and its data management system increases transparency in the judicial system." He also likes that CEO Rick Smith is a missionary leader, businessman, and innovator whose life goal is to "make the bullet obsolete." And here are Matt's three key numbers to understand the Axon business.

KEY NUMBERS TO UNDERSTAND AXON

50%	95%/25%	77B

50%: Matt says Axon is a high-quality business that will continue to grow and increase margins. More than 38 percent of net sales comes from software and services, and unlike bodycams with 40 percent gross margins or TASERs at 60 percent, the software business enjoys 80+ percent gross margins.

The main source of software revenue comes from Axon Evidence and Records. Matt believes it has the potential to become 50 percent of total revenue over the next decade. The bigger the software business becomes, the more it will substantially raise the total company's overall gross margins.

95%/25%: It has 123 percent net revenue retention thanks to the seamless interconnectivity of the Axon system and the subscription bundles of products and services it sells its customers in contracts that are five-plus years long with low single digit price increases annually (figure 12.5).

"The biggest subscription package is the Officer Safety Plan 10 Plus Premium, said Matt. "Axon will sell you just TASERs or body cams, but you can buy the whole thing with the Officer Safety Plan and automatically get product upgrades whenever a new device comes out and all the software. It costs about $325 per month per officer. That gets you all the goodies they offer."

If that sounds expensive from a budget perspective, Matt checked the expense as a percentage of police officer salaries. "The average salary with benefits for an LAPD officer is about $100,000, so $325 per month is less than half a percent of that salary. And if someone says Los Angeles police officers make a lot more than police in other parts of the country, go to Alabama or Louisiana. There it's still less than 2 percent of average police salaries. And they get all this equipment and the software services to protect the communities they serve. Plus, it helps

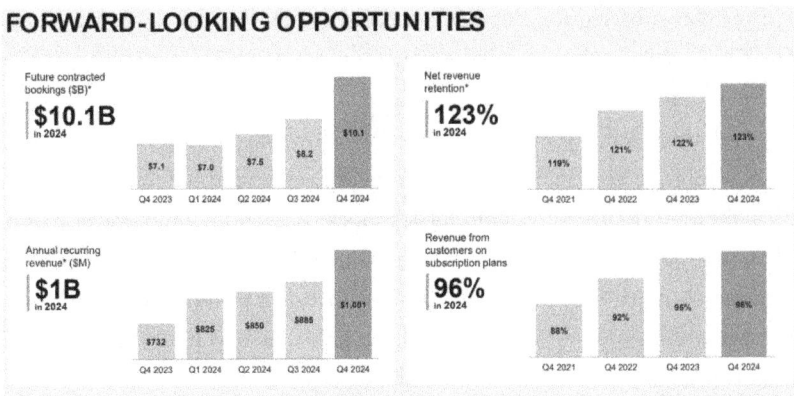

12.5 Axon had 123 percent net revenue retention in 2024.

these departments, which are usually 70 to 80 percent of where they want to be in terms of manpower, become much more productive."

And for Axon's business, as police departments lock into large subscription businesses, Matt says "it moves from being a simple profit margin play to a lifetime value creation play."

It reminded me of the time an ecommerce expert told me about the incredible long-term value of a customer who buys diapers on Amazon.com. The ecommerce giant would discount diapers to get "lock in" with mostly young mothers, who they knew would then become prime members and long-term customers not only for their baby but for their entire household. In this case, police departments start with TASERs and then grow into more products and an entire software solution. And those solutions store tremendous amounts of video and evidence that makes it very hard to move to another solution.

"There are high switching costs for software solutions," Matt noted, adding, "It keeps customers on network and drives recurring revenue." In 2019, Matt said 73 percent of the company's total revenue was tied to subscriptions. By 2023, it has grown to 95 percent, a 44 percent CAGR on recurring revenue over that period.

All that recurring revenue comes with an adjusted earnings before interest, taxes, depreciation, and amortization (EBITDA) margin of 25 percent. It allows the company to continue to invest in its growth while delivering cash flow.

$77B: More than 85 percent of their net sales are made in the United States. Public safety spending has historically remained stable over time, regardless of economic conditions (such as the financial crisis in 2008) or pandemics. Matt also believes there is enormous potential to grow its business by moving customers into larger subscription bundles, penetrating other US law enforcement and corrections agencies, as well as international markets. Currently only 20 percent of their revenue is international.

"It took them seven years to get into Italy. Now the company recently closed its largest international deal. And every time they penetrate a new agency in Brazil, it's like adding the equivalent of a customer two to four times the size of the NYPD." Rick Smith even recounted a meeting with a senior government leader in Europe—a place that has been slow to move from on-premise software to cloud-based solutions—who was wowed by Draft One and its ability to leverage generative AI to do reports in a hundred languages. Draft One is now increasing the company's overall pipeline for new business.

Matt says the company sees a total market of $77 billion, which includes $7 billion for TASER, $10 billion for cameras, $18 billion for software and services,

$16 billion for real-time operations and the coordination of services in live situations, and $19 billion for drones. Although he thinks the $19 billion coming from drones is a bit ambitious, he said, "What gives me more comfort though is their speed to innovation. Their customers love Rick and the guys at Axon because they keep bringing out new stuff they need or want. They talk to police and really listen to their feedback. The grip and feel of the handle matters to the police, where it is on the belt matters, each iteration from the company improves each of its products and takes them to the next level. But a bigger part of my interest level and excitement level is that Axon is also driving the change their customers need, not the other way around. They have been historically dealing with low innovation, slow moving customers. With live situation command centers, virtual reality training programs, and AI-powered products, they can significantly change how these officers serve their community. I don't know what they are building next and what will be important tomorrow, but I do know they are leading on the innovation front and creating a very powerful economic model that entrenches them in an ecosystem."

That deep rooted and enduring relationship is also helping Axon with the competition. "There's a lot of players and it's very fragmented. There are two key players. There's Axon and there's Motorola," says Danielle Menichella, Portfolio Manager at Sands Capital and an analyst that covers Axon. "However, Axon is significantly larger. And I think the reason why is because they have that model, that flywheel that ties in. They get in the door with the TASER, they then sell the body camera that is integrated with the TASER, but then it collects that data. Because they have the most customers, they have the ability to get the most data, which actually helps them create software that is better."[7]

Axon's success has translated into a steady rise in the stock price, and Rick Smith has invited controversy with the size of his internal stock plans. Although it caused a bit of consternation for Matt, it hasn't deterred his enthusiasm for the company. "The first plan was for Rick Smith, but the second version is broader and more inclusive for more employees. It is controversial because they are going to share more of the upside with employees that typically accrued to the shareholders. Every public company has a stock plan, but this one is more aggressive, almost three to five times more. And I think the value accretion of Axon's fundamentals outweighs the dilution to shareholders from the option plan. Axon is such a big winning proposition that I'd rather own a smaller piece of a much bigger company than not participate in it at all." Rick Smith topped the *Wall Street Journal's* list of highest paid chief executives in 2024, with pay of $165 million.

AT THE TABLE

Matt shared his interest in the company with his family. Everyone was already feeling a little raw after a recent break-in at their home, so discussions about a company helping policing was welcome. The break-in happened early in the morning while Matt was at the gym, but his wife, Maury, and daughter Pierce were at home with their newly adopted dog, Bourbon, and Whiskey, an English cream retriever who normally hides from strangers. No one got hurt, but it was still a traumatic experience.

> MAURY: It happened so fast. Who would have ever thought anyone would try to break into a house at 6:30 A.M.? We live in a good neighborhood, but I guess it can happen anywhere. I am so glad we had Bourbon. He went nuts when the intruder came in. It scared the intruder so much he immediately ran out of the house. We got him on the security camera flying down the hill. We are so lucky that we had adopted Bourbon only a few weeks earlier. At the time, we assumed Bourbon was "battle-tested" given he had lived on the street and had a half-torn ear and scars on other parts of his body. From that moment, we knew we had picked the right dog for us. Literally, he saved Pierce and I from something dreadful. By noon, we had someone at the house to put new locks on the door, and I had called a fence company. There is nothing scarier than having a stranger in your house. We were discussing whether we should get a gun, but I am a bit nervous how I will react with a gun and an intruder in the house. The local gun shop owner told us that having a dog is by far the best deterrent for any break-ins.

Bourbon barked occasionally as Matt explained the Axon business to his family. Here were their reactions:

> PEYTON: I had heard of TASERs, but I didn't realize Axon had created an entire product suite for police departments with body cams, fleet cameras, and now drone detection.
>
> PIERCE: It seems the new AI technology, that does the automatic police reports, is really cool and would save the officers a lot of time. By the sounds of it, Axon is not as much a weapons company but more like a

comprehensive officer safety company that makes the job easier and safer for the officers.

MAURY: The Officer Safety Plan you explained really locks in the police departments to stay with Axon—making it really difficult for any competitor to get its foot in the door. If Axon's CEO could be successful in his big goal to lower gun-related deaths by 50 percent, that would be huge and a real benefit to the US.

A CONTROVERSIAL INVESTMENT?

When Matt first brought up Axon and the TASER, I confess that I was somewhat hesitant to be involved in a company that sold, well, weapons. Don't get me wrong. I've certainly shot guns, from pistols to rifles, and just came back from a summer shooting and fishing trip to Montana with my family—but I've never actively invested in a company that made products that required a holster. The culture of a company extolling the virtues of barbed cartridges that send electric currents into a person's body can certainly rub someone the wrong way. And many states and police departments still need to adopt policies on how best to use TASERs and routinely check the data logs Axon provides to make sure they are being used correctly and humanely, as the *New York Times* pointed out in their 2025 story about the lack of oversight at many Mississippi police departments.[8] But as I learned more about the company, and what it is trying to do to replace guns while providing more lifesaving technology for police departments and the communities they serve, my initial hesitation started to dissipate. I then learned that the body cam footage of the George Floyd murder, made public by a Minnesota judge, was from cameras made by Axon—and after the incident, the company said its employees were so horrified by what they saw that they brainstormed ways to try to help prevent this from happening again and to maximize transparency when it occurs. The team built software to help supervisors sift through the thousands of hours of body cam footage they get each week to zero in on potential abuses of power. It uses an artificial intelligence algorithm that identifies keywords such as profanity, racial slurs, or other red flags and then aggregates the video on a "Use of Force" dashboard for management to view. The company notes that Derek Chauvin, the officer who knelt on George Floyd's neck for nine minutes and twenty-nine seconds, had eighteen prior misconduct complaints filed against him.[9]

Axon Chief Product Officer Jeff Kunins said, "All of these (new features) are means that would enable a department to be taking a much more proactive role in having data in their hands to see how their officers are behaving in a wide variety of circumstances and being able to drive changes to policy."[10]

Matt, ever the composed and neutral Midwestern investor, was proud to make an investment in the company, not just because he believed in its enduring model but also because of what he considers its long overdue contributions to society at large:

> Think about my 4Es, one of the most important Es is the essentiality of the product or service. What Axon does is take something that is so vital to our society . . . justice . . . so our citizens can feel comfortable and safe and not fear for their lives in their communities. They have hardly had or seen any innovation in that in a long, long time and now have a company helping police officers do their jobs better. Police have been using sticks and balls from three hundred years ago. Now they have TASERs. I wish we had a body cam on that officer in Ferguson. We did have a body cam filming George Floyd. And the body cam filming Tyreek Hill showed just how the situation escalated. Axon is trying to create a fairer world for police, victims, and per-petrators, so everybody has the best information at the time. Axon is shining a bright light on what's happening out there.

From the stone age to the nuclear age, "the story of violence is as old as the story of humanity. We're about to write a new chapter in it," Rick Smith said. "War, violence is a fact of life. We should continue to try to contain it. We should also try to make it less bad. I think there is an opportunity for us to take this awful concept of killing and tease it apart and make it obsolete."[11]

CHAPTER 13

DON'T LET THE BED BUGS BITE

Andrew Ransom is known for sending his teams on some pretty exotic missions (figure 13.1). "We were hired by Libya to go and deal with bubonic plague. That was a bit of a surprise. We've done some work in Australia with mouse plagues, where we had millions, millions of mice to deal with. We've had monkeys in Singapore. We've had camels we've had to deal with in the Middle East. I mean, you name it, snakes and everything. It's a crazy business in that sense."[1]

That business is helping people and companies get rid of unwanted pests. Ransom is the CEO of Rentokil Initial plc, a global pest control and business services company with headquarters in Crawley, England, that operates in eighty countries, including the United States. It was founded in 1925 by Harold Maxwell-Lefroy, a professor of entomology at Imperial College in London. He had been looking for ways to kill death watch beetles, which feed on the structural timbers of old buildings and had infested Westminster Hall—a medieval space erected in 1097 for William II. Lefroy and his team created something called "Ento-Kill Fluids" to eradicate the wood eating beetle larvae. "Ento" is the Greek word for insects, and Lefroy tried to register the name "Entokill," but because of existing trademarks, he decided instead to call his company Rentokil.[2] And there began a long history of pest control innovation. In 1948, for example, the company invented the "Fetcham Injector" to squirt fluids into timber, marking a significant advancement in pest control technology. A million units had sold by the late 1950s.

"Somebody once described the business to me as almost biblical; you know, the pests have been with us since the beginning of time, and they will be with us till the end of time," Ransom said in an interview with Nicolai Tangen, a Norwegian hedge fund manager.

13.1 Andrew Ransom, CEO of Rentokil Initial plc.
Source: Rentokil Initial

Rentokil got started by helping Westminster Hall with its death watch beetle infestation, but today the company (Ticker symbol: RTO) helps people deal with a host of more common pests such as mosquitos, rodents, roaches, bed bugs, and termites. Bed bugs are micropredators that feed on blood, usually at night, and hide in mattress seams and furniture. They made headlines when they were discovered in hotels around the world, from New York to Paris (right before the 2024 Olympics). Pictures of people with red-brown rashes on their backs popped up all across social media. Mosquitos have transmitted malaria, dengue fever, the Zika virus (which can cause serious birth defects), and the West Nile virus (which led to the death of dozens in the US in 2024) according to the CDC.[3] And termite infestations cause more than $40 billion in damage globally and destroy parts of 600,000 homes in the US each year.[4] Twenty species of termites in the US are classified as structural pests. They feed on wood for the cellulose and are able to break it down into simple sugars for nutrition and survival (figure 13.2). A single colony of Formosan termites can eat one thousand pounds of wood a year—the equivalent of six hundred and fifty baseball bats.[5]

13.2 Formosan termite nymphs.
Source: Rentokil Initial

CLIMATE PESTS

Climate change only adds fuel to the fire. According to the Environmental Protection Agency (EPA), warmer temperatures accelerate mosquito development and the incubation of a disease within its body.[6] It also increases the reproductive cycle of bed bugs.[7] And termites will be able to decompose deadwood—the dead parts of trees that contain carbon—at a much higher rate, which actually adds to the overall problem. As they munch away, the carbon they release into the atmosphere drives a further increase in global temperatures.[8] It's a creepy-crawly doom loop of sorts, where one negative factor begets another. In addition to global warming, there are other accelerants for pest control.

"Rising standards, I mean, I remember when I used to travel to parts of the world years and years ago and I'd go out to dinner and a cockroach would run across the tablecloth, and you'd just flick it to the floor. You wouldn't accept that today in a nice restaurant," said Andrew Ransom. "They don't look so good in social media, and that's a big part of why their companies hire us. Well, they need their health protected, but they need their reputation protected as well and that's a key part of what we're doing, particularly for the businesses."[9]

Urbanization is yet another factor. Rentokil says global population is growing 1.1 percent a year, and 68 percent of the overall population will live in cities by 2050, up from 55 percent in 2021. Alongside that, the global rat population is set to increase to seven billion. In the United States, 29 percent of Americans have experienced a rodent pest issue at some point, and 35 percent have in the northeast. For anyone who has seen the YouTube video of "Pizza Rat" moving a whole slice of pizza down the staircase in a New York subway station, you know there's a problem!

"If you take rats and rodents, for example, they go where the food is, and people go to the cities. The cities are typically not so clean. Restaurants put the trash out the back, they leave it around and rats, in particular, will find those sources of food, they'll find places to live. So, the bigger the cities, the more urban they become, the more likely they're to be an attractive place for rats to come and move into. So that's one of the key reasons that urbanization has an impact, quite a big impact on growth in the pest control industry."[10]

Evolving regulations in Europe and California, for example, combined with Gen Z demands for more sustainable solutions with less harmful chemicals, also benefit large pest control companies that continue to invest in innovation. Rentokil even offers a surveillance service, which uses machine learning to identify pests and live streams video of them to its headquarters for real-time analysis to help teams decide where and how to hunt them down.

"And the technology will always identify which rat has come back, where are they feeding, where are they sleeping, who's causing the damage, which part of the building are they coming from, where are they getting into the building from, whether it's the same rodent that caused the problem last week," said Ransom.[11]

THE HARD NUMBERS

"What the market doesn't understand is that this is a recession resistant business, with pricing power, and long tail growth," says Matt. His favorite quote of Ransom's is that "rats don't read the FT." In other words, this is another business that provides an essential service (that is both B2B and B2C) and grows despite what's going on in the world economically. And here are Matt's three key numbers for understanding the business.

KEY NUMBERS TO UNDERSTAND RTO

5%+	50%+	34%

5%+: Because of all the factors outlined previously—from global warming to urbanization—Matt believes there are strong tailwinds for growth. The global market for pest control is $26 billion, growing to $33 billion by 2028. The US market, which represents half of total pest control services, is growing at 5 percent per year, and the rest of the world is growing at 6 percent. Ransom believes the big cities, particularly in China, India, Brazil, and Columbia, places he calls "cities of the future," are experiencing massive growth and will, in turn, become a massive growth driver for the company. In 1994, Rentokil was hired to treat the soil around the new Petronas Twin Towers in Kuala Lumpur to safeguard what was then the world's tallest building from termites. And in 2017, *Pest* magazine (yes, that is a real publication in the UK for pest professionals!) announced Rentokil's joint venture with PCI of India to create the largest pest control company in the country.[12] In its first half 2024 results presentation, Rentokil says that per capita spending on pest control in the US has grown 24 percent between 2018 and 2023; 35 percent globally, 170 percent in India, and 468 percent in China.

50%+: In 2023, the company generated approximately $6.9 billion in revenue and $1.1 billion in adjusted EBITDA. It converts about 50 percent+ of that adjusted EBITDA into free cash flow, making Matt well up in tears of joy. With all the cash they are accumulating, they can layer on additional growth through acquisitions. Most of them are small. One of them was huge. More on that one later.

34%: Rentokil has a ton of rather small Mom and Pop types of competitors. The only large competition it has is Rollins, which you may know through its popular customer-facing sub brand, Orkin. Together, Rentokil and Rollins, Matt says, have 26.3 percent market share in the US. The next four players are either smaller national or regional players and have 7.6 percent of the market. All combined, the top seven players have 34 percent of the market share. The rest are small or Mom and Pop types of pest control companies, the ones we call because they are right in our neighborhoods. As Matt likes to say about this business, "there is no barrier to entry, but there is a barrier to scale." And many of these companies are ripe targets for a scale player such as Rentokil and all the cash it's constantly accumulating. It's done 284 deals since 2018, representing almost $1.2 billion of acquired revenue. In the first half of 2024, Ransom, a former M&A lawyer, and his team did sixteen deals in pest control (including a wildlife exclusion company called Xceptional that operates in the Midwest and Southeast that tackles everything from unwanted armadillos to bobcats) and has a strong M&A pipeline in place. But what surprised me was that the company also bought seven hygiene and wellness companies (figure 13.3). As my niece who is not allowed to curse yet says, "What the . . .?"

Matt comes to the rescue with an explanation. In addition to commercial pest control, the company has diversified into other business services, including Initial, which provides washroom services to companies and helps them make the workplace more hygienic (and that was before COVID!). It also owns Ambius, which helps companies with air purification, plant design, and green walls, as well as ambient scenting, corporate artwork, and holiday decor. Although pest control,

13.3 A technician and a Rentokil truck.
Source: Rentokil Initial

hygiene, and plant services appear to have nothing in common, Matt explained that they are all route-based businesses. People go out to provide their service in trucks and follow a route from client to client each day. The more Mom and Pop businesses each of these verticals buy in a geographically contiguous manner, the more clients they can serve along the same routes, and the more productive the employees servicing them are. No time wasted on daily schedules; maximum revenue per employee and per van; shared back-office services that lower costs; a shared brand that requires less marketing spend; and increased profit margins. Matt says the company calls it "densification," and he points to a graph that shows its impact on each branch's profitability within a local market (see figure 13.4). Once Rentokil gets over 20 percent market share in a particular area, each branch improves its own profit margins to 25 percent. That then creates more cash flow for the company to go out and buy more businesses. And they are running the same playbook across all the different business services they provide.

Impact of density on branch profitability

- Our model
- 5 year track record

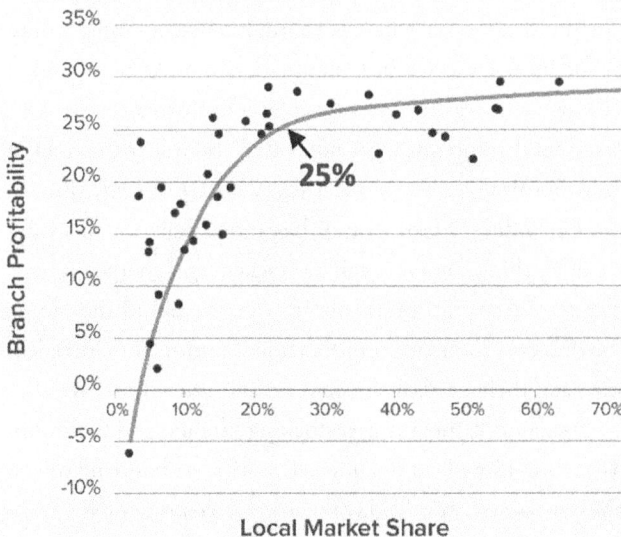

13.4 More density of branches drives local profitability.

Source: Rentokil Initial

"Rentokil is an acquisition machine with capital to compound," said Matt, adding: "It's designed to drive density and improve margins, leading to even more capital that can be used to compound value." Hygiene, by itself, is a $55 billion market, growing 4 to 5 percent a year, and Rentokil is just getting started with 2 percent market share. "The markets Rentokil operates in are massive and enjoy solid growth," said Matt.

Andrew Ransom took over the company in 2013, and earnings per share (EPS) grew in every year with a CAGR of >12 percent, according to InsiderMonkey. com. "He is still running the same playbook today, growing revenue 9 to 10 percent (equally split between organic and bolt-on acquisitions) coupled with margin expansion." "Margins are guided to reach >19 percent by 2026 (vs. 16.7 percent today)," it added.[13]

A POINT OF COMPARISON

Mark Twain is often credited with the aphorism, "History never repeats itself, but it does often rhyme." In this case, Rentokil "rhymes" with Cintas. You will remember that Cintas was one of the previous 100-baggers identified in Matt's research. It's a B2B company with a rags to riches story, literally. The company was started in the depression when Richard Farmer, a circus worker, started cleaning rags for local factories in Cincinnati, Ohio. As it expanded, it asked itself what else it could wash? The answer was uniforms. Today it's America's largest uniform rental company, from hotel and hospitality clothing to mechanics overalls and hospital scrubs to even the white, full body, lint free outfits employees at semiconductor fabs wear. It has 21,000 delivery vans, puts barcodes on every piece of clothing so that it can be tracked, and charges as little as $2 per day per employee. Companies prefer the service instead of the more expensive alternative, buying and then cleaning their own uniforms. Cintas learned a lot about its clients and their needs over the years and started to diversify into other essential business services, including restocking kitchen and bathroom supplies, cleaning carpets, providing first aid and safety kits, and making sure fire alarms and sprinklers were up to code. Today the average customer has been with them for twenty-five years; and it pays off, as the company generates $10 billion in revenue and $2.2 billion in operating profits.

"It earns 50 cents of annual profit for every dollar of capital it invests in its operations. That's a very good return," said Delian Entchev, a portfolio manager at Aoris Investment Management, in an interview with *Business Breakdowns*. "But it's five times the return than its largest peers earn, let alone the small mom and pops that it also competes with day to day. And that's because it earns a much higher operating profit margin than its peers, about three times the margin. And it turns over its assets faster because it has a denser route network."[14]

Since going public, Cintas stock is up over 60,000 percent, making it a 600-bagger! Matt believes Rentokil, adopting a similar playbook, is a candidate to be a future 100-bagger too. "Rentokil offers essential service out in the open, executes well, and creates tremendous scale economies from a route-based business."

NOT SO EASY?

Rentokil certainly has large ambitions. Like a lion preying on an elephant, Rentokil made its biggest move when it completed its acquisition of Terminix at the end of 2022 for $6.7 billion. It's a company with 375 locations across forty-seven states, 2.9 million customers, and fifty thousand customer visits per day. Rentokil has been especially strong with commercial clients, but Terminix is a leader in residential pest control (especially with termites). Matt said it helps "Rentokil substantially increase its scale in North America, providing an enlarged platform for profitable growth with game changing density. But it also created challenges."

Just about every company that makes a big acquisition goes through integration challenges. Rentokil has a three-year plan to realize $150 to $200 million in cost synergies—colocating Rentokil and Terminix branch offices, cobranding marketing efforts, reducing duplicative back-office functions, deciding what the new management structure looks like, deciding who stays and, unfortunately, who goes, etc. It's a laundry list of cost savings activities investors applaud, and Rentokil was on track with its plan. But along the way, over several quarters, Rentokil adjusted downward the organic revenue growth of Terminix because the cost of acquiring new customer leads via ads on digital channels such as Google was much higher than expected. The company said it would launch a new brand campaign called "Terminix It" (figure 13.5), shift some of its marketing spend to door-to-door

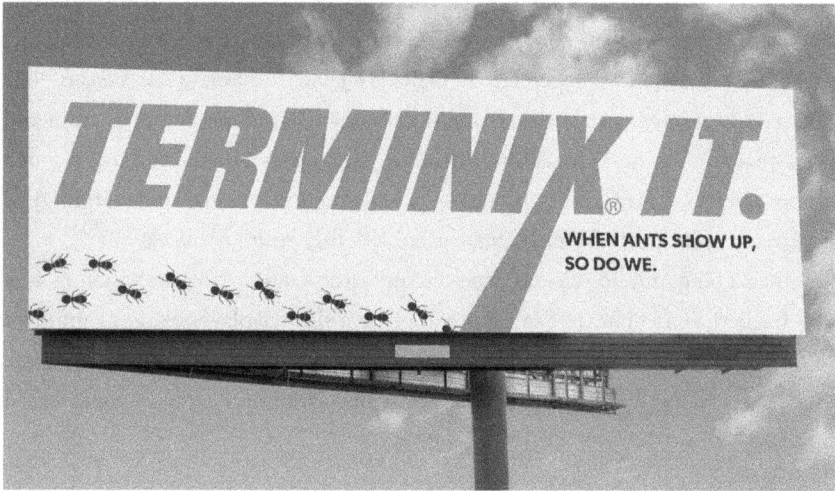

13.5 A Terminix billboard.
Source: Rentokil Initial

campaigns in local communities to improve the quality of its leads, restructure its digital marketing team, improve SEO (search engine optimization tactics to drive organic, unpaid search results), improve retention by adding forty colleagues to the Customer Saves team for at-risk clients, create an innovation center to develop solutions to address customers future needs, and so much more. Suffice it to say, Wall Street punished the stock to the point where Rentokil was trading on a PE multiple that was less than half that of its main competitor, Rollins.

"Matt, there's trouble in the jungle!" I said during one of our routine calls. "I thought this company was going to be a smooth ride. What's happening with Rentokil's stock?"

Matt responded by saying:

The funny thing about Wall Street investors is that they think management knows everything and can just hit a switch to make it better. However, it is much more nuanced than that. Even though I believe Rentokil has accurately identified its problems and is taking the necessary steps to address them, it takes longer to see the results. For example, improving your leads and shifting them from purely digital to door-to-door is a lot more time-consuming and complex. You must hire the right people (it takes time running an ad, interviewing, training, etc.). Then you have to create the funnel of leads from which you eventually build the sales. Again, not difficult, but not simply hitting a switch either. Given my time horizon, I am not concerned. I believe this is a temporary problem, not a structural issue. Rentokil's management team didn't simply become buffoons after leading a well-run company. They didn't become stupid overnight; they've been running pest control for one hundred years. However, the market gives you opportunities to make more money because its time frame is different than mine. This is definitely one of my greatest advantages relative to my peers!

And Matt took full advantage. While the market was saying "sell, sell, sell," he was thinking "Buy, buy, buy!" He felt the market had overcorrected.

"Rentokil closed on the Terminix acquisition in Oct 2022. Just prior to the acquisition, Rentokil had a total enterprise value of $13.1 billion. The acquisition cost was $6.7 billion, implying a total valuation of $19.8 billion post the close of the acquisition," said Matt. "Today, after the stock drop, Rentokil has an enterprise value of $15.6 billion. Thus the value the market is applying to Terminix is less than $2.5 billion, which is inconceivable. Markets can be brutal in their assessment of missteps."

He added, "This is not rocket science. I strongly believe management will get the ship righted, but it is taking longer than the company imagined." The bottom line for Matt was twofold. "First, historically, he said the company has had a ROTA of 27 percent for the last twenty years; management is clearly experienced in value creation. Second, Rentokil issued $2.2 billion of net debt to buy Terminix and is not only de-levering quickly, it is also *not* slowing down the pace of its smaller bolt-on acquisition activity. Third, moving forward, the pest business is only going to get bigger. Pests are profitable, and Rentokil is operating a compounding machine in a resilient industry."

RBC Europe analysts, who also took the long view, told the *Wall Street Journal*: "We continue to believe in the fundamental strength of the North America business. The substantial structural growth opportunities, enhanced by the benefits of the Terminix transaction, means the value creation opportunity remains intact, albeit taking longer to realize than anticipated."[15]

So, over several quarters, in two tranches, Matt bought Rentokil stock for the coffee can. He is long-term confident! Not just in Rentokil, but in the industry itself.

In fact, he had a longer-term plan . . . and was even contemplating what can only be called a side hustle.

PLANS WITHIN PLANS

Once Rentokil fully digests Terminix and returns to its normal growth rates and operating margins, he predicted two things would happen. First, "if a year from now Terminix is growing not at 2 to 3 percent but 4 to 6 percent, they get improving operating profit and a re-rating on their valuation. You get the double upside." He added, "As an investor, your value add is not to own it after everything is proven, your value add is to know where it is going."

Second, Matt believed Rentokil's capable competitor, Rollins—trading at twice the PE multiple—would normalize too. He felt some of the air in Rollins valuation would come out of the balloon if investors regained confidence in Rentokil. And when that happened, he would likely buy Rollins as well. Wait, he would want to own the two largest public players in pest control?

"I owned Visa and Mastercard at the same time. I owned S&P and Moody's at the same time. The hard part is picking the right industry. This time, I am long-term bullish on the pest control industry, the route-based industry, and the ability to improve economics through densification. I will buy Rollins once Rentokil starts to fix things. Remember, there are eighteen thousand pest companies just in the US, and there is a long tail of acquisitions for both of these companies," commented Matt.

And possibly others. Matt likes to chew on ideas as part of the intellectual investigation otherwise known as investing. Charlie Munger liked to talk about how big insights only come once in a lifetime: "Take a simple idea and take it seriously." He is also often quoted saying, "Good ideas are rare. When you find one bet heavily." David Senra, who studies founders and considers himself a walking, talking business encyclopedia, said his favorite tweet of all time came from Cedric Chen, the author of the Commoncog blog that routinely talks about "earned secrets."[16] Chen believes that when you find an "earned secret," you exploit the hell out of it for a good part of two to three decades. Senra said Chen was referring to Constellation Software and the power of vertical SaaS businesses. Senra also said it could easily be applied to the "shared scale economies" that Nicholas Sleep focused on with his concentrated holdings of Costco and Amazon. To me, it may also apply to Matt and his thesis on densification in a resilient industry.

AT THE TABLE

After Labor Day weekend, I asked Matt, "How was your weekend? Did you do anything fun during the last glorious weekend of summer?" I could tell from his face that his brain had been actively working on all sides of a mental Rubik's cube. He told me, as part of his due diligence of the pest control industry, he had spent the weekend browsing opportunities on bizbuysell.com. It's an online marketplace for small business owners to buy and sell local businesses. He said he was looking for privately owned pest control businesses for sale in Kansas City. Given how many Mom and Pop businesses there are, he said he could start to buy up contiguous businesses in his local area, increase local market share, and then apply Rentokil's densification strategy and slowly raise overall margins up to 25 percent. They would then throw off cash for him to buy more local businesses. At a certain scale, he could even sell the group to Rentokil or Rollins for a higher multiple. He was dead serious. But he needed to find the right first business to buy, an anchor tenant, if you will, with strong management that could then operate the roll up. Matt certainly didn't have the time to go house to house killing bed bugs. He did identify some pest control companies to buy, but as the long weekend ended, he concluded that in order to get to 20 percent+ market share it would take a ton of time and capital. And he needed both to find and buy more stocks to put into his daughters' coffee can. That—more so than anything—would let him sleep peacefully at night. Plus, I could only imagine the faces on his three daughters when they learned their father left them a pest control empire to run!

Instead, the girls were happy he was investing in, not operating, a company that could do it for them.

PIERCE: Pests are not going away, not in the US, not globally. As people move up in socioeconomic status, they want to get rid of pests, no matter where they live. It is such a global opportunity.

PEYTON: Rentokil was a surprising stock pick to me at first glance. In many ways I never considered the potential growth a pest control company could have. After all, how many different ways could one reinvent terminating insects. I was dead wrong (no pun intended). As climate changes continue to increase our pest related problems, Rentokil will be of even greater need.

MORGAN: This is a rapidly growing business with an urgency like never before. With global warming, bugs are not dying off in the winter like they used to, and this poses a huge threat to human health.

Morgan, who has a growing interest in health and well-being products and companies, also liked its diversification.

MORGAN: I had no idea that 16 percent of Rentokil business comes from hygiene and well-being. I think it's smart for a company to diversify and expand its business into different realms in the same field.

As for Andrew Ransom and his team at Rentokil, who celebrated the company's one hundredth anniversary in 2025, they continue to digest their Terminix acquisition and seem to be heeding the advice of Desmond Tutu, who is credited with saying that "there is only one way to eat an elephant—one bite at a time."

Ransom, who will be retiring in 2026, concluded his conversation with Nicolai Tangen by saying:

One bit of advice that I give when I talk internally to my colleagues here. I would say when the shit hits the fan, you've got a choice. You can either take a step back, avoid it, or you can take a step forward and move toward it. And what I mean by that is throughout our lives, throughout our careers, in particular throughout our jobs, there'll be many times where there's a situation that looks a bit messy, that looks a bit complex, that looks a bit scary. And my advice is when you see those, grasp them, go toward them, take that opportunity.[17]

CHAPTER 14

DAD'S NOT PERFECT

I'm a tennis player . . . at least on weekends. I enjoy the game, especially doubles. I like to play with partners who can cover the deep lobs to the empty corner of the back court, while I use my height and wingspan to aggressively poach balls at the net. Teamwork makes the dream work! I also religiously follow the pros during major opens. Over the years, I've enjoyed watching the fiery passion of John McEnroe and the sheer dominance of Serena Williams. But there has always been something truly special about the effortless play of Roger Federer. For years I tried to mimic his one-handed backhand that he could use to shoot the ball either down the line or cross court (keeping opponents guessing), but I could never master it. Instead, I opted for a backhand slice return, which also easily disguises my drop shots. I also admired Roger's grace on the court and, of course, his incredible record: winning twenty major men's singles titles and ranked world number one for 310 weeks. The only words to describe his career would be "pure perfection." Or was it?

Here's what the newly minted "Dr. Roger" said in a commencement speech to Dartmouth students in the summer of 2024 after getting an honorary doctorate from the university:

> Perfection is impossible. In the 1,526 singles matches I played in my career, I won almost 80 percent of those matches. Now, I have a question for you, what percentage of points did I win in those matches?
>
> Only 54 percent.
>
> In other words, even top ranked tennis players win barely more than half the points they play.
>
> When you lose every second point on average, you learn not to dwell on every shot.

You teach yourself to think: "Okay, I double faulted . . . it's only a point." "Okay, I came to the net and I got passed again . . . it's only a point." Even a great shot, an overhead backhand smash that ends up on ESPN's top 10 playlist—that, too, is just a point.

So, here's why I'm telling you this. When you're playing a point, it has to be the most important thing in the world. And it is.

But when it's behind you, it's behind you.

This mindset is crucial—because it frees you to fully commit to the next point and the next point after that with intensity, clarity, and focus.[1]

I never quite heard the accumulative metrics of winning and losing individual points in tennis over a career. The margin of victory over the long term is, well, tiny. And somehow winning only 54 percent of your points can lead to tennis immortality. It also means Roger made a lot of mistakes but was able to push past it. It certainly gives me hope for this year's annual doubles tournament!

Roger's insights into the math of winning and losing also made me think about Matt. How does the investment world think about and embrace losses, or mistakes? The first example Matt cited was similar to Roger's track record.

"Citadel, one of the most successful hedge funds in the world, had a hit rate of 52 percent. Yes, 52 percent—the analysts were right only slightly better than half the time—a coin flip," Matt said. "However, their winners were up on average about 20 percent and their losers were down about 12 percent. With leverage, Citadel has been able to consistently deliver 14 percent–15 percent annualized returns for the past 20+ years."

I asked Matt to zoom in . . . on his own career. He didn't have the scale of Citadel, nor a strategy to make up for losing almost half the time. I was curious: What were his major mistakes? Every investor clearly makes them . . . even the greats. I wasn't asking him to commit hara-kiri, but instead to be frank and honest about his mistakes so we can all benefit from the painful lessons he learned over decades as a fallible investor. And in typical Matt fashion, he let it all pour out.

MOVING ON FROM MISTAKES

"I have made a tremendous number of mistakes in my professional investing life and my personal life. However, I do not have any regrets," Matt said.

"For every decision I made, I made it with the best available information I had. I would have preferred that a lot of decisions turned out differently. Outside of the relationships you have with your family—your spouse, siblings, children, parents—an individual's relationship with their money is probably their most important. It feels very personal, because it affects your personal situation, not simply your socioeconomic status, but also your ego. When it comes to investing, mistakes should not only be tolerated but should be an accepted part of the process. It is painful, but it is how you learn."

It's not just lip service. Matt actually writes down all his mistakes. He does what the Marines call "after-action reports," so he never forgets them, let alone repeats them.

"For me, every mistake is agonizingly analyzed and cataloged in my mind to not repeat. It doesn't always work this way, but the greatest investors are the ones who don't make the same mistakes again. It is being intellectually honest with yourself, a very hard thing for most of us, knowing what you don't know, your circle of competency, and expanding your knowledge by reading and engaging as much as possible."

It's a sentiment that he adopted from Charlie Munger, who famously avoided tech stocks and once said, "The single most important thing, if you want to avoid a lot of stupid errors, is knowing where you're competent and where you aren't. Knowing the edge of your own competency. And that's very hard to do because the human mind naturally tries to make you think you're way smarter than you are."[2]

Matt believes his mistakes have formed him into the investor he is today. He doesn't pretend to be an expert on every subject, but he clearly rolls up his sleeves to investigate each area he is contemplating for an investment. Just think about all the stocks in the coffee can. Each one takes you into a completely different field. But what makes these investments something he is expert in is that they were all selected because they share common quantitative and qualitative traits with the previous 100-baggers that he has diligently researched. That is the basis of Matt's wisdom: a combination of dogged research of historically and current outstanding quality stocks, an unwillingness to compromise on companies that don't show a true capacity to finish the long-term race of doubling every five years, and, of course, making sure he is learning from his mistakes and building pattern recognition from a lifetime of investing. All of it compounds his knowledge base like the many companies slowly and methodically growing in his portfolio.

I'm going to start his walk down "mistake memory lane," however, with an investment he made outside of public stocks—because many of us, usually on walks with our dogs in our neighborhood, have considered doing the very same thing he did: buying a small real estate property . . . and becoming a landlord.

Time Is Money

Purchase of His First Rental Property

Mistake: Matt bought a single-family home near the University of Denver campus to rent to college students. It sounded like a no-brainer given half the students live off campus. He prepped the house for student living (low-maintenance exterior, added a bedroom, other small improvements) and asked his wife, Maury, to be the property manager. It turned out to be a lot more difficult and less profitable than they had anticipated.

Learning: Two things really stood out to Matt: (1) one-off properties are very difficult—they don't provide any scale advantages, and dealing with young renters is quite challenging and time consuming. The return on investment is quite low, and you must consider all costs, including personal time; and (2) "don't make your wife have to deal with all the BS—it never ends well."

What Happened: Matt sold the property about one year later at break-even (almost to the penny). Although it was a poor use of their money and time, it resulted in one of the most important lessons that enabled Matt to make one of his best nonstock investments.

How It Changed His Approach: This investment caused Matt to rethink the value of time invested (both his and his wife's, in this case) plus the powerful advantages of scale. For multifamily apartments, the larger properties (100+ units) can typically generate 50 percent to 70 percent operating margins (versus smaller, one-off properties that are highly variable and typically have less than 20 percent margins). These larger properties allow for on-site management, maintenance workers, and advertising budgets (to fund the operating aspects of the business). Plus, if a tenant moves out, it is a small percentage of the total revenue in any given month or quarter. "If a tenant leaves a single family or even a duplex, as the landlord you can lose 50 percent to 100 percent of revenue in that given month, quarter, or longer . . . and your costs don't go away. That can be devastating to the finances of the business." His approach is now to seek businesses that have already demonstrated scale advantages with a very direct route to making money without stripping him of his most important asset—time. In 2013, Matt bought 50 percent of an apartment building with 210 units in Colorado Springs. He bought three more, each with at least one hundred units, in the same area as well as Albuquerque, New Mexico. Not only did he get scale in a multiunit apartment, but he also got multi-multi's in the same cities, allowing him to leverage his operating team across more buildings in the same areas. Or, as Matt likes to say, "Hyper local means hyper scale." With property values up and distributions from the rent he and his partners are collecting, Matt has already made 3.5x on his initial investment . . . and is still collecting cash.

On weekends, he and Maury have started visiting Kansas City multifamily units. Pierce, who just took her SATs and knows she doesn't want to study medicine or computers but hasn't ruled out a career in business, also tags along. She peppers Matt with questions about the ideal neighborhoods and the ideal buildings. Matt is more than happy to pass on his learning. Time will tell if Pierce, who is starting to become interested in the art of marketing, wants to help her Dad increase occupancy and eventually become the real estate Queen of Missouri.

Easy Come, Easy Go

Exodus Communications, PSINet, MacLeod Communications, NextLink, Metromedia Fiber, Qwest Communications, Level(3), and Others

Mistake: In 1997, early in his career at Janus, Matt covered companies building out the internet's infrastructure; these included web-hosting firms, internet service providers, competitive local exchange carriers (CLECs), and others. These were capital-intensive businesses as they were laying fiber, switches, and the fiber optic equipment necessary to enable the explosion of data traffic on the internet. (Cisco, one of the companies that achieved 100-bagger status, and had a different business model, sold routers to many of these companies.) Initially, Matt made his fundholders a lot of money (Exodus was up twentyfold in eighteen months), but he held on too long, and many of these players eventually went bankrupt.

Learning: The short version, according to Matt, is that none of these businesses had proven business models. There were too many overleveraged players chasing an unproven market. Today Matt says that "solvency or staying alive" is more important than generating the highest returns.

What Happened: Each of these investments were up anywhere between five and twentyfold in eighteen to twenty-four months from his initial purchase price. As money kept coming into the funds, the funds kept buying more of each of these stocks. They were very capital-intensive businesses and thus required a lot of debt and equity to keep growing. As these were new players in an emerging, high-growth industry, the companies did not generate anywhere near the cash flow to support the debt, let alone deliver a risk-adjusted return to the equity; however, these investments were like "call options on the future of the internet—if you won, you won huge and investors didn't want to miss the opportunity." Since each of these players was betting on the same steep customer growth curves, Matt said, they were all susceptible to the same risks. In other words, "if/when one fell, they all would fall." Eventually the market rolled over and supply far outstripped demand, leading to bankruptcy and forced consolidation for many of these firms. "Even the best-intentioned managers cannot overcome the crippling effects of debt when a slowdown occurs."

The same can be said for investors like Matt. "I made a fair amount of money at first; I consolidated down to just the winners. We sold Qwest but kept Level(3). We lost money on PSINet, but got out before it fell apart. We held onto McLeod in Iowa versus NextLink, which had competition in big cities. But they both went down. Net-net, we lost money . . . but, thankfully, it was a tiny percentage of the hundreds of billions being managed at Janus."

How It Changed His Approach: Everything is 20/20 in hindsight, but this experience forced several powerful fundamental changes to his investment approach: (1) He won't invest in highly capital-intensive businesses, no matter the growth opportunity; (2) He won't invest in businesses that have not proven out a sustainable, high-return business model. He "only invests in high-quality companies with high returns on capital, strong balance sheets, and businesses that throw off predictable free cash flow;" (3) He avoids any company that has a highly leveraged balance sheet (and, if any of his companies has any debt, he tracks bond prices very closely); and (4) He "seeks boring over exciting—this sector was so hot, it was in the news every day."

Locking in a Profit and Selling a Phenomenal Company

Mettler-Toledo/Fastenal/Progressive/Moody's

Mistake: Each of these world-class companies were in funds Matt helped manage, but the team sold each of them for some trivial reason (in hindsight). And worse yet, they never bought back in as the stocks continued their relentless climb higher.

Learning: "When you discover these one-of-a-kind value compounders, buy and hold on as long as you can," Matt says. "Try to see through one-off issues (like earnings misses, for example), and bet on the long-term future (not short-term trading mentality). Investors, Matt says, forget that management teams can adapt and address issues if their competitive advantage still exists. "Incumbents with great management teams have the time and ability to respond, and they have tremendous advantages that they can utilize, including size, resources, and customers to bounce back."

What Happened: They sold these companies and never repurchased the shares, missing out on multi-multi bagger performance. In the first example, Mettler Toledo, a B2B company that makes precision instruments such as scales, Matt met with management on the IPO and bought the shares but sold them after a 30 percent gain because his team felt the valuation was a bit high for a "niche scale company." Mettler Toledo went on to become a 100-bagger, and they missed out on all the real upside. Another example, as discussed earlier in the book, was Fastenal, of which they owned nearly 8 percent of the total company in 1998. They loved the management, felt there were tremendous barriers to entry, and that the company could continue to grow for decades. But in April 1998, after Matt did his routine due diligence checks, he believed Fastenal would miss its numbers and others believed Amazon would get into the industrial business. They sold the stock. In the short run, they were justified: the stock went down 55 percent. However, Amazon never entered the business. And based on the price they sold it at, Fastenal has gone up nineteen fold since versus the S&P500 (up 4.3-fold), outpacing the index (including dividends) by approximately 500 basis points per year for twenty-six years. "That is a lot of Alpha we left on the table," said Matt. "That one investment likely would have placed our fund in the top quartile for the thirty-year period." Progressive Insurance was another one that got away. Matt owned the stock and had done very well with the investment. Then, when electric cars came out with cameras, algorithms, and advanced safety features, he was shaken out of his position. The stock subsequently has gone up nearly eightfold since his sale eight years ago. And he never bought back in. Same for Moody's, the bond rating agency. In 2008, during the financial crisis, ratings agencies were accused of misrepresenting the risks associated with mortgage-related securities and their stocks went down. "I sold, and then the thing was a huge homerun," said Matt: "there was nothing wrong with their business, and I missed their climb back up."

How It Changed His Approach: The most meaningful change to his approach is that Matt now more deeply understands the power of compounding and how few truly great companies there are. And that's why, for Matt, valuation is less of a consideration for high-quality, growth companies that are enduring and well managed. "When I find one, I learned to buy and hold on as long as I determine the company maintains its competitive advantages and has real growth opportunity with the right management team. I have a very high hurdle to invest in a company, but today I have an even higher one to sell," Matt said. "These are the mistakes that hurt the most—we were right, but then we chose action over inaction. We let the fear of a market drop shake us out of a great investment. It was a short-term mentality. We didn't act like owners of a business; we acted like renters of pieces of paper. Worse, we never bought back in even though we knew it was an amazing company." In the end, Matt believes a fear of the future always needs to be considered and vetted, but fear itself is never a reason to make snap decisions. Thoughtful consideration and research are a much more powerful response.

The Lesson of Historical/Backward-Looking Bias

ABInBev, Liberty Global, Dentsply

Mistake: Matt invested in several names that historically were market leaders, dominant players in their industry, that had fallen on hard times. His investment thesis was predicated on these companies returning to their previous glory.

Learning: "The sad truth is historical competitive advantages can dissolve—often slowly and in unnoticed ways," Matt said. And it usually is a result of change from new entrants or through new innovations that forces a market to compete differently. Matt believes its critical to constantly reevaluate your original assumptions and thesis.

What Happened: The best example Matt points to is Anheuser-Busch InBev, which had powerful distribution into retail stores through a network of wholly owned and independent distributors in America (a clearly dominant position). Its returns were exceptional, and it delivered excellent efficiency (measured in revenue per hectoliter), particularly relative to its competitors, which allowed it to invest more into its distributors, driving its advantage even higher. "Unfortunately, as InBev kept acquiring companies around the globe, it lost focus in the US," said Matt. "The company experienced high management turnover, and its brand managers pulled away from its core customer. In addition, new competition from artisan craft brewers and a shift to higher priced alternatives such as flavored hard seltzers changed the overall marketplace dynamic."

The stock was approximately $125. Matt bought the beer company at $71.83 and sold it at $71.01. "It had fallen due to concerns about debt/lower returns. ABInBev was an aggressive acquirer, and there was some fear about the ability to recover some market share losses to Truly and other hard seltzer companies as well as artisan beer. I felt that the Truly-craze would pass, and its strong competitive position would allow the company to return to its prior glory and higher multiple. I was wrong but got out of it with minor losses."

Eventually, Bud Light lost its top spot to the Mexican beer Modelo, and the stock has dramatically underperformed on the S&P500 since he sold it.

How It Shaped His Philosophy: It's simple, Matt says never get comfortable. He reminds himself to be open-minded and flexible to all ideas or incremental information. And he learned to recognize that size and success can drive complacency.

The Lesson of the Risk of Regulatory Capture

ITT Education, Strayer Education, Corinthian Colleges, Career Education and DeVry Institute (for-profit education companies), as well as Sallie Mae, Fannie Mae, and Freddie Mac (government sanctioned financing companies)

Mistake: During his career, Matt was an active investor in the for-profit education sector (and Sallie Mae and government sponsored enterprises [GSEs]). On the surface, these businesses fit all the "quality" criteria Matt seeks—very high returns on capital, high free cash flow, negative working capital (that generates more free cash flow with growth), pricing power, etc. However, the primary competitive advantage was driven by regulation (access to Stafford loans, specifically) or implicit government guarantees (for the GSEs and Sallie Mae). Thus the companies were "captive" to the generosity of the government. When the Obama administration came in and chose to remove this advantage, this easy access to loans, the entire value of the companies collapsed. He believed these for-profit schools were saddling students with debt and not landing them the jobs they were hoping for. Republican administrations, such as George W. Bush before him and Donald Trump after him, had much more lax restrictions on the multi-billion-dollar for-profit school industry. Republicans, citing the few numbers of students who can get into exclusive Ivy League schools, believed these for-profit schools give students the opportunity to succeed, not the guarantee that they will succeed. When Biden's

Secretary of Education came in, he introduced new regulations to hold these schools accountable for student outcomes. Back and forth like an old-fashioned tug-of-war, Democrats tried to protect students and Republicans tried to ensure open access, and investors like Matt got caught in the crossfire.

Learning: "What is given, can be taken away even if there is little basis for the change," said Matt. "Politics/Government can be a dangerous and highly unpredictable partner."

What Happened: The example Matt cites is ITT Education (Ticker symbol: ESI)—a company that closed its doors after a government crack down. As an investor, he felt there was some cognitive dissonance in this action—the government and the Department of Education claimed ITT was providing no value to its students, but the largest employers of ITT students were the FBI and CIA.

How It Changed His Approach: This forced Matt to better understand the basis for a company's competitive advantage and to avoid companies benefiting solely from regulation. It's similar to having too much customer concentration. When that customer leaves, there's a big revenue hole management has to fill. "I learned to avoid politically charged names, companies that benefit from a given party in power, because eventually that will change," said Matt.

The Lesson of Dogmatic Thinking and Market Timing

Mistake: At various points in his career (2000 and 2008/2009), Matt developed a strong conviction on the market decline. He can't forget the time "someone who looked like they just came off the beach like a surfer dude came into pitch a dot com and couldn't even explain his business model." Another time, he was working on Fannie and Freddie during 2008 and remembers "the craziness going on." Each time, Matt saw the frothiness early. He turned out to be right in both cases, but that was probably more luck than anything. He acted on his research and overall thesis and moved a relatively large percent of his portfolio into cash. He looked like a genius for the first six to twelve months as the market declined. However, he didn't buy back again at the bottom(s) and missed a lot of upside he should have enjoyed.

Learning: Matt says bull markets grind higher for long periods of time as stocks typically follow earnings and cash flow and most well-run companies deliver growth (at various levels) more times than not. Bear markets, however, he says, drop hard and fast, driven by overstretched expectations, slowing growth, higher rates, an outside shock, or some combination of these. "The risk of missing out on the market are much greater than the savings you can make by trying to time the market."

How It Changed His Approach: "Don't waste energy trying to time the market. Build a portfolio of exceptional companies, one company at a time, without regard for the overall market," said Matt. "Always remember that the returns of the business will determine the returns of the stock over time; the market has no impact on this rule."

Dad's Not Perfect: The Lesson of Existential Threats

Alibaba (BABA) Perhaps the most personal mistake Matt made was an investment that involved his daughters. As we know, Matt shares his investment ideas with his girls and leaves it up to them if they want to invest as well with the $10,000 he and his wife gave each of them. In late October of 2022, he wrote an email to all of them with the Subject Line: "Alibaba—I am selling my position." The email started the following way:

> Girls, I am selling my Alibaba (Ticker symbol: BABA). The stock is down dramatically from where we purchased it. Although the market is down about 19 percent YTD, BABA is down 47 percent.
>
> There are three reasons you should sell a stock:
>
> 1. you have better opportunities to invest your money (i.e., you found a better stock);
> 2. the valuation has risen so high that you can't justify owning it from here (i.e., the future returns to the stock are low); or
> 3. you made a mistake in your evaluation.
>
> For BABA, I made a mistake in my assessment of the stock.

Matt then went into a long explanation. He said he had tracked Alibaba for years because it was the "Amazon of China," and it was a bigger market than the US and spilled out into the Asian region. The stock was always too expensive for Matt, but when the stock declined from $300 to around $150, he became more intrigued. Then, when he learned Charlie Munger (Warren Buffett's right-hand man) took a large position in the stock, he did his normal analysis and thought the stock was cheap enough to own. What he missed was the risk of the Chinese government and its impact on Alibaba and every other successful Chinese company. Specifically, China has grown into one of the world's great superpowers over the past 30+ years by unleashing its people's entrepreneurial drive. He explained that "some have thought China was more capitalistic than the US during this time (as the US began implementing many more regulations, more taxes, and more bureaucracy)." However, the Chinese Communist Party (CCP) decided it did not take kindly to the power these successful entrepreneurs (many of them now billionaires) enjoyed. The CCP started taking steps to rein in their power. First, it levied huge fines on the companies. Then it started arresting or detaining the entrepreneurs. Recently, it even went so far as to effectively undermine the IPO of Didi, a ride sharing company that didn't seek government approval to list in the US. Didi had to eventually de-list. "In fact, this weekend, Xi Jinping, paramount leader of China, consolidated his power and dispatched any non-loyalists. Because of this, there is real risk to any investor who owns Chinese companies that Xi could destroy all to demonstrate his power and drive other's loyalty to the CCP." Matt explained to his daughters that this was a "real existential risk."

Existential risks are the ones that worry Matt the most. He can't see them coming. He told me that to this very day, while he works on his stock picks, he usually wakes up in the middle of the night, at least once a quarter, in cold sweats. It's because his brain is processing existential threats. What can't he see? Who else can he converse with to solidify or debunk his thoughts about potential existential risks? Is artificial intelligence a threat or an accelerator for the business he is studying? What other financial figures can he look at to reveal a risk he's not thinking about? On his nightstand, he keeps a pad and pen that lights up when he pulls it out of its sleeve to write down his thoughts, additional questions, or areas to investigate. Maury usually urges him back to bed.

But he was cool and calm about it when he ended his email to his daughters. And not surprisingly, he listed out all the learnings from his investment mistake so that his girls would fully absorb them:

1. Not all countries have the same laws/mindset as the US—when you invest in other countries, you are taking risk that may not be evident at the time of the investment. You thus should require a higher rate of return for taking on this increased risk.
2. Even smart investors (like Charlie Munger) make mistakes.

3. Size investments appropriately—even though this one stings, it is not a big hit to our overall portfolio.

4. Always keep learning—you are early in your investing, learn from these mistakes so that you don't repeat them. The greatest investors became great more by not repeating mistakes than they did by finding the next home run.

5. Don't hold onto losers hoping they come back; rather, reevaluate the stock and if the company does not justify investment at the new price, accept your losses and move on. You will be far better served to focus your energy and money on an investment you are confident in than hoping one you are not bounces back.

6. When the facts change, reassess the situation and change your opinion if appropriate.

    Please let me know if you would like me to sell your position. I am not sure my timing is correct; in fact, the stock could rally strongly from here as the fear subsides. However, for me, I am not betting on hope and am licking my wounds and moving on.Your always learning analyst,Dad

Matt lost about $40,000 on his Alibaba investment. Maury and the girls, who lost about $200 each, reacted with short, consoling replies: "That makes sense, Dad," and "We're sorry the investment didn't work out after all the work you put into it."

The email was as much a teaching moment for his girls as it was a mental postmortem for himself. In fact, after selling Alibaba (which hovered just below $100 per share for much of 2023 and 2024), Matt declared to himself that, if he was going to start managing the family's assets full time, "he needed to get serious, really serious," and would redouble his efforts to get even smarter, to spend more time reading, or "deep reading" as Matt calls it, and learning, or as he calls it, "compounding his own knowledge." He wanted to get into a better mindset, a similar mindset to the one that Roger Federer talked about after losing a point:

When you're playing a point, it has to be the most important thing in the world. And it is. But when it's behind you, it's behind you. This mindset is crucial—because it frees you to fully commit to the next point and the next point after that with intensity, clarity, and focus.

He went into his office with single minded determination and almost monk like devotion to his craft, and after a few months emerged with an idea after reading two things that sparked his interest: Robert Kirby's 1984 article in *The Journal of Portfolio Management* about "Coffee Can investing" that ended with an invitation for someone to "repeat the experiment"; and Thomas Phelps's 1972 book called *100 to 1*, which provided a look at the 100-baggers of his time. What if he could do proprietary research on all the 100-baggers since 1980 to see what they have in common, and then apply those learnings to future stock picks that he would hold in a "coffee can" for his girls?

Today, years later, his mistakes have transformed into well-learned screens for quickly eliminating stocks.

"A good stock picker is experienced in learning," Matt says. "I don't spend time on over leveraged companies, or government dependent companies, or businesses that have high customer concentration, or no real recognizable or discoverable competitive advantage. If I can't figure out what makes them special, I won't invest. And for the ones I want to invest in, I try to avoid dogmatic thinking. As they say, have a strong opinion loosely held." For Matt, eliminating high probabilities of future failures drastically increases the probabilities of future success.

And Matt also knows his daughters have not forgotten the lessons of his mistake in China. Each time he briefs them on a new company he wants to invest in, one of the girls inevitably teases him by lovingly asking him, "Dad, are you sure this isn't another Alibaba?!?"

CHAPTER 15

"THE ROAD TO SUCCESS IS ALWAYS UNDER CONSTRUCTION"

—Lily Tomlin

Succession. So many of us, particularly insiders in the media industry, were mesmerized by the HBO black comedy drama that chronicled the greed and dysfunction of the fictional Roy family—owners of a global news and entertainment behemoth—as it navigated succession from an ailing patriarch to his largely unworthy adult children. In real life, Rupert Murdoch, now in his nineties, finally struck a deal with his children to give control to his son, Lachlan. And succession in corporate America, even in nonfamily-controlled businesses, can be equally difficult. Finding someone who can manage movie studios, sports networks, and theme parks as deftly as Bob Iger has been and will continue to be a tall order. Starbucks has gone through six CEOs since its IPO in 1992. Will its latest hire, Brian Niccol—the rockstar executive who spent six years at Chipotle and helped navigate a company reeling from a food poisoning outbreak back to recovery and then growth—turn around the beleaguered Seattle-based coffee chain?

Of course there are success stories, and the most notable and surprising one to me is Reed Hastings, now chairman, passing the torch to not one but two CEOs. So far Netflix, under Ted Sarandos (who drives content) and Greg Peters (who drives product), continues to out distance the competition in the streaming wars.

When Matt told me about a company that was built by five brothers and had to find a nonfamily member to be its new CEO for the first time in forty years, I was hooked. But before I tell you the outcome, let me tell you the origin story . . . and why Matt added this family-run company's stock to his family's coffee can.

BENTLEY (NO, NOT THE CAR)

The company is called Bentley Systems (Ticker symbol: BSY), and it's the world's leading provider of infrastructure engineering software—the kinds of digital tools engineers, architects, and designers use to build many of the world's biggest and most difficult infrastructure projects. And the Bentley brothers—Greg, Barry, Keith, Ray, and Scott—credit their success to the early influences of their parents, a clear sense of mission and purpose over decades, and an occasional sense of self-deprecating humor (figure 15.1).

"We say we were five guys with bad haircuts," says Ray.[1] "We are a year apart in general and we like to solve problems together," says Greg. It was a DIY approach that began in Delaware in the 1960s. "Our mother was a schoolteacher and very creative person and throughout childhood, it seems, we were always doing things that were a little bit out of the realm and the norm, if everyone else would have a book cover that looked a certain way, we made

15.1 The five Bentley brothers: (from left to right) Greg, Barry, Keith, Ray, Scott.
Source: Thanks to the Bentley brothers, of Bentley Systems.

ours from scratch in a different way. There was always paper mâché and there was no end of different ways to try things and learn things," recalls Greg in a recently released video by the company.[2]

"I very much learned from my father about when you took something apart, fixed whatever was wrong, put it back together, and then the problem was solved," said Keith.[3]

"My father was a true handyman, he could build everything, he could fix anything. I think that's where a lot of it came from," remembers Ray.[4]

They all came together as teenagers when their father agreed to let them buy a set of wheels . . . with conditions, of course. "When I was 15, he said, you can have a vehicle, we can use it here. And he said, it has to be a pickup truck . . . and you can only pay $25 for it. And we did find a truck worth $25 and millions of dollars' worth of labor went into making it a viable vehicle, including by all the brothers. We've worked on it together," said Greg.[5]

In junior high school, the kids were also exposed to the brand new world of computers. "There was one at our school and if you signed up, you could get an hour on the computer. I did that every hour I could, and I found that it was just amazing that you could type things into this computer and cause something to come back out," said Keith. It "didn't have any screens or anything in those days. You had to write the program, and say, 'save to paper tape' and it would punch out a paper tape. I wrote a program that played blackjack, and that was my first experience with computers," remembers Barry.[6]

Those experiences led Keith to think about a career in engineering. He got his bachelor's in engineering from the University of Delaware and his master's in electrical engineering from the University of Florida. He was hired by the DuPont company, where his father had worked his entire career. There was an opening in the CAD group, which stood for computer aided drafting.

"There were rooms of drafting boards, and people bent over drafting boards, and you could watch them do it, and they were artists. Pencils, erasers, straight edges. I remember the first time I saw a real draftsman look at a computer screen and be able to just change a mistake, move it from here to there. With (paper) you would have had to erase the whole thing. So, I started working on computer aided drafting at DuPont. It was the most fun you could have and get paid for it."[7]

Meanwhile, the other brothers were pursuing their degrees and their dreams—none of them were slouches! Ray got a bachelor's in mechanical engineering from Rensselaer Polytechnic Institute and a master's degree in computer engineering from the University of Cincinnati. Both Scott and Greg got degrees from Wharton. And Barry, who got a bachelor's in chemical engineering from the University of Delaware and a PhD in chemical engineering from Caltech, set off to start a software company called Dynamic Solutions that collected data from chemistry instruments and analyzed it. He then called Keith and asked him if he wanted to join his company. He was surprised when he said he'd think about it. "I thought it was kind of cool. My mother was distraught. She thought it was the dumbest idea ever. She did not understand how you could make money at software, something you could not see."[8] Keith decided to quit his job at DuPont and went out to Pasadena, California, to join his brother's chemistry company.

"At the time, I didn't know if I was leaving the greatest job for the dumbest idea ever and, uh, it turned out a bit of both. So, I began working for Dynamic Solution, Barry's company. You know, interesting programming challenge, but we never made a nickel. It was very difficult. So, I told Barry, I said, look, chemistry ain't the way for us to, you know, make a living. This CAD thing is a bigger opportunity. I've seen it from the other side. Let's see if we could start marketing the software that I had written for DuPont."[9]

They said DuPont agreed to let them market the software Keith had written for them. Together they launched Bentley Systems. Barry remembers putting together the plan. "We started with the spreadsheet of the day, which was a piece of green engineering paper, and we drew out a business plan that went out seven quarters." Keith added, "Bentley Systems started doing well from the very beginning. We sold more CAD software than chemistry software from the first month."[10] They then decided to move back to the east coast, to Philadelphia, to recruit people to work for them.

Keith told *Engineering News-Record*, "the only piece of business advice I ever got, someone told me, make sure you always hire people smarter than you. And I thought that's easy; I'll hire my brothers!"[11]

BROTHERS UNITE

And that's exactly what Keith and Barry did. First they hired Scott to start making deals with people, and then they hired Ray to do programming. The personal computer entered the scene, and the team knew there was a large opportunity afoot. Instead of just selling CAD connected to large hardware stations, they could and should be building new CAD software, separated from the back system, for personal PCs. "I knew, that's where we should be working," remembers Keith. They moved quickly, started experimenting with state-of-the-art computer graphics and doing things no one had ever seen before. They didn't have a business plan for this new era of personal computing, and Barry said they realized they "needed more drive, you know, and Greg was the supplier of drive, for sure."[12]

Greg and two of his colleagues had founded a financial trading software firm, which then was sold to SunGuard Data Systems for $40 million in 1987.[13] He was serving on the public company's board when he showed up at Bentley Systems in 1991.

Ray says, tongue-in-cheek, "We weren't sure we wanted to work with Greg, because we knew when Greg showed up, we would end up working for Greg!"[14] That's what younger brothers always say about the oldest!

That's what eventually happened; Greg was the final piece of the puzzle, the final brother to join the company. "I was just inclined to help," Greg remembers, "and I decided I would rather have brothers than partners or be in a corporate environment."[15]

"Greg started applying what I think he now calls financial engineering, because, you know, it's cool to be an engineer at Bentley Systems. At the end of the week, he knew more about all of our users, what they do, how they made money, how they used our software better than anybody else at Bentley Systems," Keith said.[16] Keith was happy to give Greg the financial reins so he could focus on the technology development.

"I was the worst!" Keith said modestly. "Greg is very good at it."[17]

"And it fell to me to decide that we should go from being entirely indirect in our commercial model to being almost entirely direct, and we heard lots of advice to broaden horizontally, but I have always thought we should set our compass by that which would be of greatest value to professionals accomplishing something important," said Greg, who eventually became CEO of Bentley Systems in 1995.[18]

FROM DIGITAL TO PHYSICAL

"Something important" meant creating software to assist teams working on some of the biggest infrastructure projects around the world. That includes

Europe's largest construction project, Crossrail, a sixty-two-mile-long east/west rail line through Central London; the expansion of Reliance Industry's largest oil refinery in Jamnagar, India; Keystone Engineering's efforts to design and analyze underwater support structures for America's first offshore windfarm; China's South/North water transfer project, which will deliver clean water to nearly five hundred million people through the six-mile-long Shahe aqueduct; and Abu Dhabi's airport, which according to Sulaiman Daoud Al Siksek, chief program officer, "It is the front of house for our Emirates. So we wanted to do something spectacular, something iconic, something everybody will remember." Mark Davis, SVP of Design, Midfield Terminal, Abu Dhabi Airports, added: "It will be one of the most recognized buildings on the planet."[19]

The project that brought out Matt's young, inner "Lego Master" was the fifty-story Leadenhall Building on a crowded street in London: it looked like a massive cheese grater that had no staging area for equipment while the building was being built. Rogers Stirk Harbor + Partners architect Dirk Krolikowski said, "We were very constrained on site because the footprint of the building is actually the site. So, there is no room for storing any components. They just have to be driven in right into London and lifted into place. We built the building many times digitally before we actually built it. We wanted to use technology, digital technology to do it in the best possible way. For this, we used Bentley software to simulate the assemble as much as we used it to design the building."[20]

Matt said Bentley Systems software showed the architectural and engineering teams responsible for Leadenhall "how to build it day by day, floor by floor, so they could get the right equipment and the right people at the right times."

Bentley Systems spends 22 percent of its revenue on R&D, constantly engaging its users (the company won't call them customers) about their needs and innovating incredible new features and platforms tantamount to what a Hollywood producer working on a science fiction franchise would call "world building." As much as Silicon Valley has evolved from the early days of MS DOS, so, too, have Bentley Systems programs. What started as an enormous opportunity for Computer Aided Programming to model designs on PCs evolved over the decades into programs to assemble structures, as we saw with the Leadenhall Building. The programs also evolved into beautiful and intricate multidimensional drawings, or worlds if you will, that would allow a user to not only stress test designs through different conditions and simulations in a predictive manner but also to maintain them into the future.

"With manual drawing, if you had to change something, you would have to redo the whole thing. Then with 2D digital, if you want something to be twelve feet instead of ten feet, it was easy to change. When Bentley gave you 3D digital drawings, you got to look at something from this angle or another angle. You got to see reflections from other buildings or how something looked from the ground versus somewhere else in the city," said Matt. "What 4D does is add the dimension of time: how the building can change with degradation, how roads will change with certain amounts of cars driving over them for a certain number of years, and how the environment will affect infrastructure over time."

Matt says the software helps infrastructure asset owners make decisions after a project is complete as well. He used the example of a cell phone tower. "Say you own cell phone towers, and a service company wants to shift from 4G to 5G. You, as an owner of the tower, want to know what the new equipment will do to the tower. What if wind blowing at 25 mph can now blow down the tower because of the new equipment? What do you need to do to the structure to make it stable? The software helps you figure it out. It's a powerful use of existing data and design to easily re-simulate and evaluate the tower every time a new product is added to it."

The idea of a living, breathing design that can be stress tested and then help asset owners optimize the maintenance of their properties with intelligent insights is what Bentley Systems calls a "digital twin." It leverages a variety of sensors installed across a bridge, building, or railway to offer real-time operational analytics and predictive maintenance. Remember the Crossrail project in London? Well, Malcom Taylor, Head of Technical Information at Crossrail Limited, said, "We talk about building two railways. A physical railway and a digital or virtual railway. It's that virtual or digital railway that will be managing and maintaining the physical railway."[21]

Not to sound like an engineering student indulging in a late-night thought experiment, but I couldn't help but wonder how the digital twin can then change itself over time to mirror the real-world changes happening to, say, a physical plant over time? Well, I quickly found out that it's going to be damn hard to stump Greg Bentley.

"If it is going to be a twin, it needs to change continuously as does the ever-green nature of the actual plant, and that requires change synchronization. On the physical side, it's continuous, frequent surveying of the plant with drones and cameras. On the engineering/information side, it's a hub with distributed databases and change synchronization so the engineering information is also always up to date," he said in a conversation with Andy Chatha, president and CEO of the ARC Group, a leading technology research and advisory firm for industry, energy, and infrastructure. He added that his digital twin cloud ser-vice was made to address this. "It can be continuously synchronized and be an evergreen digital twin."[22]

THE HARD NUMBERS

Wow! Eat your heart out, world builders at *Star Wars* Universe! Based on its products, it's not surprising Matt believes Bentley Systems is a potential 100-bagger. As for the financials, here are his three key numbers to understand Bentley System's business.

KEY NUMBERS TO UNDERSTAND BSY

9/10	$1.41	108%

9/10: Bentley Systems is the leader in "horizontal" infrastructure, projects that span large areas such as roads and bridges, electric grids, rail and transit, and water and waste. They say nine out of ten of these broad infrastructure projects are designed using their software. Their most known competitor is Autodesk. Matt says the San Francisco–based company is the market leader when it comes to "vertical" infrastructure, or buildings. Their respective dom-inance in the two separate areas may be a result of the way the companies' software was built.

"Our principal competitor is Autodesk, and Autodesk is most concentrated in vertical infrastructure in buildings, and that's because Autodesk started on the PC, and the PC had small address space and buildings are smaller projects that don't last long. In horizontal infrastructure, we started on the UNIX workstations. Those are more challenging in terms of data requirements and so forth. And each of we and Autodesk overlap between horizontal and vertical to some degree, but that's kind of how things break down in terms of the competitive landscape for us," said Greg Bentley in an interview with William Blair & Company analyst, Dylan Becker.[23]

But given Autodesk's strength in vertical, why not buy Autodesk stock too? "Autodesk has a $57 billion market cap. It's already a 100-bagger, and it will be hard to multiply a hundred times again," said Matt. "Bentley Systems has a market cap of $15 billion. And there are even smaller companies in this space that are really good companies too. It's a great market: rational competitors, underlying growth, and management teams that make great decisions." Matt is talking about upstarts such as Aveva, Hexagon, Trimble, and Esri (a mix of public and private companies) that he said he would be keeping his eye on over time. Sometimes when Matt goes deep in a particular sector with a strong thesis, he finds a gushing oil well he can pump for years!

$1.41: Half of Bentley's revenue comes directly from the asset owners and the other half from design and engineering project delivery firms contracted by the asset owner. Matt says the design firms usually bill an asset owner about $150/hour. The cost of the software is just $1.41 of that $150/hour they are charging. In other words, it is such a small percentage of their costs that there is ample opportunity for Bentley to upsell the design firm into more powerful and useful products to assist their structural and artistic efforts without becoming a burdensome toll on their profits.

If anything, Bentley believes it actually helps grow the margins of the users using their products. It says it helps increase their users' efficiency, accuracy, and collaboration, leading to tremendous cost savings to complete projects. Based on a survey of its clients at a recent Bentley conference, the median engineering hours saved per project is 18 percent.

108%: About 92 percent of revenue comes from subscriptions, and it has had profitable growth since its founding. A big driver of Bentley Systems consistent revenue performance is its stable net recurring revenue (NRR) of 108 percent. "First, if a client uses Bentley to make a design, they will need to go back to it for decades when things break down. Second, they are hesitant to switch to new software because they will have to retrain their entire team on how to use it. It makes the software very sticky," Matt said. And the Digital Twin software adds a whole new dimension to the essentiality of the product through the power of network effects! "With Digital Twin, they've got an emerging competitive advantage, which makes it even harder to switch software. Not only are the engineers using it, but Bentley is creating a growing ecosystem of users. Asset owners such as governments or municipalities are using it; design firms are using it; construction firms are using it; it's a much broader ecosystem of users all using it at different times during the project build and maintenance thereafter. As more users collaborate, it creates a network effect whereby the system becomes more valuable as more users are on it."

Matt was particularly moved by its commitment to annual margin improvement of "100 Bps in Adjusted OI w/SBC margin." Moved? And what is SBC margin? Well, SBC stands for stock-based compensation (or the stock a company rewards employees with), and Matt says many companies don't include that expense when representing their operating income. "The Bentley brothers include it in their calculation. These are guys you can trust. They're not going to screw you. They're old school in a good way. I would let my sister date a Bentley brother!" It's fun listening to Matt get moved by accounting transparency. And for the record, his twin sister is already married!

The company is also cash flow efficient: 70 percent of its revenue is paid annually in advance. And it converts approximately 80 percent of adjusted EBITDA to free cash flow. And with the cash spigot open, the company can make acquisitions to further add to their revenue growth. And the team at Bentley has certainly taken advantage of that opportunity in a unique way. Over forty years, the company has made one hundred acquisitions. Matt called the company's investor relations office and asked, "How do you make so many acquisitions? Don't you have to rewrite code each time to make sure the software you're buying integrates with the software you've built?" The IR team explained that they have an open platform, and they are acquiring companies that have already written applications for their platform. In other words, Matt says they know which ones are providing real value to their existing users and they are already "pre-integrated."

Greg Bentley told *Diginomica*, which writes about business enterprise computing, "So, most of these one-hundred acquisitions that we've done are among this ecosystem who have started with our platform. They had something in common to start with, so the integration was not as burdensome as it would otherwise be if it were a hundred random acquisitions."[24]

Two of their notable acquisitions are the $700 million acquisition of Power Line Systems (design software for overhead power and communications lines) and the $1.1 billion acquisition of Seequent (3D modeling software for underground modeling and risk analysis).

Matt said Bentley Systems told him, "Power Line systems were kicking our ass, so instead of competing, we just bought them. They are the winners in that space and will benefit from the 'electrification of America.' Seequent is the cool one. It lets you see underground. An engineer using it can learn, for example, twenty years from now, we could have water or a sink hole in a certain location . . . and either choose to avoid that location or remedy the situation and make sure to build a more resilient structure."

All combined, Bentley's ARR (average revenue run rate) is growing through a mix of pricing, volume, upsell, and cross sells into new software products and acquisitions, yielding a 16 percent CAGR on adjusted operating income w/SBC. (And don't snicker about the stock-based comp!)

INFRASTRUCTURE AND MORE INFRASTRUCTURE

The global infrastructure opportunity for Bentley has been large. Although the company is facing headwinds from the China real estate bubble bursting, Matt says the company is in pole position as the country resumes its investments in pure infrastructure. "China went out and built a whole bunch of buildings no one needed. Bentley is in water, power lines, bridges, all the core things a society needs to invest in. Unlike real estate, infrastructure is generally well thought out and is a long-lasting contributor to the companies involved."

Perhaps the greatest growth opportunity is here at home. Everyone remembers the old black and white films of the roads being built after President Eisenhower enacting the Interstate Highway Act in 1956. The impact on the country was enormous . . . and a very long time ago. Well, at the end of 2021, President Biden and Congress implemented the largest federal investment in infrastructure in decades. According to experts interviewed by the Council on Foreign Relations (CFR), "The U.S. population has almost doubled since the 1960s, when most of the country's major infrastructure systems were designed. Many are reaching the end of their lifespan and are dangerously overstretched."[25] The American

Road and Transportation Builders Association says one in three bridges need to be repaired or replaced.[26] Amtrak has a repair backlog of more than $45 billion, notes the CFR, citing the American Society of Civil Engineers.

Electric grids need investments for security and output. Nuclear power plants are being debated again. Three Mile Island is planning to reopen, and Microsoft is in need of fuel to power its growing number of data centers and has agreed to buy as much power as possible from the nuclear plant for the next twenty years. Amazon and Google are focusing on a new generation of smaller reactors. And Eric Schmidt, former CEO of Google, said we don't even have the power to match the multi-hundred-billion-dollar ambitions of Open AI.

"I told him I'd done the calculation about the amount of energy required," Schmidt said, referring to a conversation he had with Sam Altman of Open AI. "Then in the spirit of full disclosure, I went to the White House on Friday and told them that we need to become best friends with Canada because Canada has really nice people, helped invent AI, and has lots of hydropower. The alternative is to have the Arabs fund it. I like the Arabs personally, spent lots of time there, but they're not going to adhere to our national security rules, whereas Canada and the US are part of a trumpet where we all agree."[27]

Matt notes the need for civil engineers is skyrocketing and the rates of retirement are larger than new students are graduating, fueling the demand for even more productive tools. That may just be the legacy of the Bentley brothers: arming the next generation with the tools to build a new era of infrastructure, along with arming their company with a new generation of leadership to continue advancing its capabilities. It's something they have been planning since they went public in 2020. Tucked into one of their letters to shareholders, the brothers wrote:

> we take most seriously our responsibility for similarly qualified succession in BSY's executive leadership. We have suitable plans and prospects in mind, including having recently recruited successfully from top levels at leading public software companies. Our successors will have the continuity benefit of many years of anticipated overlap with our Board tenures, but we also have ambitions to improve upon own leadership, and certainly in dimensions beyond engineering. Indeed, spending all of our careers working with brothers (who are certainly not easily impressed with each other) has hopefully

inclined us toward humility rather than hubris. While we are proud of our many next-generation Bentleys in various roles at the company, we have programmed against dynastic succession.[28]

It's worth repeating the last line, "We have programmed against dynastic succession." Could you ever see Rupert Murdoch writing something like that? Of course not!

MAKING THE TRANSITION?

Regardless of whether it's family or nonfamily, installing a new CEO is an incredibly difficult process. In 2020, *Forbes* wrote: "Research from the Corporate Executive Board (CEB) estimates that 50 percent to 70 percent of executives fail within 18 months of taking on a role, regardless of whether they were an external hire or promoted from within. At the highest level, the 'turnover rates of CEOs of major North American corporations' jumped about 50 percent from the 'last half of the 1990s' to 2000–2007, and the average CEO tenure dropped 17 percent between 2013 and 2017."

Why do they fail? *Forbes* continued:

> A survey of 2,600 Fortune 1,000 executives conducted by Navalent found that 76 percent said that formal development processes were inadequate, and 55 percent rated coaching subpar, if it existed at all. Research by McKinsey senior partners Scott Keller and Mary Meaney also reveals that three-quarters of executives consider themselves unprepared for a position because of inadequate onboarding processes. I've seen a lot of executives come and go during my business career, including some who've failed spectacularly. Much of this blame lies with companies that fail to properly onboard new executives, clearly communicate their culture, and provide leadership training and development for them and other leaders.[29]

That very year, Bentley Systems started the transition . . . and they were intent on doing it methodically. Just before their IPO, they recruited Nicholas Cumins as Chief Product Officer. A dual citizen of France and the US, Cumins had come from SAP Marketing Cloud, where, as General Manager, he had full P&L responsibility and direct supervision of product management, engineering, product marketing, and business development. Before that, he had served as Chief Product Officer at Scytl, a platform for online voting to power democracy, and as Senior Vice President of Product with OpenX, a pioneer in programmatic advertising.

Steeped in the product roadmap, what users were looking for, and the culture of the company, Cumins was then promoted into the COO role in 2022. Two years after that, in the summer of 2024, he was promoted to chief executive.

Scott Bentley is now running a company that builds underwater robots; Keith, Barry, and Ray are all retired but serving on the board; and Greg is now executive chair of the board. In other words, the brothers managed an orderly transition for Cumins and themselves and will continue to help the new CEO, from a board level, steer the ship.

Greg, now sixty-nine, said, "I'm the oldest of the five brothers, but I am the last to retire. And the standard I've had for myself is to get the whole succession completed, and then I can retire. As I mentioned, Nicholas and those who report to him are all in their forties. It's a cadre twenty years younger, which is a big advantage. The average tenure of a CEO in a public company in the US is five years. We don't want to look like just any company. What has benefited us is to have continuity in our management."[30]

What started as a start-up between five brothers, now has five thousand employees across forty countries, $1.2 billion in revenues a year, and a never-ending thirst to embrace the next great leap in computing. By the way, if my two younger brothers—already accomplished executives in banking and advertising—are reading this, it's not too late to start brainstorming ideas for a family business!

"Sometimes I wish I was thirty years younger because it's a great time at Bentley Systems. The future is amazing," said Keith.[31]

Cumins is already determined to seize on the next big wave in computing. When he took over, he said, "Every owner-operator in the world is looking for a simpler and more effective way to understand the condition of their assets. Think what the power and possibilities of AI imply for improving asset performance and making infrastructure more resilient. This is the moment for our generation to apply its ingenuity and build upon the legacy of innovation to continue advancing the world's infrastructure for better quality of life."[32]

Matt loved the overall transition. One of his 4Es focuses on management and culture, and the Bentley brothers—from accounting transparency to really treating their clients like partners and not just a transactional customer to the way in which they brought in, trained, and elevated a new CEO—scored high marks in Matt's report card. "As the brothers were retiring, they hired a guy four years ago, who is forty-seven years old, and they want him to be there another thirty years. They got him from SAP and a start-up. Again, they took their time moving him up in the organization, from CPO to COO and then CEO. He has an engineering background and even more sales prowess."

AT THE TABLE

When Matt told his daughters about Bentley Systems, they were impressed by its track record of powering the lion's share of horizontal infrastructure projects. It was also not surprising that the sisters liked "the brothers" part of the story, both on a personal as well as a business level.

> MORGAN: Finding out that Bentley was started and ran by five brothers for over 40+ years makes it more of an appealing investment for me because it proves that it is well run.

When I asked the sisters if they could work together like the Bentley brothers, the response was unanimous:

> MORGAN: I think . . . no, we value our sisterhood friendship more than working together.
> PIERCE: We might be able to work together, but based on our very different career aspirations, I don't think it would be best.
> PEYTON: I think there may be too many chefs in the kitchen, if you know what I mean!

All kidding aside, Peyton went on to talk about the legacy of the Bentley brothers. She saw deeper meaning in what they were trying to accomplish. Part of it could have been her psychology training. Part of it could have been the example her own father sets in his approach to life.

15.2 Nicholas Cumins and Greg Bentley.

PEYTON: I think what really stood out to me about Bentley Systems,
beyond the strong position they have in the horizontal architectural
world, is that they are building things that last—both product and
company. By incorporating digital twins and stimulations they're telling
the world that they don't just care about making infrastructure, they
care about making infrastructure that is safe and that will stand the test
of time. By doing so they are proving that they care about people, and
I think nothing is more valuable than a company that values the well-
being of others.

As for the new CEO, they thought Cumins (figure 15.2) might be the first top
leader at Bentley Systems with a good haircut!

CHAPTER 16

SOMEWHERE, SOMETHING INCREDIBLE IS WAITING TO BE KNOWN

—Carl Sagan

T his next company struck a chord with me personally because it reflected a path I'd walked earlier in life. I wasn't supposed to be a reporter. For much of my youth, I wanted to be a doctor: to help people, to study the frontiers of science, and be a part of a new generation of medical advancements. I grew up in New York City in the 1980s and saw firsthand how AIDS victims were ostracized. In junior high school, I volunteered in the emergency room of a local hospital in Queens, and everyone was so afraid of the virus that, out of an abundance of caution, I was told to wear a full body suit when an AIDS patient came in—even though transmission was known to happen through blood, either by sexual contact or the sharing of needles. As much as the experience haunted me, it only emboldened my desire to further my studies in science. When I told my parents I had been accepted to Stuyvesant—a specialized math and science high school in lower Manhattan—my mother, Mohini (which means beautiful and bewildering in Hindi), celebrated the occasion by giving me a cake with a medical symbol on top (figure 16.1). No pressure, Mom!

During my time there, as a junior I decided to try my hand at research. Several times a week after school, I would get on the L train at 1st Avenue and 14th Street and head west before transferring to the 6 train up north to 68th Street. I would pick a seat with a heat vent below it, trying to keep warm on winter days, while pouring over my graph-paper-filled lab notebook, planning that day's experiment. Once uptown and up the stairs from the subway, I would emerge onto the bustling city campus of Hunter College, one of the constituent schools in the City University of New York. I made my way past scores of racially and economically diverse college and grad students, traversed the beautiful glass walkways that connected the campus buildings high above the hot dog and pretzel carts

16.1 The author's parents, Mohini and Lal Khemlani.

and taxi cabs roaring by below, stopping into the faculty lounge to get a cup of coffee and some store brand Oreo knockoffs while donating the suggested 25 cents into the jar (which was used to buy more cookies), before taking off my black and white varsity fencing jacket and settling into a biochemistry lab. The professor I was interning for, who had been studying the outer protein shells of the AIDS virus, explained to me that if scientists could find a way to block the receptors on its shell, it wouldn't be able to bind to other cells in our body. It's akin to putting a mitten on a baby's hand so it can't scratch itself. The second thing he explained was that the protein shell on AIDS had certain similarities to the protein shell on harmless yeast cells. That's right, the single cell fungus that we use to help make bread rise. The idea was if we could find something to block the receptors on yeast, we could then try to see if it also worked on the AIDS virus. It was a two-step long shot. First test a whole bunch of stuff that would block a yeast cell from interacting . . . and then see if it would do the same with

AIDS virus, essentially putting the killer into a biological straight jacket. I spent my afternoons slowly testing different potential blockers. I got to use pipettes that injected tiny amounts of liquids—think microliters—into different vials. I had to mix chemical solutions that took time to blend. Instead of doing it by hand, I was introduced to magnetic stirrers, or little magnetic capsules that you would drop into a beaker that would start to spin when you turned on the power of the electromagnetic plate below it. I thought it was the coolest thing, in a nerdy sort of way, and fantasized taking it to college with me to make a never-ending supply of margaritas in my dorm room like a slushy machine at a 7-Eleven! I also got to use a machine called the Western Blot, which entailed injecting a solution into a well on a dense slab of gel. You would hit the switch and proteins within the liquid would start to move through the charged gel in a race to get to the other side, with the smaller ones moving further than the larger proteins. Sort of like me coming in way behind my six-time-marathon running wife in a five-mile race. You then use known antibodies and other markers to attach to the different bands of proteins to identify what proteins were in the solution. I was also given the grunt work of buying solutions, reagents, proteins, yeast cells, antibodies, and equipment each week from a thick phone book sized catalog of lab supplies that had everything. I remember thinking at the time how amazing it was that some company was making all these highly technical things somewhere. In the end, I made some headway on blockers on the yeast shell but never got close to a definite answer, let alone testing it against the AIDS virus. As an intern, schoolwork and applying to colleges got in the way, not to mention the lack of a PhD in biochemistry! But I brought my work to the New York City Science Fair and explained what I was attempting to do, and I was awarded a first-place prize for trying and being able to explain the process. I was interviewed by a local television station for the eleven o'clock news (which my parents taped on a VHS cassette to show relatives), and the US Navy presented me with a brown leather brief case that I kept for years, until the clasps broke from carrying around too many papers. NYU granted me admission into an eight-year program with automatic acceptance into medical school—but I turned it down to go to Cornell, where I could study chemistry and write for the daily paper, the *Cornell Daily Sun*. You see, I was also interested in journalism, which gave me a wider birth to learn how things work while also helping people. (Surprisingly, my parents supported me!) Ultimately, I switched majors to communications and then went to the Columbia Graduate School of Journalism, where I met my wife. But I have never stopped loving science. Over the years, I did stories about genetic algorithms, profiles of Dean Kamen and his Segway and water purification machines, GM's billion dollar bet on hydrogen powered cars, the rise of many internet start-ups, and even NASA's plan to build a highway in the sky, if and when flying cars ever really materialized. More recently, I commissioned many stories about the growing impact of global warming, Elon Musk and his incredible inventions, as well as COVID and its devastating impact on the world when I was at Hearst Newspapers and then CBS News.

BACK TO TODAY

All those memories flooded back when Matt told me he was looking into potential investments in the growing field of biotechnology; a lot has changed in the expanding field since my early internship in the lab. Gene therapy aims to replace defective or missing genes in a cell with healthy ones. According to the Mayo Clinic, the FDA has approved gene therapy products via clinical trials for certain types of cancer, spinal muscular atrophy, hemophilia, and sickle cell disease.[1] Precision medicine, also known as personalized medicine, targets the right medicine to the right person at the right time based on their genetic makeup, environment, and lifestyle. Spatial biology allows researchers to visualize molecules in 3D to better understand their context within individual cells or tissues. The area Matt was zeroing in on was drug development, notoriously known for an incredibly long discovery cycle, littered with failure after failure after failure before finding something with a hint of promise. On average, it takes ten to fifteen years from discovery to testing to regulatory approval. According to the *Journal of the American Medical Association*, "Studies have estimated that the R&D cost for a new drug ranges from $314 million to $4.46 billion, depending on the therapeutic area, data, and modeling assumptions."[2] But powerful computers and artificial intelligence hope to streamline that process and bring costs down along the way. Matt thought the most successful companies doing this just might be a good 100-bagger candidate for the coffee can.

The media was also looking at the feasibility of all of this. Would it have an impact in the near term or long term? David Remnick, the iconic editor of *The New Yorker* and former Pulitzer Prize winner, published an incredible piece in the fall of 2024 by Dhruv Khullar, a writer, a practicing physician, and assistant professor at Weill Cornell Medical College, called "How Machines Learned to Discover Drugs."

Khullar began the piece by visiting a chemical biologist at Rockefeller University in Manhattan who discovers medicine by sifting through dirt samples from around the world for new kinds of antibiotics. "Dirt is one of the richest sources of medicine, because its microbes have been waging a war with one another for millions of years," he wrote. He scooped his own sample of soil, went into the lab and added a detergent that broke down the bacteria's cell walls, causing their DNA to spill out. The Rockefeller University team then sequenced the genes, picking a promising section, and then manufactured a chemical they could test against a harmful bacterium. Let's just say his sample didn't win. But that wasn't the point. The Rockefeller team tests more than a hundred molecules a month, and "a tiny fraction might show antibiotic activity, and a tiny fraction of those perform well enough—and are nontoxic enough—to advance to animal testing and clinical trials."

There's a lot to test. Khullar says, "The number of chemicals that theoretically could prove useful as drugs has been estimated at ten to the sixtieth power—a quantity greater than the number of atoms in the solar system. Some of these potential medicines can be found in nature. Others have already been discovered but we haven't yet found their uses. Still others have never been imagined."[3]

To tackle a challenge that big, Khullar visited James Collins and his team at MIT, who have introduced AI to the drug discovery process, training models to rank different molecules in their databases by their likelihood of inhibiting E. Coli. They then did real-world tests on the top ninety, and one is headed into preclinical trials. According to Khullar, "antibiotic-resistant infections already contribute to 1.5 million deaths annually, and by the middle of the century, they could kill ten million people a year."

"For twenty billion dollars, you could have it solved," Collins told Khullar. "For twenty billion, you can get ten or fifteen new antibiotics. That would get you a lot of the way there."

Jon Stokes, who used to work with Collins at MIT, and is now a professor at McMaster University in Ontario, is now using AI to conjure up new molecules instead of just testing the ones that have already been discovered.

As much as the top of the funnel of drug development—the discovery phase—is being accelerated beyond our wildest imaginations, the clinical trial phase still requires enormous amounts of real-world testing.

Khullar wrote: "Techies often get overexcited about what it means when AI can identify a molecule," Peter Lee, the head of Microsoft Research and a coauthor of a book about AI in medicine, told me. Is the molecule potent, or do you need impractically high doses to see an effect? Is it selective, or does it attach to off-target cells and inflict collateral damage? Is it stable, or does it degrade in the body? Is it soluble, or will it clump up in your bloodstream? Sometimes medicinal chemists can tinker with a molecule to improve its performance. Often, they cannot. "The techies are just waking up to the sheer magnificent complexity of human biology," Lee said.

It's a good thing that each new discovery requires rigorous testing—after all, human lives are at stake. The disruption within the discovery phase made me wish I could buy stock in MIT's labs! But obviously it's not a public company, and that's why Matt was busy researching companies that were actual investable opportunities. He studied, probed, and analyzed companies as if he was doing his very own clinical trial. He was interested in companies that were breaking ground in bio-simulation software, companies that could identify and design molecules, companies that attempt to predict what molecules would do in the human body and even offer recommendations for dosing, and companies that can help drug developers with the regulatory approval process.

For months, the routine was the same. Each morning Matt started with his daily and somewhat religious workout at the Carriage Club: a family-oriented club founded in 1956 that sits on more than six manicured acres in Kansas City and features an ice rink and pools for his daughters, pickle ball courts for his wife, and a fitness center for him to invest in himself. He would combine cardio exercises on either the stair climber, elliptical or treadmill, with free weights and some bench pressing. It's a regimen he has been doing for a very long time, but after a drunk driver rear-ended him, his mother, and sister while they were on their way to church in Wisconsin in 1988, he has had to replace three discs in his neck over the years, and thus he has reduced his bench pressing to seventy-five-pound dumbbells with each arm. The rest of the day, he canvassed the drug discovery space. He looked at company financials and business strategies, attended an AI roundtable, and spoke to medical experts.

But one afternoon he pushed back from his desk in his home office and decided to stop the pursuit. He had come to a few conclusions, and it was time to change tack. After all his research, Matt explained that the technology being deployed in these public companies "wasn't as proprietary as I need. In fact, money—a lot of money—could put anyone into the competition. There was, so far, no strong competitive barrier. That is not a sustainable investment . . . for us long-term holders." Furthermore, Matt learned that some of the smartest people at the companies he was researching were constantly being recruited by Google.

That's right, Google. The company, known for its moonshots, reportedly spent between $400 million and $650 million for DeepMind, an artificial intelligence research lab led by Demis Hassabis, a decade ago. DeepMind spun a commercial venture called Isomorphic Labs to work on drug discovery. Its product, known as AlphaFold, is the standard bearer in the business. In a Google blog in May of 2024, it described the latest iteration, AlphaFold 3:

> Inside every plant, animal and human cell are billions of molecular machines. They're made up of proteins, DNA and other molecules, but no single piece works on its own. Only by seeing how they interact together, across millions of types of combinations, can we start to truly understand life's processes. In a paper published in *Nature*, we introduce AlphaFold 3, a revolutionary model that can predict the structure and interactions of all life's molecules with unprecedented accuracy. For the interactions of proteins with other molecule types we see at least a 50 percent improvement compared with existing prediction methods, and for some important categories of interaction we have doubled prediction accuracy. We hope AlphaFold 3 will help transform our understanding of the biological world and drug discovery.[4]

AlphaFold 3 provides open access to over two hundred million protein sequences, and Hassabis (and his DeepMind colleague John Jumper) won part of the Nobel Prize for Chemistry in 2024 for protein structure prediction. It is an astonishing library backed by one of the most powerful tech companies in the world. So, would Matt put Google (Alphabet) into the coffee can? Well, Matt is already a long-time investor in Google, but he believes that the $2.36 trillion market company is unlikely to multiply one hundred times again.

As he sat at his desk, he knew Google, as well as the other companies he researched, would continue to make advancements in the drug discovery space. And those advancements would lead to even more clinical trials. Artificial intelligence will make those who know how to use it even more productive. It's then when he remembered the old Mark Twain quote: "When everyone is looking for gold, it's a good time to be in the pick and shovel business."

He quickly grabbed his original 100-bagger study that detailed all the previous companies to enter the hall of fame. As he went down the list, he found the one he was looking for: Bio-Techne (Ticker symbol: TECH). It was a 100-bagger stock that sold proteins, antibodies, and diagnostics equipment and tests—all the ingredients and tools needed to facilitate the testing of what would soon be a Tsunami of drug discovery. He smiled as he thought to himself, "Could Bio-Techne, with a market cap of only $12 billion, multiply one hundred times . . . again?" He shifted all his research efforts to answer that question. He would also have something new to think about while pumping iron at the gym.

THE HARD NUMBERS

A few weeks later, he called me and said he was ready to add Bio-Techne to the coffee can. He believed it was poised to multiply one hundred times again. It was the only one on his original list that he thought had a strong chance of doing it a second time. And, no, it had nothing to do with the fact that the company had the best ticker symbol ever: TECH! Here are Matt's three key numbers for understanding the business.

KEY NUMBERS TO UNDERSTAND TECH

81%	$800	150+

81%: The Minneapolis-based company, which was founded in 1976, has two main lines of business: consumables and instruments/diagnostics kits. The consumables, not to be confused with food or, say, toothpaste, are products that are intended to be used up relatively quickly. In this case, the consumables are an incredibly large catalog of six thousand proteins and four hundred thousand antibody types. Together it makes up 81 percent of the business. It brought me right back to my internship ordering lab supplies. Hey Door Dash, I want three Fluorokines, two Heparanase enzymes, some buffers and substrates, and a six pack of recombinant antibodies! And there's ten bucks extra for you if it gets here on time! Matt calls these core products, most of which are made in the company's factories, the "juice" that researchers use to create and test new breakthrough medicines. And most of that juice is made in the company's factories.

Matt asked the investor relations team about the impact of the explosion of technology at Google and other places. They replied by saying that Alpha-Fold "is a great tool for the individuals that truly understand protein biology, enabling them (us) to design 'super' proteins that don't exist in nature. That said, biology is tricky and unpredictable and does not behave the same way for everyone. Regardless of any type of computational biology/computer algorithm tools, there will ALWAYS be a need for experimentation in the lab. Tools like this might allow you to predict how a reaction/biological pathway might respond to a therapeutic, but you never know until you know (which can only be solved in the lab). Sorry to sound like an old guy, but I'm skeptical of the ability of this tool to disrupt our business for the foreseeable future."

$800: Now for the incremental margins. "Say the company charges $800 for a vial of juice," Matt says. "The incremental margin on that vial is between 90 and 95 percent. In other words, it only costs them around $40 to make that $800 vial."

"You have all these chemists with big vats of stuff, like they are creating new kinds of beer, but they're proteins (figure 16.2). They must ensure quality, keep

16.2 Bio-Techne technicians making proteins and reagents.

it in minus 81 degrees or whatever is the right temperature, and their incremental margins are off the charts. With software you build it once and sell it a million times. It's not quite as good as shipping code on the internet, but each vial costs $40 to make and it sells for $800. That's better than . . ." Matt paused and then added, "most businesses do." I thought he was going to say better than drugs, the illegal kind, but Matt is too much of a boy scout to say something like that. Instead, he explained why their customers value their products so much. "TECH offers the widest selection and highest quality material that ensures consistent results that researchers can be confident are dependably accurate." In other words, the company offers one stop shopping. Why order from multiple places when you can get most of everything you need in one place? Second, he explained that most drug trials are longitudinal and go on for several months or years. Consistent product (that doesn't differ from batch to batch) and quality control (i.e., proteins that don't break down) are essential constants when measuring for other changing variables in any given test. Experiments in early stages cost less than a $1 million and are significantly higher in later stages, Matt says. "An $800 vial is a tiny fraction of the cost, and if it ensures consistent, reproducible results that could lead to a breakthrough, it's worth the price."

"Quality is the driving force," says Kevin Callahan, the senior director of scientific support at Bio-Techne. "The fact that we can control the process from beginning to end really sets us apart, and quality doesn't end when the product leaves the facility. We're really known for the support that we offer after the sale. You call into our technical service lines; you can many times get right to the researcher who developed a product. We understand our customers. We really care about their research, and we want to make sure that their experiments are successful."[5]

In addition to the "juice" that they sell, they also offer diagnostics and instruments (figure 16.3). The diagnostic kits they develop help people detect inherited genetic disorders and cancer diagnosis. And instruments, that's when I was reunited with my beloved Western Blot—the machine that separates proteins in bands on a dense gel. But now it's automated, much faster and feeds the results into software. It's like using ChatGPT instead of your library card. All their "ProteinSimple" instruments have names like "Jess," "Leo," and "Peggy Sue" and look like cute Japanese rice cookers, white and blue or yellow, but they offer researchers powerful tools for their research, spanning immune-oncology and vaccines to cell therapy. They help researchers isolate single cells and even help

16.3 Bio-Techne's analytical instruments.

detect subvisible particles because of the risk they pose to patient safety. "While these instruments do not have margin characteristics like the consumables, they actually drive more pull-through demand for the consumables used in these high-tech machines," says Matt. "And as the installed instrument base grows, it creates a growing captive customer base for all the reagents." In other words, by inventing and acquiring the new instruments needed in modern day labs, they ensure a continued demand for their "juice."

Bio-Techne is incredibly disciplined about its M&A. Matt said they won't buy a company unless it believes it can achieve gross margins greater than 70 percent, an adjusted operating margin of at least 30 percent at scale, and a return on invested capital in the double digits within five years. Oh, and by the way, it also has to leverage Bio-Techne's core consumables!

Consider the ProteinSimple Devices. Bio-Techne bought the company in 2015 for $300 million. According to Matt, "The trailing revenue and EBITDA at time of acquisition was $57.1 million and $7.9 million, respectively. Thus TECH paid a multiple of 5.25x revenue, or 37.5x EBITDA. In 2024 (or nine years later), the instrument was generating ~$300 million in revenue and (best guess) about $120 million in adjusted EBITDA. Thus the acquisition valuation on F24's numbers is 1.0x revenue or 2.5x EBITDA. Assuming TECH did not have to dump a huge amount of capital to grow the business, this was likely a huge homerun for the company."

Buying companies in the biotech space is not for the faint of heart. Companies routinely feel they are worth more than what Bio-Techne is offering. There, too, Bio-Techne has a novel approach to acquisitions—consider, for example, Wilson Wolf. When it comes to cell and gene therapy, immune cells

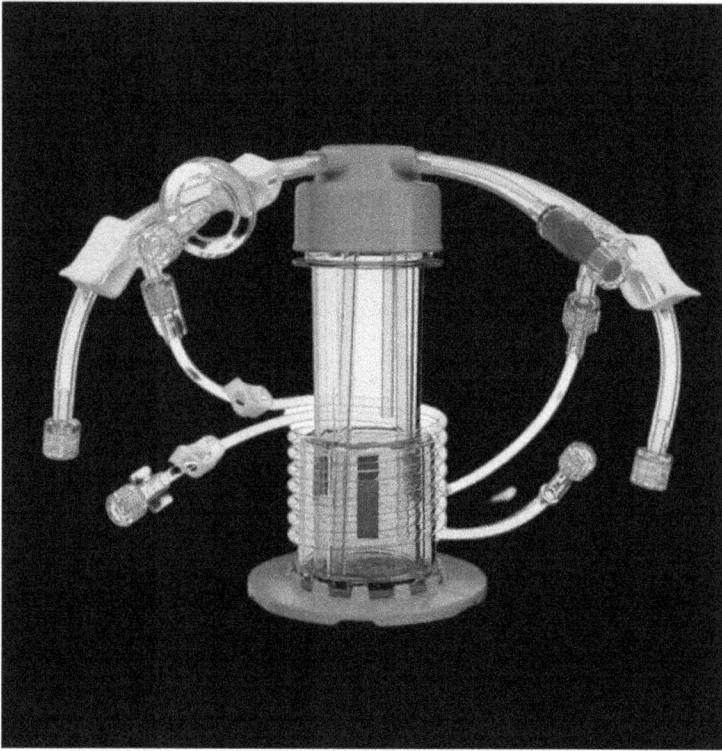

16.4 Wilson Wolf instrument to assist in immunotherapy.

are grown outside of the patient's body. These cells are then put into a patient to restore their capacity to fight things such as cancer, infections, or auto-immune diseases (figure 16.4). Well, Wilson Wolf's products provide those immune cells with the ideal amount of oxygen and nutrients as they need it, turning them into strong, highly capable cells ready to do their job. Serious stuff for serious treatments that would also position Bio-Techne in new high growth markets. It's why they made an early investment for 20 percent of the company. But when Bio-Techne went to buy the rest, Wilson Wolf said it would cost $1 billion dollars.[6]

According to Matt, Bio-Techne's reaction was essentially, "I know you think this is worth a billion dollars, we agree with you . . . but only if you hit these numbers."

Matt explained that Bio-Techne has an agreement to acquire the rest of Wilson Wolf "for $1 billion when it reaches $226 million in revenue and $136 million in EBITDA. Or, if not reached by the end of 2027, Bio-Techne may acquire Wilson Wolf for 4.4x trailing revenue. It's a good example of Bio-Techne's M&A approach to partner/invest with potential targets."

In other words, the onus is on Wilson Wolf to keep growing the business to realize the billion dollars. If it does, Bio-Techne would consider it a good purchase. If not, it has a deal in place to buy it at a lower valuation. It's an innovative acquisition structure and a win-win for both sides.

Acquisitions have fueled Bio-Techne's financial and geographic growth over the decades. Today it generates $1.16 billion in revenue and $365 million in adjusted operating profits and has about $5 billion in dry powder for even more acquisitions to drive continued growth well into the future.

150+: On Pinterest, there is a T-shirt with a green space alien shaking hands with an astronaut/scientist. The alien says, "one hour on this planet is 7 years on earth." The astronaut/scientist says, "Great, I'll do my PhD here!" Seriously, though, it's no joke getting a PhD. The dissertation alone and low pay along the way is enough to cause many to walk away from pursuing the degree. Those who do are usually determined to make an impact over the long term. Although many get hired by the tech giants, many pursue research. Working in a lab can be lonely and full of failure. But they aspire to contribute something new to the world, even if it takes a helluva long time. Bio-Techne employs more than 150 PhDs around the world. They work on everything from reagents and assays to new instruments. They need to understand where biotechnology is going and how they can help their customers, also PhDs, make the next big discovery.

But a company that employs 150 PhDs does not mean Bio-Techne operates in slow moving committees common to academia. Quite the opposite. Matt admires how Bio-Techne organizes and propels itself forward. Each year the organization, from the PhDs to the business leaders to the area managers, comes together to work on a strategic plan. They brainstorm countless ideas, but then score them based on how they weigh against strategic filters (strategic growth, enhancing the core business, customer experience, and revenue), available resources, known risks, and, unlike most academia, return on investment. The best ideas get funded and deployed. "The prioritization process has proven to be a relatively accurate determinant of future revenue for the company," says Matt, pointing to a graph comparing projected revenue to actuals over the last five years (see figure 16.5).

bio-techne

Prioritization Process

Prioritization Projections
Have Been Predictive of
Revenue Five Years Out

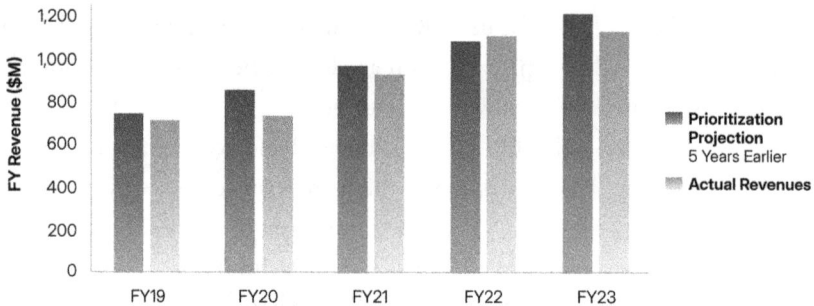

16.5 Graph of Bio-Techne's prioritization projections versus actual revenue.

Looking out, the company's current strategic plan has it nearly doubling revenue, to $2 billion, by 2028. It would have happened earlier, but some of their products have faced longer than expected regulatory approvals.

Doubling in size every five years is the basis of Matt's 100-bagger trajectory. I asked him to lay out his case for the company to be a 100-bagger . . . again.

He points me first to its stock chart, which was a rocket ship up and to the right . . . until October of 2021 (figure 16.6). Matt explains that after COVID hit, governments around the world drastically increased spending on vaccines and treatments. The stock rode up along with it . . . and then came down with it as well as the world slowly recovered.

"It's a coiled spring," Matt says, "The decade before COVID, the company was growing operating profit at 16 percent a year. The market thinks it's pricing it as if it will be growing much slower. I think it will be 16 percent again. Health care is too important to society globally and the stock will bounce back like a spring."

Second, Matt points me to the total addressable market (TAM). Bio-Techne only has 10 percent market penetration in its core products as well as its instruments. They have only 2 percent in cell and gene therapy and spatial biology. There is a tremendous amount of upside.

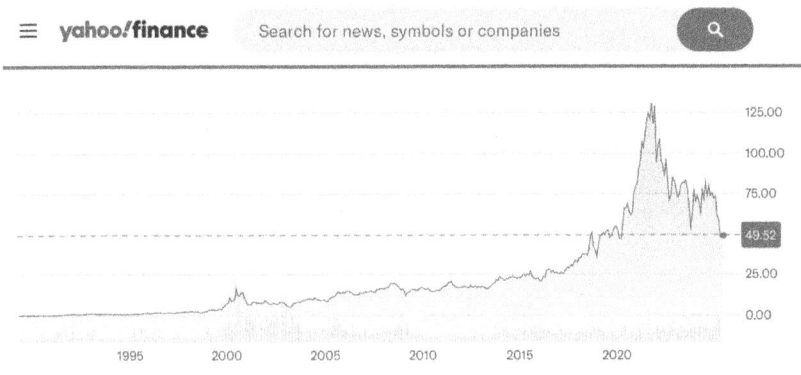

16.6 Stock chart for Bio-Techne.
Source: Yahoo Finance.

"The industry is highly fragmented with hundreds of players across the globe. Bio-Techne's large catalog of reagents makes it easier for a customer because they can get all their specific proteins/immuno-assays/etc. from one vendor. Bio-Techne's consistent quality makes Bio-Techne the go-to choice if you are looking for quality," said Matt.

Third, he believes the company is well-positioned in high-growth markets to capitalize on health care mega trends. "I believe it can be a 100-bagger again because of its market opportunity/growth and return profile. I believe Bio-Techne can continue to grow top-line by 12 percent+ for next ten to thirty years, and still has reasonable margin leverage, which should allow it grow free cash flow 14–16 percent+ and possibly a little valuation improvement as well to get to 100-bagger in thirty years."

And what's the biggest risk to it becoming a two-peat, a dynasty, or whatever sports metaphor you prefer? I wasn't expecting Matt's response.

"Most likely, the company will get bought out." So somebody will snatch the trophy just before they cross the finish line? Although the company doesn't have any direct major competitors, Matt says that companies like Thermo Fisher Scientific or Danaher, giants in the life sciences industry with market caps of over $200 billion each, may want to tuck it in. "Bio-Techne competes against Thermo Fisher and Danaher by having the best, most consistent and broadest catalog of products. Thermo Fisher and Danaher are huge in other areas of Life Sciences. This is a very small percentage of their offerings." Matt said.

So, there you have it, ladies and gentlemen. If its left to its own devices, Bio-Techne, Matt says, can multiply one hundred times again. And if someone acquires Bio-Techne, they will pay a premium for it. Matt and investors will do well, but the company will not get a second ring on its finger. "Where Bio-Techne really shines is that it offers the next leg in the value-chain (diagnostic instruments), so customers buy the more efficient/higher accuracy instrument, then buy the reagents that are needed to conduct an experiment."

Matt's reminder about cutting edge diagnostics brings me to my final note.

DEGREES OF SEPARATION

Dr. Johan Skog, a Swedish scientist, was working on his second postdoc at Mass General Hospital in Boston in the neuroscience group, studying brain cancers. He was isolating tumor stem cells. "And what was interesting was that you had these larger vesicles coming off from the stem cells, but also smaller type of vesicles that was only around 100 to 200 nanometers in diameter. So those I obviously didn't see in the light microscope, but in the electron microscope, they were very obvious. And they were present not only on the tumor stem cells, but also on other non-stem cell tumor cells," said Skog.[7]

They were exosomes, cells that specialized in waste management. Cell debris. They're the garbagemen of our biology (and I say that with respect). They normally are full of proteins and lipids. But upon closer inspection, he noticed they also carried RNA, which creates the template for protein production.

Ordinarily, to diagnose someone with malignant cancer, you need to do a biopsy of the tumor. But if exosomes carry the RNA from the cell they came from and are swimming around our body, Skog thought there could be an easier way to test for tumors. In other words, Skog wanted to use exosomes as a noninvasive biomarker for tumors and create a "liquid biopsy."

He left Mass General to start a company and raised $20 million during the financial crisis in 2008, a very hard time to get anyone to back you. One of his first products was a urine test for prostate cancer. The current method is a twelve-core transrectal biopsy of your tumor and then repeated testing to

16.7 Kim Kelderman, CEO of Bio-Techne.

understand its severity. Just the term "twelve-core transrectal biopsy" is enough to make many men simply run in the opposite direction. And here Skog was asking men to just pee in a cup.

In 2018, Bio-Techne bought Skog's company.[8] Kim Kelderman (figure 16.7), now CEO of Bio-Techne and the previous president of the diagnostic and genomics division, commercialized the "ExoDx prostate test" (figure 16.8). More than 150,000 men have now used Skog's invention to help inform their diagnosis (figure 16.7). Bio-Techne sold the test to Mdxhealth in 2025 but retained access to the proprietary exosome-based technology for ongoing kit development in its precision diagnostics growth pillar.

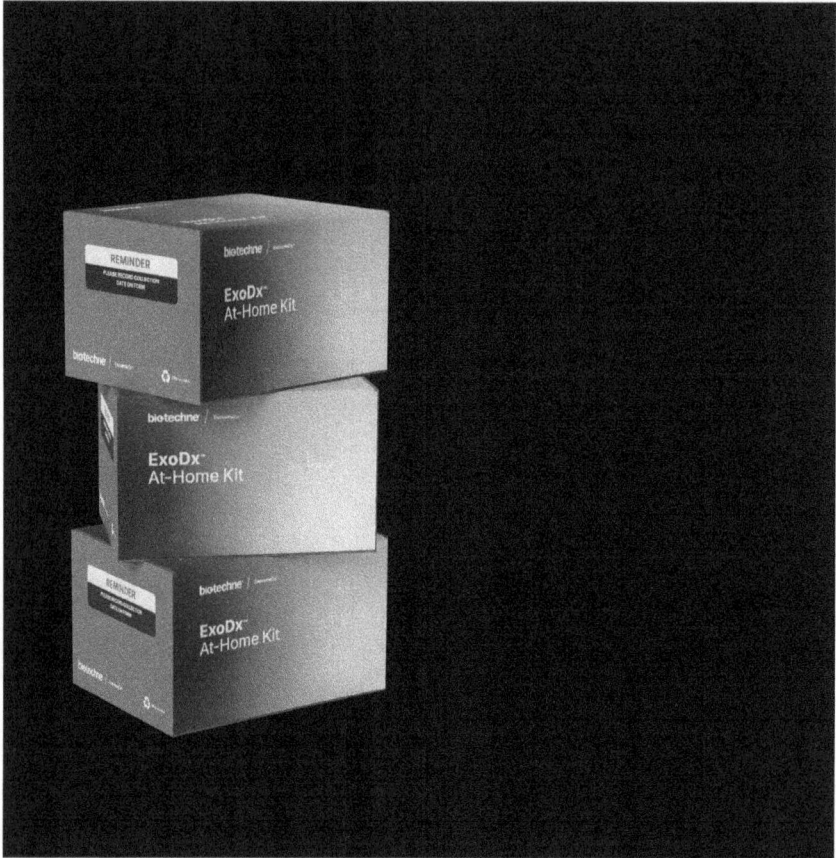

16.8 Bio-Techne's ExoDx prostate test.

I bring up this story because of Matt's uncle, Dr. Robert Nieland, who went to college and medical school at the University of Iowa. He interned at the Sacramento Medical Center at UC Davis and then served in the US Air Force as a flight surgeon at Shaw Air Force Base in South Carolina. He then went into private practice at the Medical Arts Clinic in Hickory, North Carolina.

"My uncle died of prostate cancer, and he was a doctor and couldn't do anything about it," said Matt. "Most prostate exams come up with a questionable result. They test you again and again. Most are wrong, and now they have found a way for it to be a lot more accurate."

16.9 The late Dr. Robert Nieland.

Dr. Nieland was survived by his wife Andrea (but everyone called her Andy), his sister Jonel Ankrum (Matt's mother), his two sons Danny and David (a secret service agent), and four grandchildren.

This chapter is dedicated to Dr. Nieland, for his service to his country and to the countless patients he has helped over his professional career (figure 16.9). It is also dedicated to all of the PhDs quietly working every day in their labs inventing ways to make tomorrow a better day for all of us. May it also serve as inspiration to Matt's daughter, Peyton, and my daughter, Samantha, as they both embark on careers in psychology and science.

CHAPTER 17

NETWORK EFFECTS TIMES TWO

"**A** million dollars isn't cool. You know what's cool? A billion dollars." That was one of my favorite lines from Aaron Sorkin's movie, *The Social Network*. Justin Timberlake, playing the slick Napster cofounder Sean Parker, said it to Jesse Eisenberg, playing a young, impressionable Mark Zuckerberg, over lunch one afternoon soon after he launched TheFacebook. Zuckerberg's cofounders were pressuring him to put ads up on the site. Parker thought the company would get a bigger valuation if they delayed putting ads on the social network and stayed cool. The more people who joined would make the social platform exponentially more valuable thanks to network effects, and it would lead to an explosive increase in valuation—from one million to one billion dollars. As Timberlake walked away from the lunch table, he turned around with one other piece of advice and said, "Drop the 'The.' Just Facebook. It's cleaner." Shaking his head in complete and utter awe, Eisenberg just said, "Shit!"

Simply put, network effects make a product more useful as more people use it.

COMPOUNDING NETWORKS

Go back to the telephone or the fax machine. The first person with a phone didn't have anyone to call. With two phones, the product becomes more valuable; with billions of phones, it becomes invaluable. And according to Metcalfe's law, the value of a network increases in proportion to the square of the number of connections. If that sounds confusing, just think that each new person has a disproportionately positive impact on the growth and value of the network.

William Brian Arthur, the Belfast-born economist best known for his work on network effects, told the team at Andreessen Horowitz, "Five generations ago, none of our ancestors spoke English, but we're all speaking English now." In other words, English is a network effect. "We speak English because we wanna be understood by everybody else. . . . And if small events had gone otherwise in the 1700s, it might've been French. Or, if you were betting in the 1500s, it could have been Latin or whatever."[1]

In the twentieth century, Visa (the credit card company) also benefited from network effects. As more merchants accepted Visa, Visa card holders had more places to use it. And as more people used it, more merchants were willing to accept it as a form of payment. Round and round we go!

As I mentioned earlier, Facebook created enormous network effects. If your friends were on it and thought it was cool, you needed to be on it. And the more people on it, the more powerful the utility of the network becomes. And unlike the hardware costs that go along with fax machines, telephones, or credit card readers, digital businesses with network effects have even lower marginal costs (for example, hosting and streaming). Not only does the business itself gets better with increasing returns, but the valuation also spirals upward. At Google, search results get better with higher search volume, which then drives more users to go to the simple white box multiple times a day.

As a media guy, I have often wondered whether Netflix and other streaming services could create network effects. Do more users make the product better? It's understood that they can spread the cost of a big budget show across a larger base of users. That demonstrates the power of economies of scale, not network effects—because the users are not connecting with each other. But video platforms such as YouTube and TikTok are different. There the creators and the users form a network that benefits each other in an exponential fashion. The more users they have, the more low-cost content creators they attract, making the product better, which in turn attracts even more users. And unlike YouTube or Facebook, where you choose who or what to follow, TikTok serves you up the most popular content . . . from the entire network. I'm not smart enough to know what that does to Metcalfe's Law! Putting aside all the large and serious impacts of these services on society at large for just a minute, it will be interesting to see who wins the video wars on a purely business and technical architecture basis.

So what does this have to do with Matt and his daughters? Well, so far, I've talked about the power of essential products and the incredible characteristics of business-to-business companies. Bentley Systems, as I discussed in chapter fifteen, is starting to benefit from network effects in its most recent product, the digital twin business, bringing engineers, designers, and infrastructure asset owners all together onto their platform. But just imagine the "chocolate meets peanut butter" combination of business-to-business companies where network effects are at the center of what they do! Matt has found two such companies, and he's adding both to the coffee can.

FORMS, FORMS, AND MORE FORMS

First, let's focus on SPS Commerce (Ticker symbol: SPSC). It's a Minnesota-based company (named for St. Paul Software), and its vision is to be the world's retail network. What does that mean? Well, have you ever thought about how a retailer buys and stocks products for its shelves? For example, where does Target, Walmart, or Home Depot get red hammers? And how do the suppliers of red hammers get their products to retailers? These are all simple questions, but behind the scenes the process historically has been paper driven and cumbersome to say the least. Well, SPS Commerce offers a digital solution—that leverages forty-year-old electronic data interchange (EDI) documents—to help retailers and suppliers communicate throughout the ordering, shipping, and invoicing processes.

If that sounds boring, it is. But as I have learned, with the companies Matt chooses, that boring can be excellence when it comes to growing stable returns. Let's get started, and just pretend you are a kid again listening to Schoolhouse Rock on "How a Bill Becomes a Law!"

The first thing is the retailer sends the supplier a purchase order (also known as an EDI Form 850), which also details specific instructions on how many red hammers it wants and how to ship and package or palette them as well as where they should be shipped. Despite its obscure code name, it's the most wonderful document a supplier could ever receive! It means the supplier will be generating revenue. And to show its gratitude, the supplier then sends back EDI Form 855, acknowledging that it received the order and can fulfill that order within a specified date range. It's sort of like replying with a heart emoji on a kind text. Then the supplier has to send a document (I'll spare readers all the form numbers moving forward) to its warehouse to see if the red hammer is in stock, and the warehouse has to check the inventory and then confirm the request back to the supplier.

Then the warehouse or the supplier has to check in with whomever is shipping the hammers. The warehouse could have its own trucks or may contract out to a third-party logistics (3PL) company. The 3PL has to confirm shipment plans with the warehouse or supplier. Then the warehouse and 3PL have to pick, pack, and ship the red hammers with the correct scannable labels. Once it's shipped to the retailer's stores, there's another document to confirm receipt and what, if anything, was wrong with the shipment. After that is reconciled, the supplier sends the invoice, and the retailer has to submit payment. And that's just the basics.

What if the retailer wants the shipment sent to its distribution center instead of directly to a specific store or multiple stores? Or, to compete with online retailers, the retailer may want the supplier to ship to a customer directly from its warehouse after the customer purchased it on the retailer's website. What if the retailer wants all three, as is becoming more commonplace in a world of omnichannel sales? What if the supplier is selling goods to Target, Walmart, or Home Depot, among others, and has to go through this for every retailer with very different requirements or rule books? All of this increases the number of touch points in the system that need to communicate with each other. Can you see "network effects" starting to rear its head? And, by the way, timing for each step of the way is critical. For example, one of the forms a supplier has to send a retailer is an advanced shipment notice (ASN), notifying the retailer of a specific delivery date and time.

"Well, they want that document because when your truck of product arrives at their store or at their DC (distribution center), they know when it's coming, they can quickly unload the product and get it on the sales floor faster," Emily Curran, senior product manager at SPS Commerce told Startup CPG. "Whereas, for example, without that advanced ship notice, without that EDI document, that retailer-distributor is essentially blind. We've had retailers tell us that without an ASN, that product can sit in the back room for up to six days. Whereas with the ASN, they can actually process it and receive it that same day. So, you're avoiding those missed sales."[2]

SPS Commerce's system also helps take the boring out of the boring. The supplier isn't hit with a whole bunch of unnatural EDI codes. Instead, the platform translates the documents into clear, easy to understand language. "We're going to take care of translating, getting rid of any of the EDI code segments. You need to know nothing about that. And you're going to get a human readable order just like you would an email," Curran said.

SPS Commerce also helps automate some of the steps for repeatable orders, Curran added:

> So typically, if you're always accepting your orders, you're good on your inventory, that can just be something that we automatically send out on your behalf. You don't have to think about it. But if you know there are situations where maybe you might not have the inventory to fulfill and you just want to communicate some adjustments to the quantity, again, our solution makes it super simple for you to be able to communicate that back and do all the heavy lifting of getting it back into the distributor or the retailer's EDI format.[3]

THE HARD NUMBERS

According to SPS Commerce, every day thousands of retailers are in contact with hundreds of thousands of suppliers about millions of products. Given the complexity, retailers consider the old way of communicating—phone calls, faxes, and emails—a giant time suck. They are requiring their suppliers to be on the digital EDI system. And that means, Matt says, the company is hitting its tipping point, because suppliers are starting to get the message. If English is a network effect, digital EDIs are the language of retail. And we all know Matt's lingua franca. Here are his three key numbers to better understand the SPS Commerce business.

KEY NUMBERS TO UNDERSTAND SPSC

95+	120,000	94%

95+: EDI doesn't charge the retailers for providing this service. Instead, Matt says, they charge suppliers $100 per month per retailer. The good news for SPS Commerce is that this charge can add up pretty quickly. Matt says the average supplier/customer pays $12,850 a year. In 2024, it is projected to generate more than $635 million in revenue and $185 million in adjusted EBITDA. Since 2012, revenue has grown at 19.1 percent CAGR and adjusted EBITDA at 28.7 percent. Overall, it has had ninety-five consecutive quarters of revenue growth.

"It's amazing how few institutional investors own this company," Matt exclaimed. "It's an overlooked gem that does something so freakin' boring that nobody understands it." (By the way, if Matt is calling something freakin' boring, it means he believes it's a very, very good investment!) He continues, "It keeps going like the Energizer Bunny, with ninety-five consecutive quarters of revenue growth, almost twenty-five years of revenue growth each and every quarter. Show me how many companies can do that. The growth is enduring. And if I am right about the tipping point, I expect to see even more growth." I told you!

120,000: SPS Commerce has forty-five thousand paying customers and one hundred twenty thousand connections with clients. Many of those clients are using the platform to validate orders but are doing the rest of the process manually, with their own teams.

"Many of the companies on the one hundred twenty thousand list are spending money building their own EDI systems or using a less full-service version of SPS Commerce, and they have 'Bob, Jane, and Suzy' running these operations for them. They may or may not know SPS Commerce is a better solution, but they like 'Bob, Jane, and Suzy' too much to let them go. At some point, these companies will say, 'I don't need to do this myself,'" says Matt. "The question these suppliers should be asking themselves is whether managing EDIs is a differentiating, strategic function that the supplier must internally own and control. That is becoming increasingly less likely given SPCS's role and its ongoing efforts to advance the technology, along with the push by retailers to be more agile."

Matt explained that the larger suppliers, companies as big as P&G, have historically had their own EDI teams . . . and used them to their advantage:

P&G has been running its own EDI team and technology for decades, and historically that has been a huge differentiation for them as they can guarantee a Kroger or Walmart that they can keep up with their retailer rule playbook that smaller players could not. That is no longer the case anymore with SPSC. But, in the past, that is partly why P&G (and other big suppliers) gobbled up smaller players and leveraged marketing dollars to control shelf space at the retailers. *Today*, with internet competition and consumers' thirst for all new brands (through introduction by the internet or other marketing channels), the retailers no longer cling solely to the biggest suppliers. With SPSC, the retailer can know that the smaller suppliers can keep pace with the retailers' pace of innovation and change.

94%: The clients that are on the system tend to stay on the system. Around 94 percent of SPS Commerce's revenue is recurring. That's music to Matt's ears. Attrition, he says, usually happens when a retailer drops a supplier.

"To get new customers," Matt said, "SPS Commerce has one of the best go-to-market strategies." It basically waits on retailers to make changes to their rulebook. And that happens a lot. In other words, every time a retailer changes its preference for a shipping label, adds a new form or a new field to an old form, or wants to know the dimensions of a palette so they can optimize space in their distribution centers, or wants to stock a new in-store promotion, or wants to start drop-shipping, or whatever it wants to change, it's an opportunity for SPS Commerce's sales team to talk to its suppliers that are only using the service for validation and upsell them to come fully onto their platform. The more change, the more complexity, the harder it gets, Matt says, for Bob, Jane, and Suzy to keep up. The chain reaction also attracts new suppliers that can meet the retailer's exacting demands—all in the name of serving the customer, of course.

The company has forty-five thousand paying clients and one hundred twenty thousand in the system, but Matt says the company sees two hundred thousand potential clients in the future, each paying $25,000 a year versus the current $12,480 because of new features and upsells in their platform (more on that when we get to acquisitions). That's a $5 billion opportunity. The number of nodes or new clients increases the value of the network. "Remember Metcalf's Law," says Matt. "Like with any power law, the winner in this space will accrue most of the benefit." It's also why the team at SPS Commerce likes to say, if we win a new client today, the whole network wins tomorrow.

To help further accelerate its journey up the curve of this law, SPS Commerce, Matt says, converts 21.5 percent of its revenue into free cash flow and uses the capital to compound via share buybacks, and, you guessed it, acquisitions. In the past five years, they generated $400 million in free cash flow and used $103 million of it to do share buybacks and $289 million to make acquisitions. Its ROTA is a Warren Buffett friendly 27 percent.

Some of the acquisitions get them into new geographies (Europe is way behind) or into new kinds of retail markets, such as GCommerce, which they bought in 2022 and put them into digital EDI's for the auto aftermarket industry. In 2024, Chad Collins, the CEO of SPS Commerce, made the company's largest acquisition, paying $206 million ($119 million in cash, net of cash acquired, and

$87 million in stock) for SupplyPike, an Arkansas-based retail tech start-up in the shadow of Walmart.

Christian Hassold of *In/Organic*, who regularly comments on mergers and acquisitions (M&A) transactions of hypergrowth SaaS companies, explains:

> And what SupplyPike does is essentially help brands recover what are called chargebacks or deductions from a retailer. So, let's say that you are a brand like Coca-Cola or Mondelez and you're doing business with either Amazon or Walmart, some portion of the transactions that you do with them will have some sort of a dispute. Walmart will say, you didn't send us the right product, or you didn't send us the whole order on time and in full, which is a term they use, OTIF, in the retail industry. You didn't meet with our compliance requirements and therefore we're going to charge you back. Some 10 percent of those charge backs are considered to be errant and the old way of fixing them was accountants essentially talking to one another and saying, you owe me a dollar and here's why, and there's paperwork flying around in terms of the companies trying to decide who owes who for what reason and what's all the backup. The system was really so inefficient.[4]

Hassold, who applauded SPS Commerce's CEO and corporate development team on buying a company that digitized and automated his whole process, added, "SupplyPike is essentially helping those suppliers do right by themselves financially in terms of making sure that if a deduction is right, then they pay for it, and if it's not, then they get to reclaim that deduction from the retailer. So going back to what SPS said on their conference call, they reported this as high customer overlap, highly complementary to their business, expanded the TAM. You can see all of the pieces coming together."

What supplier or retailer on SPS Commerce wouldn't pay extra for this new feature? And that expanded TAM from SupplyPike is yet another $750 million on top of the $5 billion opportunity we learned about earlier. Matt explained, "In a network, the owner of a network has a captive customer base. This allows it to monetize that by acquiring future capabilities that bring substantial value to its customers and the entire network. It's fun watching them creating higher and higher fortresses around the castle, making it even more interesting for new customers to join the network. It's watching network effects multiply in real time."

Matt, thrilled about his calculations, said: "Over the next fifteen years, if SPSC can approach its target of 200K (a ~fourfold increase) and wallet share of $25,000 (a ~twofold increase), revenue growth should compound at 14.9 percent CAGR (an eightfold increase)."

He added, "The real power of a network B2B is the sustainable advantage— your customers won't go to another vendor because you have all the people, resources, and connections they need. This probably leads to better growth and definitely should result in higher margins—due to lower customer acquisition costs and higher retention. SPS has substantial margin leverage as the network expands, which should lead to adjusted EBITDA margins well above 40 percent."

Perhaps the biggest risk is if Amazon swallows up the entire retail market. In other words, no more Walmart, Target, or Home Depot. No more Dick's Sporting Goods stores, Ralphs groceries, or Hudson shops at airports. And no more websites from any of these brands. Although Amazon is clearly winning the ecommerce race (with 37.6 percent of the online market), ecommerce accounted for just 22 percent of all retail sales in 2023. What we are seeing is the growth of omnichannel businesses, where customers buy from brands both in stores as well as online. A case in point is Walmart, which is benefiting from its "buy online and pickup at the store" strategy, which also allows returns at the store. In 2024, Walmart's stock increased more than 72 percent (before dividends), which was a 63 percent higher return than Amazon's stock (which was up 44.4 percent during the same period). "If anything, Amazon is forcing the rest of the industry to become more digital, and that's a positive for SPS Commerce," Matt says.

AT THE TABLE

When Matt explained the company to his daughters, they liked that SPS Commerce was leveling the playing field.

> **PEYTON:** SPS is giving the power back to the little guys, smaller companies from real people who are looking to give their customers the convenience of Amazon with the quality of their own. A lot of us debate whether to choose to buy a product from a company we care about more or from a company that's more convenient. This way we don't have to make that choice, and that's what I think makes SPS really special.

For Morgan, the proof is in the pudding.

> MORGAN: Learning that SPS Commerce has over 95+ consecutive
> quarters of revenue growth is remarkable.

She was also struck by her father's explanation for the company's go-to-market strategy. For her, it was the company's way of continuing their winning streak.

> MORGAN: I was really interested to find out how SPS recruited other
> companies to join their customer list. It is a brilliant strategy they have.

Without telling them, Matt then made a digital transaction of his own, buying SPSC for the coffee can. A few seconds later, he got an email confirmation saying, ironically, that the purchase order was complete.

But this wasn't the only network effects driven B2B company Matt was purchasing. The other one was Descartes (Ticker symbol: DSGX), a company based in Waterloo, Canada (one of America's largest trading partners). It has much in common with SPSC: it, too, operates in the world of commerce, focusing on supply chain logistics; it, too, is building up its fortress around its network via acquisitions (even more so than SPSC); and it, too, is not widely known.

"It's completely under the radar," says Matt. "Not a lot of managers own this stock. If you ask them about it, they then ask, 'Who is Descartes? I don't know them. Is it some French company?' Matt says it's a stock that's hard to buy because it always feels expensive, but it's easy to own because they just keep creating value . . . year after year after year."

YET ANOTHER NETWORK

If SPS Commerce manages the communications between a retailer and a supplier, Descartes focuses on all the players involved in getting products made and shipped globally. How do you have something made in another country and get it here? How do you cross borders? Which ports of entry do you use, Los Angeles or Newark, for example? Do you use ground, ocean, or air transportation? Are there expeditors or 3PLs involved? Well, Descartes, has all these parties on the same platform—pulling together a network of more than twenty-six thousand customers all looking to improve their supply chain logistics.

"The way I think about it is SPS is the intranet, connecting the supplier and retailer and all their communications. Descartes is like the internet," Matt said. "This is the outside network. Descartes is helping businesses move their goods around the world."

It's a world I grew up in. My earliest experience learning about global supply chain logistics was sitting down with my father Lal Khemlani after he returned from overseas business trips. Over the years, he worked with various fashion designers, including Egon von Furstenberg, Diane von Furstenberg, and Guy Laroche, to expand their global production capabilities. Always on a plane, he was often among the first garment producers to try to do business in new international markets and was a pioneer in the field now known as "global sourcing." He bought cloth and materials for his designers from across Asia, Africa, and the Middle East. He determined which factories could make high quality clothing without exploiting labor. I still remember him waking up in the middle of the night in New York (because of the time zones of the countries he was working with) to call and fax suppliers and shippers to make sure the orders arrived on time. There was no email yet. It was stressful. If the shipments were late or damaged, sales would suffer. Fashion only stays fashionable for a short amount of time. But he relished exploring and connecting the world and took great pride in what he did. In fact, I will never forget the first time he came back from Dubai. After dinner, he unrolled a map of the Middle East on our dining room table and told me the UAE would become a powerful global player someday because Dubai was investing in its shipping ports, had a business friendly government, a free trade zone, and access to the Persian Gulf to the west as well as the Gulf of Oman and the Arabian Sea to the east. Today it is one of the busiest ports in the world and a transshipment center for global trade. Lessons like that not only opened up the world to me, but it also made it feel real. It reinforced the importance of geography when it comes to global trade. And it also contributed to my interest in global affairs and economics as a reporter (figure 17.1).

Descartes is a tool I wish my father had. It was all in his head, in his folders, in his big briefcase full of samples, and on his maps. Today the world is so much more complicated, and the need for a digital logistics platform is increasingly necessary.

17.1 The late Lal Khemlani with his three sons: Neeraj, Dhiren, and Sanjeev.

"People don't understand how complicated and how outdated the supply chain is today." Matt adds:

> Governments tell companies which countries they can deal with and which ones they can't. Governments also say which individuals you can deal with and which ones you can't. It's hard to keep track of all these growing lists, especially when so many of these individuals create all kinds of shell companies to disguise themselves. Then there's tariffs. When Trump increased tariffs on Chinese goods, a company had to suddenly figure out how to manufacture and get their goods from Vietnam or India. All the attacks in the Red Sea by the Houthis are now causing ships to go a longer route and come into a different port. All of this stuff in the world is getting more complicated and more challenging. But as supply chain logistics gets more and more digital, it has a transformative effect. Companies can deal with getting their

products from Point A to Point B in faster and easier ways. The flow of information between trading partners is as important as the movement of goods. And Descartes essentially provides everyone on its network a sort of Bloomberg terminal for logistics.

That terminal has grown in value every time there's been a shock to the global system.

The hideous attacks on the World Trade Center in lower Manhattan on September 11, 2001, led to a tsunami of regulation around global supply chains. "Governments of the world since 9/11 have increasingly said, I need to know what's coming across my border in the form of an electronic manifest before the plane or the ship or the truck set sail to come into my country,"[5] said Ed Ryan, the CEO of Descartes.

That additional complexity, and the tools required to share documents with greater transparency and frequency, led more customers to use Descartes. The same thing happened when the COVID-19 virus spread across the world and completely ground global supply chains to a halt. I was the president and cohead of CBS News and Stations at the time, and I remember LA correspondent Carter Evans doing countless stories about shops with empty shelves, the impact on small businesses, and whether certain toys would make it to our homes in time for Christmas. To highlight the shortage of truck drivers, Norah O'Donnell went to trucking school. Bill Whitaker at *60 Minutes* investigated logjams at California's largest shipping ports. Ed Ryan said one of the first things his customers did was to make investments in technology—like Descartes—to get a quick sense of the return on investment (ROI) for alternate shipping routes and solutions.

THE HARD NUMBERS (AGAIN)

When Biden came into office, we did reports on the world's reliance on Taiwan and its computer chips; the impact of the war in Ukraine on wheat prices; and how China's belt and road initiative around the world was enabling it to corner the market on certain natural resources, such as lithium for electric car batteries. All of it made me feel that we would continue to see a global strategic realignment between countries around supply chain needs. Today, as a country, we are constantly debating what industries and resources we need to own and how best to connect to and be dependent on to the rest of the world. These are heady issues, and I wanted to get Matt's point of view on their impact on his investments. But let's start with his customary three key numbers to understand the Descartes business . . . a business that almost didn't make it.

KEY NUMBERS TO UNDERSTAND DSGX

35%	46	15%

35%: In 2004, saddled with debt, Descartes almost went bankrupt in the post dot com bubble collapse—a true existential event. Newly minted CEO Arthur Mesher, who worked on a shipping dock during his university days and had a photographic memory for purchase orders, did two things to turn the company around. First, soon after his appointment, he fired his sales staff during a restructuring. He believed the product needed to sell itself. He said he "didn't want to sell; he wanted to serve . . . his customers." In other words, continue to invest in the product, and word of mouth would take care of the rest. Second, he changed its business model. Descartes used to sell software via large upfront license fees. But it moved to a subscription service, now commonly known as a SaaS service, because it would allow the company to start building a base of recurring revenue. Slowly but surely, Descartes turned the ship.

In 2013, Ed Ryan took over as CEO and has continued to build on those foundational moves by embracing technology shifts along the way. First there was universality of mobile and then there was the internet of things. The company put sensors on everything, from trucks to ships to planes, to illuminate all the points of the supply chain. And the resulting rich data repository of information, combined with real-time cloud scaled computing, helps all the members of the global logistics network.

"The more information that we can get, you know, we're big in the optimization business, so the more information we can get about where things are and what they're doing, the more we can help our customers optimize those assets and take better advantage of them. And, you know, in a lot of cases, save an awful lot of money," said Ryan. "If, you know, you just think of our routing applications, to put it in perspective. If a customer of ours has 1,000 trucks and they're making 15,000 deliveries a day. If I can show them how to do that with

900 trucks, take 100 trucks off the road. You know, each truck costs them about $250,000 a year by the time you're done paying for the driver and the gas and the maintenance and the vehicle lease itself. If we take a hundred trucks off the rest, $25 million a year in savings without having to do very much, right? You install some piece of software, and I'll just show you how to do it more efficiently."[6]

As word continued to spread about its ability to help its customers be more efficient, Descartes saw more customers join the network, including a "who's who" list of companies including Delta and American Airlines, to Ocean Network Express, to trucking companies XPO Logistics and Schneider, to intermediaries such as DHL, to retailers Home Depot and Crate & Barrel, to manufacturers Coca Cola and Toyota, and to distributors Fresenius and US Foods. The ballooning of customers has helped the company deliver eighty consecutive quarters of revenue growth. And the small incremental cost of servicing those customers has also meant improved margins. When Ryan took over, the company had an adjusted EBITDA margin of 29.4 percent. It had a 44 percent margin for fiscal 2025.

Matt also loves Descartes's revenue to free cash flow conversion of 35 percent. He says the main drivers of that include a very solid operating margin, getting paid upfront and paying vendors/employees later (effectively, the company holds cash for about 233 days), and a very small capex spend each year (just 1 percent of revenue).

"This is profoundly powerful for any company, because as you grow, you bring in more cash, which is typically not the case with most companies," Matt said. "In fact, most growth companies need to spend money upfront to generate future revenue. This causes these companies to need more and more cash to grow, requiring the company to issue more equity or debt to fund the growth. In DSGX's model, similar to most SaaS companies' models, once established (moved past the tipping point of clear utility), the faster they grow, and the more cash they generate. And let the compounding begin!"

46: Descartes has used the free cash flow to make forty-six acquisitions over the last ten years. Since 2016, they have made twenty-eight acquisitions for a total consideration of $1.1 billion. Most were in the $10 million to $30 million range, two were over $200 million.

"Descartes operates a powerful M&A approach that is strategic to its long-term success," Matt explained. "M&A is a clear core competency for Descartes. It is strategically focused on acquiring capabilities and geographies that extend the value of its global logistics network and bring more value to its customers."

Smaller acquisitions such as Pixi in Germany (which optimizes warehouse processes and ecommerce fulfillment) or 4Solutions in Australia (that provides B2B supply chain solutions for the health care industry) expand them into new regions and specialty sectors. Larger acquisitions such as Visual Compliance (for $250 million) help their customers deal with international trade regulation and avoid dealing with unauthorized parties on government watch lists. Descartes, which is already experimenting with machine learning and artificial intelligence (AI) to predict when shipments will arrive or surface the most important or problematic messages a member needs to address at any given time, is currently looking to add further AI-driven logistics start-ups to its portfolio.

Each time Descartes buys a company that solves a different aspect of logistics, they introduce it to their entire network of customers. It uses that M&A event to upsell and cross sell that new feature from the acquired company and increase overall wallet share from each customer in the network. That then multiplies revenue, further increasing margins and profits like a whirling network-effects cash machine gobbling up the supply chain market.

And because of those network effects, Matt believes Descartes has become the strategic buyer of choice in the markets in which it participates. Smaller companies believe it can hit long-term earn out targets much easier through organic growth if they are acquired by Descartes and exposed to its network of paying users versus private equity companies trying to run routine consolidation plays in the space.

"These guys know what they are doing. They are logistics guys solving logistical problems for their customers by acquiring targeted solutions. They are just like their customers; they know how hard it is. That helps them find the right software specifically for them. They know how to do software in the world of dock workers. And they are a trust-worthy, entrepreneurial management team that understands how to create value," Matt said. "They're not private equity guys simply doing roll ups to keep the acquisitive revenue growth game going."

15%: These guys mean business. And to prove it to shareholders, according to Matt, they don't get paid their bonuses unless they can grow adjusted EBITDA by 15 percent a year. That's a large and serious hurdle for any company. But it's the kind of self-discipline Matt respects. The good news for the team, and more important, for investors, is that the company makes those hurdles the same way fellow Canadian and Olympic runner Edwin Moses consistently cleared his four-hundred-meter hurdles on the way to winning 122 consecutive races over a ten-year span—albeit a little bit more slowly and over a longer time frame.

"We're a slow-and-steady wins the race company," said Ryan. "A lot of tech companies they are very focused on growing rapidly. We've always been focused on making money and making sure that everything we do, you know, we do profitably, if not for our own benefit and our shareholders benefit, but for our customers as well. It gives us the money to invest in more R&D for them, and acquisitions that we can bring to the table, so that we can help them solve business problems maybe more quickly than they have in the past."[7]

Since 2014, that slow and steady approach has led Descartes to post some incredible stats. It has grown revenue at a 14.2 percent CAGR, adjusted EBITDA at an 18.7 percent CAGR, and free cash flow at a 17.5 percent CAGR. I can only imagine the celebrations at the pubs in Waterloo on bonus day! Molson and Poutine for everyone! And the party doesn't seem to be ending.

"I think you'll see us continue to get more profitable every year. We have a lot of businesses that have a very low incremental cost to operate, and the revenue keeps growing," said Ryan to the Schwab Network in September of 2024, after hitting an all-time high stock price for the company. "So, I think, you know, if you've watched us over the last 15 years, we've just grown our EBITDA and our cash flow a little bit every quarter and, you know, for, I don't know, 80 some quarters in a row. And I think that's because, you know, the way our business operates. We're almost all recurring revenue. We just keep getting a little better every quarter and that shows up in in the bottom line and I, yeah, I think that continues every time."[8]

It's also important to note that Descartes generates a 56 percent ROTA, higher than any other company highlighted in this book.

"Descartes enjoys all the quintessential benefits of a SaaS company model—build it once, sell it a million times, plus low capital-intensity—which means limited spend on property, plant, and equipment, and acquiring new customers and negative working capital," said Matt. "In addition, due to Descartes's powerful global logistics network and captive customer base, Descartes is smartly acquiring companies with additional capabilities to sell into their customers, leading to higher revenue and more cash flow, but also more deeply locking their customers into Descartes and its network. These business model attributes, and Descartes's successful execution have led to a rising ROTA over the past twenty-plus years. Descartes's ROTA is very high and should be sustainably higher than most companies due to its competitive power of network effects, coupled with its disciplined acquisition strategy and disciplined financial management."

AT THE TABLE

Matt stated that Descartes's 15+ percent growth is enduring, and management has numerous levers to achieve it. He added that Descartes does not provide an estimated TAM; however, the supply chain/logistics market is trillions of dollars with software solutions likely in the $50 billion to $200 billion spend per year range.

The company was appealing to Matt's older girls for completely different reasons. For Peyton, it was as if her father had just illuminated a completely hidden world.

> **PEYTON:** Descartes systems as a company really excites me. I think what makes them so interesting is the behind the curtain effect that they provide. Behind all the family brand names we know and trust, from Delta to Coca Cola, Descartes is pulling the invisible strings to get us what we need, when we need it. As our world continues to become more interconnected, logistics isn't just a need, it's everything.

For Morgan, it was much more about the bottom line.

> **MORGAN:** It's absolutely insane that their adjusted EBITDA growth is 15 percent almost consistently. This proves how great of a company they are.

The biggest risk to the company, Matt believes, would be a dramatic slowdown in global trade. I asked Matt if the tariffs announced at the beginning of President Trump's second administration qualified as a risk:

There's a difference between tariffs and the threat of tariffs. President Trump has been known to use them as a bargaining tool. If implemented, tariffs (and anything that causes disruption/change to the supply chain) force Descartes's customers to respond and demand more digitization, which plays into Descartes's sweet spot. Players in the industry may have to reroute packages, or simply reprice for the tariff; they will need to have an updated list of what items qualify for the tariff and from which country (because you know other countries will apply their own tariff or other response). If burdensome enough, companies may need to change their sourcing locations for items. Over time, these are positive for Descartes because change requires digital solutions, which Descartes provides. It may be tumultuous in the short-term (as you might recall, the industry is still dominated by manual processes), but Descartes should be a major beneficiary of change.

Matt believes Descartes has already built the platform to manage all the ongoing changes. And he believes that if countries continue trading with each other—fairly—it will only serve to maintain and raise the standard of living . . . for everyone:

How we interact, communicate, and comply with our international partners is going to be very important. What these network businesses, whether its Descartes or SPS Commerce, or tax database companies such as Vertex, are already doing is building a global structure for how to work together—manufacturers, shippers, retailers, and governments. That's why they are so powerful. People and companies want to be a part of it because it solves problems as the world gets more complex. We should want more collaboration, more connections, not less. Our standard of living will suffer dramatically if we don't. That's not a world I want for my girls. My goal is for my kids and my grandkids, your twins and your grandkids, for all the citizens across the world and their kids and their grandkids, to benefit from a growing standard of living. And that comes from trading with each other, allowing countries to market what they do best, in a fair and organized system. And if we can get there, if we can optimize the globalization of trade, with all of its messy tradeoffs, we should live more prosperously and more peacefully.

CHAPTER 18

DRIVE TIME

As much as Matt's head was spinning from network effects and tariffs, he couldn't help thinking about finding his next investment. But before he could start screening for the next stock, he wanted to visit his father, Charles (who preferred being called Chuck). He was turning eighty-seven and feeling a little lonely. Matt's Mom, Jonel, had passed away on April 29, 2022 (the same day as Matt and Maury's nineteenth wedding anniversary), and Chuck was now in a nursing home in Appleton, Wisconsin. Matt's sister, who lives nearby, "does the yeo-man's workload with him," and his brother also visits and calls him several times a week. Matt wanted to make a special trip from Kansas City to celebrate his birthday.

"My Dad is a phenomenal engineer," Matt said.

He was the chief engineer for Fairbanks Morse, a manufacturer of diesel engines for nuclear submarines. In his free time, he would buy a car and fix it up. We had a light blue Renault, which was the pure definition of a crappy car, a pale-yellow station wagon, and a bright orange Dodge Omni with plastic black seats, and in summer you would burn your legs almost to the point of getting blisters. We had a Volkswagen with a hole in the floor, and we would stick our legs out so we could purposely wear out our shoe soles to get new shoes. My dad would always say, 'Why would you buy a new car when these other cars are just fine?' As I got older, whenever I would go to an auto body shop I would get my dad on the phone and have him listen to the car, and he would say it's just a timing belt issue, and he would get on the phone with the mechanic and suddenly the estimate price would come down from $900 to $75. I remember every Sunday afternoon, he would take me outside to fix cars, change the oil, whatever was needed, and we would just talk and listen to the Packers game on the radio. He's amazing. I wish I had spent more time learning from him.

When Matt got to the nursing home, his dad was dressed and waiting. He always wore the same uniform: some variation of a button down long-sleeve shirt, khakis, his tennis shoes (no laces now, just slip-on), and either a United States Marine baseball cap (Semper Fi!) or an Irish paddy cap to cover his nearly bald head. Matt brought him a Wisconsin Badgers vest (in honor of his daughter studying at the university just two hours away) that he can now wear over his shirts as he gets cold more frequently.

The nursing home has a lovely residential feel, with a lot of things to do from reading in the library, working out in the gym, and playing piano to meeting other residents for a free drink at happy hour every Friday at 4:30 P.M. before dinner.

Chuck uses a walker now and suffers from neuropathy, so celebrating his birthday would be a subdued and practical affair. They ran some errands in his dad's old blue Subaru, which he can't drive anymore but still owns (figure 18.1). They bought a new electric chair for his room that helps him get up and down and worked on his finances before going out for an early dinner. The afterparty was back at the nursing home, where they spent a few hours watching *Roadkill Garage* as they transformed an AMC Gremlin into a muscle car.

The next day, before Matt headed back home, Chuck said he was in better spirits and thanked Matt for making the trip to see him . . . and the power-assisted chair (ever so important for any aging dad)!

TIME TO DRIVE

My Dad couldn't fix cars, but he sure loved everything about them. As an immigrant who came to this country with nothing, he slowly saved to buy his first car, a Chevy Celebrity. When I went to college, he told me, "Every man needs to have a candy apple red car once in his lifetime, so why not now? Get it out of your system!" So I picked out a red Mitsubishi Eclipse with the cool bump on the hood to give the cam gears a little bit more clearance. Over the years, as my dad's income grew, he traded in his Chevy for an Oldsmobile and then eventually a Buick.

18.1 Matt with his father Chuck in 2024.

He was working his way up the GM lineup to get to a Cadillac but passed away before owning one. I always wanted to surprise him one day with a beautiful red Cadillac in the driveway, but I never got the chance.

Back in Kansas City, Matt was also thinking about his father, and all the cars he had fixed and driven in his lifetime. It triggered a desire to look at potential stock investments in the world of automobiles. His own 100-bagger study called out companies such as AutoZone and its empire of auto part retail shops as well as Copart and its growing salvage auction business. He knew he wouldn't invest in an ordinary car manufacturer given all the competition in the space globally. On the electric side, Tesla already had a giant market cap, so the odds of multiplying one hundred times again were low. But perhaps there was a tangential business such as the two previous 100-baggers that would be worth considering? After a series of screens, calls, and research, he found CCC Intelligent Solutions (Ticker symbol: CCC), a B2B company that is largely hidden from the public, an invisible technology layer that kicks in after something horrible happens that we rarely see coming, a car crash.

I still relive car accidents from my youth. First is the initial shock, the fear someone was hurt, standing in the middle of the road and seeing the damage to the automobile, exchanging your information with the counter party while discussing who's at fault, worrying how your parents will react when they find out, anxiously waiting for an auto body shop repair estimate, and then waiting again for your insurance company to respond to your claim, the cost and the time without a means of transportation while parts are ordered and your car is repaired, and overwhelming and alternating feelings of anger, guilt, or regret. All of it is a constant reminder that life can change in an instant.

"Our mission is to keep people's lives moving forward when it matters the most. So as an example, an auto claim, when that happens, is a pretty traumatic event for people," said Githesh Ramamurthy, CEO of CCC Intelligent Solutions who has degrees in electrical engineering as well as computer science (figure 18.2). "So now the question is, how do you deliver an incredible experience for someone who's really been through a very rough situation?"[1]

What he and his team have built is a technology platform that connects more than thirty-five thousand parties so they can all communicate with each other: 300+ insurers (including twenty-six of the top thirty), 30,000+ repair facilities, and 5,500 parts suppliers (including all major OEMs). And their goal is to make this whole process of getting a car repaired while dealing with insurance simpler for you . . . without you even knowing their involvement in the process.

One of the things that blew Matt away was how much they have expedited the process behind getting a repair estimate. "Normally, after an accident, you take your car or have it towed to a repair shop and ask for an estimate. They tell you, okay, go out to lunch and come back and they will have an estimate ready, or they will call you the next day after they have a chance to get to it," said Matt. "Today,

18.2 Former CCC Intelligent Solutions Chairman and CEO Githesh Ramamurthy.

the autobody shop that uses CCC Intelligent Solutions can give you an estimate based on mere photographs in anywhere from thirty seconds to two minutes!"

Wait, what? Thirty seconds?

You see, the company says it has collected over $1 trillion of data and billions of images over the years, and they can use artificial intelligence to prepopulate estimate forms for technicians in a repair shop. By ingesting photos from customers, repair shops, tow providers, and salvage vendors, it provides early insights into vehicle damage, including repair or total loss recommendations (figure 18.3). This helps insurers streamline work flows, reduce manual effort, and make more informed decisions earlier in the claims process.

"We were buying our own Nvidia GPUs ten years ago, before it was cool," said Marc Fredman, the former CCC Intelligent Solutions Chief Strategy Officer. In fact, Nvidia called his business out as an example of an enterprise company with strong demand for AI and accelerated computing in its Q1 2024 earnings call.[2] "We've always had the benefit of having a lot of data that runs through our platforms, so we processed over a trillion dollars of historical data, and we call it hyperlocal data. So, you think about a specific part price, a specific cost

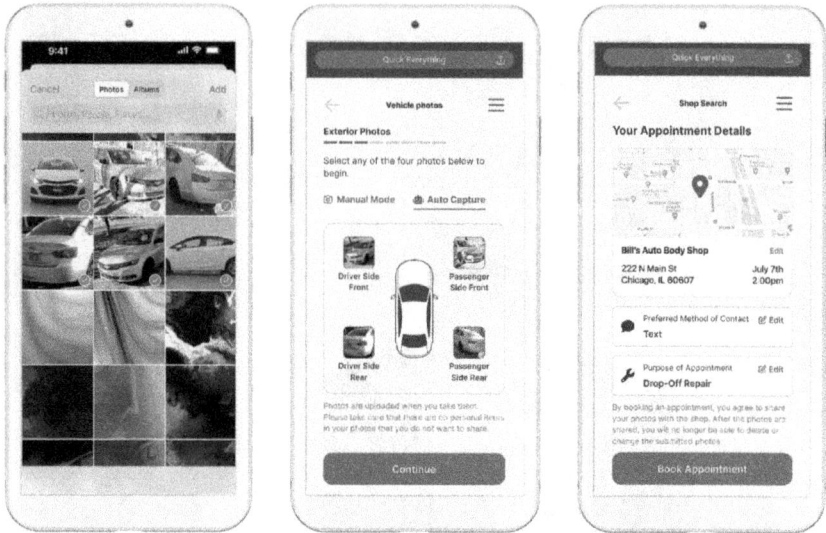

18.3 CCC First Look is an AI-powered solution that uses advanced photo analysis to accelerate the auto claims process. Shown are the kinds of data collected in this process as well as appointment details.

for something, a specific amount of hours or minutes to repair something and a specific geography, that's how hyper specific we have to get."[3]

And providing estimates is getting more complicated as cars get more complicated. "A bumper, for example, is no longer a bumper," said Ramamurthy. "Today, you could have sensors, you could have cameras, you could have so much just in one component." The company says most cars have between twenty thousand and thirty thousand individual components, and Ramamurthy said the mission of the company is to "design and deliver capability for the industry that makes that frontline decision-making process a heck of a lot easier and brings down the cognitive load for the person making those decisions."[4]

THE HARD NUMBERS

CCC Intelligent Solutions has invested more than $1 billion dollars of R&D into its platform over the last ten years—and it's not just to create whiz-bang features, but to become the operating system for auto repair and the property and casualty insurance that goes along with it. Here are Matt's three key numbers to better understand its business.

KEY NUMBERS TO UNDERSTAND CCC
INTELLIGENT SOLUTIONS

2 B	96%	80/20

2 Billion: CCC Intelligent Solutions said there were twenty-six million automotive claims in the US, and if you add up all the time to get the cars back on the road, from estimates to repairs to resolving insurance claims, it totals to two billion days.[5] If ever the phrase "time is money" could and should be used, this is it. Digitizing this industry across every single piece of the process provides enormous value to all the players on the platform, not to mention the customer. Within repair shops, not only does the platform handle estimates but also diagnostics, instructions for repair, and back-office operations including payroll. With constant labor shortages and mechanics with thirty years of experience retiring, these shops welcome the automation. The platform also connects the shop to parts suppliers and is starting to facilitate digital payments. On the insurance side, it is helping route and handle claims. It is even using AI to access accident severity from photos to inform casualty claims. And for people like you and me who have been traditionally frustrated by how little visibility we've had into knowing just how long it will take to get our cars back and claims processed, Ramamurthy said, "We pump out, you know, on behalf of our customers, 50–60 million text messages that proactively shares the movement of your particular claim across the supply chain."[6]

All of this get even more complicated the moment there is a change somewhere in the process. It's why the company built the platform using something the chief strategy officer calls event-based architecture, a system that can react to supplementary pieces of information as they occur.

"So, I'll give you a very practical example," said Fredman (figure 18.4). "A supplement basically means when you start fixing the car, you find out that there's more damage than you thought there was. So, it's supplementary to what you initially thought. Now, that sounds like a very specific and simple thing, but

18.4 Former CCC Intelligent Solutions Chief Strategy Officer Marc Fredman.

it actually kicks off all kinds of different things downstream." The ramifications hit just about every part of the ecosystem. Insurance companies must review and approve the additional repair work while increasing the reserve of money they're holding back for the claim. The part supplier has to find and ship the additional components. New payments have to be issued. The consumer may have to extend their rental car. "And today," according to Fredman, "a lot of that happens honestly kind of manually or in an uncoordinated way, a lot of phone calls, emails, different point to point integrations and solutions, and so what you'd really like to see, if that was really going to be an intelligent experience for everyone involved is when that event was identified, it would propagate and kick off and orchestrate all those different things that I describe."[7]

Well, CCC Intelligent Solutions lives up to its middle name. The platform they've built cascades all that information. And it's a far cry from the basic computer programs I wrote as a kid with if/then statements based off a linear flow chart on the blackboard. The complexity has grown leaps and bounds, at the very same time it is offering a solution that makes things simpler, for all the members of the network.

By now, you should know where this is headed! It's a B2B SaaS cloud platform that benefits from network effects! Repair shops can move more cars in and out of their facilities and spend less time on the phone with customers, insurance companies, and parts suppliers. Insurance companies get higher quality reports and process claims faster. The insurance companies also send leads to repair shops they use on the platform, and repair shops drive business to parts suppliers on the system. Ramamurthy says the platform helps manage more than a $100 billion of transactions across its network. And saving time, by improving efficiency and performance, means more money.

96%: It's no surprise then that CCC Intelligent Solutions, according to Matt who loves to see indications of essentiality, has a recurring revenue rate of 96 percent. Most of the parties on the platform stay on the platform, signing contracts on average that last three to five years. Ramamurthy said 70 percent of its revenue comes from accounts they've had for more than ten years.[8] Matt also points to the durability and predictability of the revenue: 80 percent of the revenue CCC Intelligent Solutions receives is from subscriptions and only 20 percent from transactions.

80/20: That solid customer base has helped the company achieve twenty-plus years of revenue growth and profitability. It ended 2023 with $866 million in revenue and $353 million in adjusted EBITDA. Revenue grew at an 11 percent CAGR between 2018 and 2023. It has a 41 percent adjusted EBITDA margin, with a long-term target of 45 percent (growing at one hundred basis points a year).[9]

"CCC operates a highly scalable software business that exhibits high returns (approximately 35 percent ROTA), solid growth (7–10 percent organic top-line and 12–15 percent+ operating profit), and powerful competitive advantages (switching costs and network effects)," said Matt.

Over time, he says, the company will continue to build new products and features to add to its platform while current customers continue to adopt, and pay more for, the most recent innovations. Since just 2020, the revenue per repair facility has grown 40 percent, and there has been a 50 percent growth in customers using five or more solutions being offered. Moving forward, Ramamurthy expects that very trend to continue. He said 80 percent of future growth will come from current customers and only 20 percent from new logos. In other words, a smooth, steady sail without wild assumptions around acquiring new customers. If anything, Matt expects to see the company slowly pursue geographic expansion as it expands from the US property and casualty (P&C) insurance market, with a total addressable market (TAM) of $15 billion, into the global P&C market, with a TAM of $35 billion.

The risk to the business, of course, is autonomous cars. Waymo, owned by Google, is currently testing autonomous Jaguars in California and Arizona that ferry you to the airport, and Zoox, backed by Amazon, is rolling out robotaxis in Las Vegas. In time, theoretically, there would be fewer or no accidents. But with 280 million cars on the road in the US that still require drivers (almost a billion and a half cars globally), and the average lifespan of each car growing because they are better made, Matt says it's going to take quite a long time to cycle through the current system.

Just think about how long it took to get where we are now. In fact, Fredman likes to recall the first time an auto insurance policy was ever sold. It was 128 years ago, in 1897, and it was sold to Mr. Gilbert Loomis in Ohio.

"This guy created his own automobile," said Fredman, "and he got into a situation with a horse, and destroyed a wagon, and he was found to be liable. He had to pay seven dollars, no inflation obviously, to restore this situation. Now we know about this because this guy wrote an article about his experience in a magazine back in 1897. And my favorite part of this is the name of the magazine. The name of the magazine was *The Horseless Age*. And the reason they called it *The Horseless Age* is because back then they didn't have a concept of an automobile, a coup, a sedan, a sports car. They called a car a horseless carriage."[10]

Time is a funny thing. Sometimes time moves ever so slowly. It took a long time to get from the horseless age to the modern age. It will likely take a long time to get to a completely driverless age. Time is money, and its why repair shops, insurance companies, and parts suppliers benefit from being on CCC Intelligent Solutions's platform. Time is also the most valuable thing a person can spend. That certainly applies to the care Matt puts into helping his daughters with their academic pursuits or the months he spent researching and then investing in CCC. In his world, the passage of time is also a tool, allowing his investments in quality companies to compound over decades. And, of course, days, months, and years are slipping away. Matt wished he learned more from his dad and will continue to make trips to Wisconsin to see Chuck and, yes, talk about the Packers or watch car shows together. His daughters are transitioning into adulthood and will soon embark on their own lives. He knows he can't reverse time, but in time he wants to make sure he can leave them, and his grandchildren someday, with the lessons and the proceeds of his coffee can.

CHAPTER 19

CHOCK FULL?

With thirteen stocks in the coffee can and millions of dollars of his own money spread across them, I couldn't help but ask Matt, "So which is your favorite one?"

For Matt it was kind of like asking him which one of his daughters is his favorite. But instead of dodging the question, he showed me a chart of how he thinks about these stocks relative to each other and how he will track them over time. Yes, track them. You see, Matt is committed to holding these stocks for a very long time, but if something material changes in any one of his companies, he will swap it out with another stock. He will also add new stocks as he finds them. He is committed to spending at least $5 million in total. So, although the coffee can is brimming with stocks, chock full if you will, it may be a dynamic set of assets—not in a day trending sense but over the long term.

He likes all of his companies, but in the same manner in which he looked back at mistakes in his career, Matt is intellectually honest with himself about how each company lives up to his 4Es:

- Is it an **Essential Product?**
- Does it have **Excellent Returns, Margins, and Growth?**
- Does it have an **Enduring Competitive Advantage?**
- And does it have **Entrepreneurial Management?**

For each category, he uses a simple color-coding system: black represents strong conviction, gray suggests slightly less certainty, and white indicates some uncertainty. "I want to revisit this to see how things are changing," Matt said. "Are there any new trends that change how I view these companies, good or

Names/Potentials	HQ	Country	4E's Essential	Excellent	Enduring	Entrepreneurial
Owned Names						
Diploma PLC	DPLM.L	London, UK	UK			
Globant Inc	GLOB	Luxembourg	Argentina			
Abacus Life	ABL	Orlando, FL	US			
Vertex Inc	VERX	King of Prussia, PA	US			
Technology One	TNE.AX	Fortitude Valley	Australia			
Nice, Ltd	NICE	Tel Aviv	Israel			
Axon Enterprise	AXON	Scotsdale, AZ	US			
Rentokil PLC	RTO	Manor Royal, Crawley	UK			
Bentley Systems	BSY	Exton, PA	US			
Bio-Techne	TECH	Minneapolis, MN	US			
SPS Commerce	SPSC	Minneapolis, MN	US			
Descartes Systems Group	DSGX	Waterloo, ON	Canada			
CCC Intelligent Solutions	CCCS	Chicago, IL	US			

19.1 Table of how Matt rates each business across his 4Es: Essential Products; Excellent Returns, Margin, and Growth; Enduring Competitive Advantage; and Entrepreneurial Management. Black represents strong conviction, gray suggests slightly less certainty, and white indicates some uncertainty.

bad?" He will revisit his homemade score card and its color designations as he tracks the portfolio's performance over time.

In figure 19.1, you can see that a little bit more than half of the stocks are US based, and the rest are in other parts of the world—from the UK, Canada, and Australia to Argentina and Israel. The best way to get under the hood of this table is by going deeper into each section to see the component parts that make up the grade each company is getting in each of the 4E categories.

LET'S START WITH ESSENTIAL PRODUCTS

First, when we expand the Essential Products table to reveal the underlying components, it is interesting to note that of the thirteen stocks Matt chose, eleven of them are B2B companies (figure 19.2). The only two B2C companies are Abacus Life, which buys life insurance companies from seniors, and Rentokil, which is in the pest control business and works with both corporations as well as consumers. In his previous 100-bagger study, 68 percent of the companies were B2B. He is clearly doubling down on this key insight.

Second, as we have seen throughout the book, Matt considers recurring revenue and churn to be two indicators of a product's essentiality. Will a customer

Names/Potentials	Essential	B2B	Recurring Rev	4E's Churn	cost % of total
Owned Names					
Diploma PLC		yes	relatively high	low	low
Globant Inc		yes	70.0%	low	med/high
Abacus Life		no	??	N/A	low
Vertex Inc		yes	84.0%	4.0%	low
Technology One		yes	98.0%	2.0%	medium
Nice, Ltd		yes	88.0%	very low	low
Axon Enterprise		yes	95.0%	very low	low
Rentokil PLC		no	solid	medium	medium
Bentley Systems		yes	92.0%	very low	medium
Bio-Techne		yes	relatively high	very low	low
SPS Commerce		yes	very high	very low	low
Descartes Systems Group		yes	88.0%	very low	low
CCC Intelligent Solutions		yes	96.0%	1.0%	low

19.2 How Matt rates each business when it comes to Essential Products.

continue to buy the product year in year out? The higher the percentage the better. And what percentage of them churn out each year? The lower the percentage the better. If you were in a doctor's office, this would be like checking your temperature and blood pressure—two important vital signs to provide a sense of a person's underlying well-being.

For Matt, the top companies in recurring revenue are TechnologyOne, CCC Intelligent Solutions, Axon Enterprise, and Bentley Systems. "If you are a local government in Australia, you couldn't do your job without TechnologyOne. If you are a repair shop, you want to be on a platform that has twenty-six of the top thirty insurance carriers. If you are going to build a new highway, you can't do it without architectural software from Bentley Systems. And once Axon Enterprise is in your police department, everything is connected from tasers to cameras, to police reports. It is a part of everything they need to do," said Matt. "Budweiser is a good beer, but is it essential? Maybe to some, but not to most people. They can drink Thai beer in a Thai restaurant, Japanese beer when they go out for Sushi, and Modelo with chips and salsa."

In terms of essentiality, the lower three—the ones in gray—are Rentokil, Globant, and Abacus Life.

"Rentokil and pest control is essential given what is happening to the planet, but you have Rollins, regional players, and a bunch of Mom and Pops as competitors. Now if you are in a region where Rentokil has strong penetration, it becomes more likely you will continue to go to them for repeated service," said Matt.

"Globant is a company that other companies go to when they want to digitally transform themselves. If a company really wants to change, it is essential to go with an outside group. You could do it yourself, but it will be very hard, or it won't work. And Globant is the coolest consultant in the digital services space that manages to have 70 percent recurring revenue, which makes it unique in the consulting industry. They have a lower margin business than the others because they are in the business of people, so that's why their costs are high. But remember, their market is huge, and they are aiming to have one hundred clients each generating $100 million . . . every year," he added.

"Abacus doesn't have recurring revenue, and churn doesn't apply to their business. So it's hard to compare them to the rest. People don't have to sell their life insurance policy, but if they decide to do so, Abacus is a competitive buyer. Or a customer could let their policy lapse, like 90 percent of other people. But that wouldn't be a smart move because Abacus pays you up to eight times more than a life insurance company. They are still in the stage of growing awareness of their service."

Looking at Matt's grades for essentiality, he did not give any one company a white (or uncertain) designation. "Although there are varying degrees of essentiality, every company that makes it into my portfolio is essential to their customers," said Matt.

EXCELLENT RETURNS, MARGINS, AND GROWTH

Just in case you've forgotten, ROTA is a company's return on tangible assets. And remember that Matt considers companies that have returns of more than 25 percent to be a great business. The higher the free cash flow a company has, the more options it has to grow faster, get into new markets, or even acquire companies. The ROTA is the return the company gets on that investment (figure 19.3).

Matt points to two companies on the ROTA section, which looks at it historically, how it has increased, and where he projects it to be in the next three to five years. First look at Vertex, the global tax software solution, which he designated gray because its historical ROTA of 10 percent is low, but it's incremental

Names/Potentials	Excellent	ROTA historical	incr ROTA	ROTA Projected	4E's margin	incr proj mgns	op profit growth	predictable results?
Owned Names								
Diploma PLC		38.0%	42.5%	40.0%	19.0%	21.0%	10.0%	yes
Globant Inc		23.0%	25.0%	25.0%	15.0%	15.0%	20.0%	yes
Abacus Life		16.0%	25.0%	20.0%	24.0%	45.0%	25.0%	??
Vertex Inc		10.0%	35.0%	30.0%	15.0%	30.0%	20.0%	yes
Technology One		30.0%	40.0%	35.0%	25.0%	41.0%	18.5%	yes
Nice, Ltd		20.0%	25.0%	22.5%	24.5%	31.0%	12.5%	yes
Axon Enterprise		8.0%	35.0%	20.0%	12.0%	32.0%	30.0%	yes
Rentokil PLC		24.0%	30.0%	30.0%	12.0%	20.0%	14.0%	yes
Bentley Systems		37.0%	40.0%	40.0%	28.0%	38.5%	13.5%	yes
Bio-Techne		30.8%	40.0%	36.5%	24.0%	45.0%	15.0%	yes
SPS Commerce		25.0%	35.0%	32.5%	28.0%	34.0%	25.0%	yes
Descartes Systems Group		56.0%	65.0%	65.0%	23.0%	45.0%	17.5%	yes
CCC Intelligent Solutions		35.6%	40.0%	40.0%	19.4%	30.0%	15.0%	yes

19.3 Table of how Matt rates each business when it comes to Excellent Returns, Margin, and Growth.

returns are dramatically higher at 35 percent. That gives him comfort to project the steady state to be around 30 percent moving forward. He does the same for Axon, which was 8 percent, but it's incremental returns have increased to 35 percent, and he projects it to be 20 percent in the future.

"Vertex and Axon both have a big lift on ROTA," said Matt. "Vertex reinvested the last couple of years in their sales, product, and technology, and geographic footprint, which depressed the earnings, or operating profits, but is setting it up for long-term success as it reaps the rewards of those investments. Axon is moving from just hardware such as cameras to new, higher margin revenue from software such as cloud solutions that host all the video and evidence reports. As they do that, they are moving into a higher margin, higher return business."

Matt also calls out Abacus's margin growth because they layer on more and more policies, their fixed costs are spread across them. "We know it's coming, and then it will have to prove a sustained track record of predictability." He says Rentokil's margins will expand once they fully integrate Terminix into their pest control business; and Bentley Systems, which sells infrastructure engineering software, will add one hundred basis points a year for the foreseeable future as its SaaS model continues to mature."

He is projecting operating profit growth of 20 percent or more for the next three to five years at Axon, Abacus, and Vertex for the reasons stated previously, as well as SPS Commerce's retailer/supplier network (which he says "has grown revenue for 95+ quarters") and Globant's digital consulting services (which he says "will benefit from more and more companies that will need help implementing artificial intelligence into their businesses").

"Excellent returns, margins, and growth is a result of durable competitive advantage, an attractive industry, and capable management," said Matt. "This may sound backward-looking (and it is), but that is why I focus on the incremental and projected metrics as well, to ensure my companies maintain the high-quality I require."

ENDURING COMPETITIVE ADVANTAGES

Matt, as we know, is a big fan of Hamilton Helmer's book, *7 Powers: The Foundations of Business Strategy*, which calls out seven approaches or business models a business can leverage to achieve competitive advantage (figure 19.4). In other words, build a moat.

Names/Potentials	Enuring	4E's *source of comp adv* (per Hamilton Helmer)
Owned Names		
Diploma PLC		process power
Globant Inc		process power
Abacus Life		scale economies
Vertex Inc		switching costs
Technology One		switching costs
Nice, Ltd		scale economies
Axon Enterprise		switching costs
Rentokil PLC		scale economies/brand
Bentley Systems		switching costs
Bio-Techne		scale economies
SPS Commerce		network economies
Descartes Systems Group		network economies
CCC Intelligent Solutions		switching costs/network

19.4 Table of how Matt rates each business when it comes to Enduring Competitive Advantage.

In this case, Matt does have his favorites and can rank them ... almost like judging his boyhood superheroes (i.e., Superman is more powerful than Spiderman!).

"Network economies, then switching costs, then scale economies, then cornered resources, then process power, and then branding. That's how I would rank them," Matt said. (Helmer's seventh one is "counter-positioning," but Matt didn't use it to describe any of his companies. That one is used to describe newcomers that use new business models that incumbents don't want to mimic.)

Matt says he chose network economies, or network effects, as the most powerful superpower because once you have multiple constituencies on a platform, it becomes very attractive for future customers to join. "And from a competitive advantage, it also means your competitors go away," said Matt. "Remember, Metcalfe's power law plays into network effects, and it tends to lead to winner-take-all scenarios." In Matt's coffee can, he assigned this power to SPS Commerce (the retail network), Descartes (the global supply chain network), and CCC Intelligent Solutions (the car repair, insurance, and parts network). I must confess that the combination of B2B businesses and network effects excites me to no end! I just love the beauty of the products and the acceleration of the business model over time. I also like the combination of tried-and-true B2B software businesses taking a page from Silicon Valley network effects models. My father, who passed away in 2017, would have truly enjoyed this digital transformation of the supply chain and logistics industry.

Switching costs, which Matt also color codes black, comes next. Once you lock in a customer it becomes very hard to steal them away unless they have radically lower prices or a product that is so much better. In Matt's table, Vertex, TechnologyOne, Axon, and Bentley Systems all benefit from switching costs. "TechnologyOne, for example, is such a big deal," Matt said. "If someone wanted to switch, they would have to go through the cost of procuring a new supplier, the cost of implementing the system . . . and pay that fee upfront, and then retrain everyone on their team on the new system."

Scale economies, in gray, is another huge one for Matt. Companies that have this power benefit from being able to spread costs across a large user base, making it harder for smaller players to compete. He says Abacus, NICE, Bio-Techne, and Rentokil all benefit from this competitive advantage.

As Matt likes to say, in the pest control business, "the barrier to entry is low, but the barrier to scale is high." Rentokil has route density and can spread the cost of brand advertising in a territory, as well as buying trucks and chemicals in ways Mom and Pop players can't. And by spreading those costs across contiguous territories, it can expand margins and drive more cash flow that can then be used to buy more smaller players to further expand their territory.

NICE, the Israeli company that offers B2B customer service solutions, benefits from scaled economies in three ways: (1) They can spread the cost of the R&D on their platform across their expanding client base; (2) they have collected data from their clients for decades; and (3) they are investing in artificial intelligence technology to leverage all the data they've collected. "To compete with them, you can spend money to build a competing platform, but to get the same quality of AI you will have to get your hands on all the data they've collected for the last twenty to thirty years . . . and NICE is not going to sell it."

Abacus, also benefits in multiple ways: Matt says (1) "they've been collecting data on human mortality for twenty years, which makes them price the amounts they are willing to pay for policies better than anyone else"; (2) they can spread the cost of advertising all their informercials across a growing customer base; (3) they can further invest time and effort in creating relationships with brokers across the country; and (4) as their business grows and the predictably of their outcomes is demonstrated, perceived credit risk will dissipate and the cost of financing the policies they are buying will then go down.

Bio-Techne, which creates the bio reagents used by scientists in labs, uses its scaled catalog of quality proteins and immunoassays as an advantage. "If I am a customer, I only have to go to one place. And then the company layers on instruments such as the Western Blot, which then makes me need more proteins. To compete with them, a company would need to build up a pretty hefty catalog of proteins, and it would cost them a ton of money to do that," said Matt.

And as all of you know, in my business I see this power playing out with the streaming services. Netflix has 282 million subscribers. Other services have 100–150 million subscribers. A smaller service might have only forty million subscribers. Netflix can spread its original content costs, as well as technology development and customer acquisition, across a larger user base. So how do the smaller players compete? Whether it's through consolidation of networks, or through the rebundling of streaming services, it's going to be a long road, according to Matt. "Early winners are generally the long-term winners when it comes to scaled economies." That's good news for his investments, and a word of caution for parts of the media industry trying to compete without genre-defining IP or exclusive sports rights, essential B2C or B2B content and information services, or ownership of transformative distribution platforms with real network effects—like TikTok.

Matt uses "cornered resources" to describe Globant's source of competitive advantage. The way they attract and then retain "Globers" is key to their continued success.

He reserves process power for one company in the coffee can, Diploma. As a reminder, this is a power that has been classically used to describe the process by which Toyota makes its cars—a process even if shared with a competitor could not be duplicated, and a power that takes a long time to develop.

In this case, Matt believes Diploma, a value-add distributor of technical equipment in the UK, has perfected the art of M&A. In his historical 100-bagger study, a fair number of companies hit their growth targets through a steady set of targeted acquisitions. But what makes Diploma different from other companies that do this? Descartes, for example, has done forty-six acquisitions over the last decade. Matt reminds me that process power takes decades to achieve. "While many companies are starting to smartly use acquisitions, Diploma has been doing it for close to a century," said Matt. "Hamilton Helmer says this is a power that happens in the stability phase of a company, not in its early stages. And over the decades, Descartes developed its M&A process, not just in one sector, but across three different and unrelated ones: seals, controls, and life sciences. They reinvented themselves to pursue acquisitions in these higher growth areas. They are talking to all their end customers and know what they need and want. They have been in discussions and developing relationships with acquisition targets for all this time. And when they hired a CEO that didn't quite fit with this culture and approach, they quickly made a change."

So why would Matt give this rare power a gray shade?

Although no one can quite duplicate the process of a company with this power, it doesn't mean their offering will always be the best. Consider Toyota, for example. They had this power and for years made better, cheaper cars than Detroit. But that doesn't completely stop another player, with a different process, from offering a product that can take share. Chinese car manufacturer BYD, which clearly has a very different process, was able to take the global lead in electric vehicles. Customers don't know anything about its process power, they just want the best products. Don't get me wrong, it's a strong power, but I have to be brutally honest about how I rank these powers. Even Superman has weakness. It's called Kryptonite.

ENTREPRENEURIAL MANAGEMENT

The fourth "E," Entrepreneurial Management, is perhaps the most subjective measure on Matt's chart (figure 19.5). "Judging a management team is very hard. When I look at a management team, what I am trying to better understand is are they customer obsessed? Are they a founder or a leader with missionary zeal? Or are they just there to collect a paycheck? Globant's CEO, Martin Migoya, not only deeply cares about his customers, he also deeply cares about his employees, the 'Globers.'" Bentley Systems is another standout for Matt because he likes that they are run by engineers, and they are so customer obsessed that they refuse to call their customers "customers." Instead, they call them users, or fellow engineers, all working to build the next generation of massive, horizontal infrastructure. "I could see Ed Ryan at Descartes on a dock somewhere talking logistics," said Matt. "Their previous CEO, Arthur Mesher, said he didn't want to sell to customers, but instead serve them." The only minor criticisms Matt has is directed at Rentokil's CEO, who has announced he will be retiring in 2026. Matt gave him a white

Names/Potentials	Entrepreneurial	cust obsessed	acq/reinv strategy
Owned Names			
Diploma PLC		yes	yes
Globant Inc		yes	yes
Abacus Life		yes	yes
Vertex Inc		yes	??
Technology One		yes	yes
Nice, Ltd		yes	yes
Axon Enterprise		yes	yes
Rentokil PLC		??	yes
Bentley Systems		yes	yes
Bio-Techne		yes	yes
SPS Commerce		yes	yes
Descartes Systems Group		yes	yes
CCC Intelligent Solutions		yes	yes

19.5 Table of how Matt rates each business when it comes to Entrepreneurial Management.

label. "Rentokil's CEO is very polished, an M&A lawyer, but I'm not sure I could see that guy climbing into a crawl space beneath a house and leading the team's effort to get rid of pests way down there. It's not that he isn't a great leader, I truly respect his reinvestment strategy." And that is the second factor of entrepreneurial management. "Rentokil knows how to allocate capital, and they also know how to do share buybacks," said Matt. "They are dialed into both." We've already discussed Diploma's process power across three different sectors, and Matt also calls out Bentley Systems's use of their own platform to identify companies successfully building apps on it as a pipeline for future acquisitions. The only other companies not to receive a black rating in this area were CCC Intelligent Solutions and Vertex. "I could make them all black. But I want to be honest. Nothing is perfect. At CCC Intelligent Solutions, outside of the CEO, a lot of management is fairly new. And at Vertex, which was private until 2020, almost all of its growth has been organic, so they don't have a fully disciplined M&A process yet."

In November of 2024, Matt texted me to say that Vertex, the King of Prussia tax software company, just posted results for the previous quarter. You can see what he values from his shorthand: "Vertex reported very good quarter, organic revenue growth 'mid-teens,' adjusted EBITDA growth of 45 percent as margins improved 430bps to 22.7 percent and FCF of nearly $60MM for 9mos (now 12.2 percent of revenue, and rising). Closed the ecosio acq (e-invoicing). All good numbers. Stock +10 percent this morning."

The "ecosio acq" he was referring to was the closing of Vertex's acquisition of a company called ecosio that specializes in e-invoicing. With more governments around the world mandating real-time or near real-time tax reporting, Vertex sees e-invoicing as a critical requirement for businesses to record their compliance as they operate across multiple jurisdictions around the globe.

As Vertex starts to do more acquisitions like this and gains its "sea legs" in M&A, Matt will be watching from his home office in Kansas City like a financial helicopter dad. He may even change the gray designation he gave them to black.

With this comparison exercise of the current stocks in the coffee can now over, Matt breathed a sigh of relief. He loves all his companies—superpowers, vulnerabilities, the CEOs and where they are in their maturation cycles. He loved screening for them, studying them from every angle, and pulling the trigger to buy them. It's a feeling of accomplishment, not just as an investor but as a father.

MY TURN . . .

It was finally time for me to decide if I, too, would make investments in the same companies for my twins. I had already decided to invest in one of the first companies Matt had surfaced (Diploma—the value-added distributor in the UK). But should I invest in *all* the companies Matt identified and bought for his children?

I mean . . . how could I not? I had just spent a year of my life debating and researching each company with Matt, and I felt powerfully about his choices. My conviction was based on his research on previous 100-baggers, my own experience at Hearst (where profits from the B2B Media divisions now eclipse those from the consumer media brands), and our conversations and analysis on each of the new stock picks.

But I still went through my own risk analysis for the overall investment.

On one hand:

- The idea that every one of the stocks multiplies one hundred times is definitely a "holy grail" type of outcome.
- It's not a wholesale substitute for my current investment mix of low-fee index fund funds and Treasury bills. If I made an investment, I would only do it with a small portion of my investment portfolio.
- Although they have similar quantitative and qualitative qualities as previous 100-baggers (and that arguably gives them a higher probability of success), it does not mean there is a guaranteed outcome.
- Matt is the first to admit that the nobody knows the future. Simple statement, but clearly worth saying. Existential events are out there . . . and the full impact of artificial intelligence, for example, cannot be fully imagined yet.
- Companies can lose their competitive moats, and I need to be constantly monitoring for that possibility. If that were to happen, we will divest from any company if we learn something new about them that changes the original investment thesis. So, although these are long-term holds, they are not "set it and forget it" types of investments.

On the other hand:

- They are not hot start-ups that will quickly flame out. Two of them are almost one hundred years old (Rentokil and Diploma), and most are several decades old.

- They are unlikely to go bankrupt: they are not highly leveraged; their free cash flow to revenue ratios are very strong; and they all sell essential products. For example, twenty-six of the top thirty major insurance companies rely on CCC Intelligent Solutions to deal with auto claims and repair.

- None of the companies in the coffee can are in undifferentiated or highly irrational and competitive industries. In other words, not airlines or oil companies or automobile manufacturers.

- Matt believes some of the companies will do even better than expected. For example, if TechnologyOne, the company that builds ERPs for governments and universities, not only doubles its topline revenue every five years but continues to increase its margins, the company will grow not at 15–16 percent a year, but at 20–25 percent a year. If that happens, it could be more than a 100-bagger.

- And last, although I hesitate to compare this portfolio to venture investing, if only one of Matt's picks becomes a 100-bagger, his $250,000 investment in that stock becomes $25 million (against his entire planned investment of $5 million).

On a valuation basis, some of the companies are trading at a price that is high relative to the market, but their compounding profits help level it out over time. Armed with his deep fundamental research, Matt is taking advantage of a market that is very short-term oriented. He is not judging risk on a stock price over the next 5.5 months (the average hold time for a stock). He is investing in businesses he believes will be strong for the next thirty years. In other words, I had to prepare myself and commit myself to being patient.

I am a conservative investor, and I believe this level of transparency into my own risk calculus is a window into how I balanced any skepticism for the overall outcome (where every stock multiplies one hundred times) with a researched and rational approach to investing in a world where nothing can ever be certain.

In the end, Matt doesn't want to tell me, let alone readers, *what* to think but *how* to think.

So, after discussing the risk with our financial advisor, my wife and I decided we would also invest in all the companies. . . . and we were prepared to absorb the volatility and potentially any losses. But the amount invested would be a mere fraction of Matt's intended $5 million. I won't say how much, but I will say, in comparison to Matt's coffee can, our investment will be more like an espresso shot! But one hundred times anything is a huge outcome!

So, there was one last thing to do . . . tell our kids what we had done for them.

CONCLUSION

Happy Thanksgiving

Matt and Maury were nervous. Yes, the empty nest was fabulously full again, with Peyton and Morgan back from college, rejoining Pierce and their parents at home in Kansas City for Thanksgiving. But this was not going to be a normal holiday reunion. Instead, this was the week that Matt and Maury decided they were going to tell their children what they were quietly doing for them: buying stocks for the long term that could someday turn into an inheritance of gargantuan proportions.

And yet they were anxious that this could somehow be demotivational. They didn't want the girls to feel like they could start frivolously spending money, or would never have to work hard, or, even worse, to stop pursuing their academic and professional dreams. That would go against every value they had instilled in their daughters. Plus, Maury wanted the girls to learn how to be self-sufficient and not dependent on anyone, even them.

Matt and Maury also didn't want their daughters to change the way they looked at them. They had never revealed the size of their investments before, and this would be another big indication of their personal net worth. Nor did they want them to change the way they looked at others outside their family.

Matt cited for me a line in his favorite poem, *Desiderata*, by Max Ehrmann: "If you compare yourself with others, you may become vain or bitter, for always there will be greater and lesser persons than yourself." Matt didn't want them to ever define themselves by money, not now nor later in their lives. Instead, he wanted them to, as the poem went on to say, "Enjoy your achievements as well as your plans. Keep interested in your own career, however humble; it is a real possession in the changing fortunes of time."[1] Matt and Maury had full confidence in their girls, their respective moral compasses, and their ability to continue their individual journeys, but this conversation would have to be handled just right.

The mood at home was joyous. Both Peyton and Morgan were in full bloom, happy they were on the right track at college. Pierce was starting to bud, in preliminary stages of contemplating life after high school, and for the first time revealing her interest in potentially studying marketing in college, joining a start-up, visiting TechnologyOne in Australia, and eventually running a business someday while living in a Boston brownstone. Ambition has never been a problem in the Ankrum household.

Songs from a Michael Bublé holiday music playlist were wafting throughout the house, and everyone took turns playing with Bourbon the "guard" dog (figure C.1) and his sister Whiskey.

C.1 Bourbon the dog, on a Christmas card in 2024.

The production of Thanksgiving dinner was going to be a family affair. Morgan made the appetizer: goat cheese and pesto baked with pine nuts and served on toasted French bread. Peyton tackled the handmade cranberry sauce, which took several hours and lots of sugar! Pierce was the muscle, in charge of mashing the potatoes, garnished with grated cheddar cheese, butter, and milk. Matt was in charge of the turkey and grilling steaks. Maury oversaw the drinks: ginger beer and Italian blood orange soda for the girls, an old fashioned (a bourbon cocktail with bitters, sugar, and an orange peel) for Matt, and Prisoner red wine for herself.

The Napa red blend was a gift from her parents, Pam and Dave Murray, before they recently passed away. In fact, it would be the first Thanksgiving without Nonni and Poppi (as the girls called them). And uncorking the Prisoner bottle would be in honor of them and the great tradition of Irish entrepreneurship they so passionately pursued all their lives. The other tradition her parents presided over each year was "the giving tree," where each member of the family would hang a note saying what they were thankful for. Maury didn't feel right continuing doing that without them. Instead, she and Matt had other plans, to launch a new set of family traditions to express their gratitude in addition to words. More on that later.

But before the feast would begin, Matt and Maury had called a family meeting. The girls had no idea what the subject was going to be, but I, for one, had been waiting for this moment for over a year! How would the girls finally react to the idea of a coffee can that could someday be worth as much as half a billion dollars?

Matt opened by acknowledging the loss of his in-laws and the example they set to reinforce the idea that the girls should be chasing their own dreams.

MATT: As we approach Thanksgiving, this is a great time to give thanks
and gratitude. And we know this one's a little bit more difficult
because Nonni and Poppi aren't here. We thought this is actually a good
time to reflect on all the great things that they did for us. You know,
they brought a lot of love and laughter into our lives. We will always
remember them for who they are and what they did. People loved Poppi,
and Nonni could walk into Nordstroms and so many people would
come up and want to talk to her. They helped us figure out how to chart
our own course and where we want to go. And so, one of the things
we're looking to do is we want to help you guys chart your own course.
We are so proud of each of you on where you're going. Morgan, getting

into the MedSpa, pursuing nursing. Peyton following her passion in psychology. And, Pierce, I think what mom and I were so excited about is that you finally started expressing some of the things that you really would love to do. And so that's what we're really excited about.

With the girls feeling the love about their chosen career paths, Matt started to talk about the virtue of pulling yourself up by your bootstraps, and how it has afforded him and Maury the ability to experiment in a long-term family investment project otherwise known as the coffee can.

MATT: Mom and I, we've worked really hard to try to get to where we are at. And I think you guys know this, but I didn't come from money. We weren't wanting for anything, but we didn't have a lot of the privileges that we enjoy today. And mom's family was similar, they probably had a little bit more, but then they lost it when her uncle died, and they lost the beer business. So, everything that you guys have here your mom and I built. And so, one of the things that we were looking at is trying to build long-term security, to create a family office to compound our wealth. This should lead to advantages for you and your kids and ideally your grandkids as well. As you know, I have been investing. We have worked hard to find multiple sources of income to create various sources of value. One of the areas that can be a great source of value is stocks. I was inspired when I read the 1970s book *Hundred to One* by Thomas Phelps. He talked about companies that increased in value by 100-fold. That's why I did a new 100-bagger study. That's what you guys have heard me talk about. And I was inspired by the article Robert Kirby wrote about Coffee Can investing. And so, what we're looking to do is truly create a coffee can portfolio for this family.

MAURY: Do you know what we are talking about with the coffee can?

MORGAN: Yeah, like savers. Yeah, so you would buy a stock and stash it away forever.

MAURY: In the old days people would put their money into a coffee can and bury it in the backyard. So, it was saved because you didn't watch it all the time.

PEYTON: It was actually buried in the backyard?

MAURY: Well, because they didn't have a really good bank system . . .

MATT: One of the things that always came out of it is people were always surprised when they looked in the coffee can and they were surprised at how the value had grown.

PIERCE: There were actual stocks in the coffee can?

MATT: Yes, back in the day, individuals were issued actual certificates of ownership in the company, and they were actual real certificates in the coffee can. So, anyway, so that's what we are, in theory, looking to do. For the last year, year and a half, I have been trying to find ideas to put into the coffee can, companies that we can own for, hopefully ideally thirty plus years. The reason we're bringing it up to you guys now is that mom and I are very serious about, particularly as young women, is that you guys are very understanding of money and are very comfortable with making big investment decisions. We live in a whole different world. In fact, you guys probably will be the breadwinner for your family. And as part of that role, we talk about it as being stewards of the capital, right? And mom and I are trying to be stewards of our capital. That we don't blow it, that we maintain and grow the capital. In the past, Mom has talked about very, very rich families, that get into second, third, fourth generation and they burn through all the money. They blow it. They just burn through it because they think that they have an unlimited amount. Our thought is we want you guys to be part of the process. I will still be making the investment decisions and stuff like that, but we want you guys to have a better idea of what we're doing so that you can feel more comfortable with where we're going.

Stewardship was a concept that Matt and I had been discussing. It was important to telegraph to the kids that they weren't simply being gifted an inheritance, but that they were being given an invitation to be part of a long-term process, to learn about the investments, see how they are performing, make investment suggestions, and help decide how to spend it—essentially tiptoe their way into becoming smart and additional stewards of wealth for generations to come. Matt then shared his Thanksgiving surprise, which was nothing short of a financial thunderbolt.

MATT: We have been doing a lot of research on these companies to build this coffee can portfolio. And, surprise, we have already been putting our money to work. And, if we do this right, this could mean a lot of money long term. We've been buying these companies, looking to buy twenty companies and put around $250,000 into each of them to build a portfolio of five million dollars. In thirty years, which would put you about at mom and dad's age, if we are right on these, that initial portfolio could turn into about a half a billion dollars.

PIERCE: Wow, that's a lot of money!

PEYTON: Yeah, half a billion dollars is huge!

PIERCE: I was talking about the amount of money we are investing.

Pierce's reaction surprised Matt. She was more amazed by the size of the initial investment of $5 million, let alone the potential of it turning into half a billion dollars; $5 million was essentially all the money in the world to her. Even my own twins, who worked summer jobs in high school and felt flush with earnings of a few thousand dollars, have no real concept of truly knowing or appreciating what hundreds of thousands of dollars (or the cost of college over four years for both) really means. These numbers, for both of our sets of kids, are so outside of their day-to-day lives and frames of reference that it was somewhat fantastical. The girls, slightly dazed, regained their composure and then started to ask more questions.

PIERCE: Where are you now with that?

MATT: We have invested in about thirteen companies to this point. Our whole point is we want you guys to be understanding that this money will likely be locked up for, you know, twenty, thirty years. We have other sources of income, obviously, and we have other capital. In addition, we have the apartments and other investments too, but what we're looking to do with this portfolio, if we do this correctly, it could put you guys on a completely different trajectory and your kids and your grandkids. It's the ultimate lottery ticket. And part of why we want you involved with this is to not only help you learn how we do this, but why we do it, and why we save money so that we can do this.

MAURY: Exactly. It's why we want to spend our money on things that matter. You guys drive a crappy car. You don't have the fanciest phones. You don't have all these extravagances. This isn't an accident. It's part of how we were able to save money to invest to build for a better future instead of spending money on things in a year you won't remember or care about. With Wilbur Andy (the girls' dented car with a magnetic band aid on the door) you know that anyone who dates you they must really love you, not your car. You go to school where your classmates drive Mercedes and BMWs and all the fancy cars. We provide you what you need, not what you want. And if you guys can learn to keep that mindset, later in life money won't be something that your marriage falls apart over or you won't be forced to make awful decisions such as whether to take your kid to a doctor or pay your utility bill. We want that for you guys, but it means a lot of times you have to delay gratification on the front end of your life so that the back end of your life is more fulfilling.

MATT: We put our money on the things that matter to us, like trips, your education, and investing in the coffee can portfolio. I don't value cars. I don't value clothes, but I do value you guys, and we value where you go. One day I will not be here, and mom won't be here, and so we want you guys to feel very empowered to know how to do what we do. That was a long way of saying, we want you guys to understand what we're doing.

PIERCE: What are the companies in the portfolio?

MATT: The companies I've been talking to you all about for the last year. What you didn't realize was that I was teaching you about them, and quietly investing in them.

PIERCE: And what happens if they crash?

MATT: Each one of them is a unique situation. If they crash, I will certainly evaluate it, and then make a decision at that time. If I've done my due diligence well, and I've done the research right, we're buying really high-quality companies that will be around for a very, very long time. We will continue to own the winners as long as they have their competitive advantage, and they continue to have their growth opportunities. If that changes, I may sell. The famous economist John Maynard Keynes once said, "When the facts change, I will change my mind." So how does all this make you feel?

MORGAN: A little stressed about how much money's locked away personally, but excited.

PEYTON: No, I'm interested like, I don't know like, I'm curious about, um, well, how do we get more involved?

MORGAN: You've taught us a lot of it, and I have so much more, obviously, to learn because we're still not even half educated as we should be on this, but like, what are you talking about, like get involved?

MATT: I want you guys to follow your dreams, and that may not be to become a great stock picker. That is something that takes passion, and it takes a lot of time, it takes a lot of work. If you have that interest, I would love to help you learn more about investing. I want you to see how I make those decisions and how mom and I actually talk about it and kind of go through on how we allocate money, how we spend money as well. It is one of the reasons Neeraj and I are collaborating on this book. It isn't saying to buy these stocks necessarily, it's saying, what is really important about what you look for in evaluating a stock or business or other big financial decision. Another way to think about it, Morgan, is your interest in the MedSpa and what questions you have to answer to be successful. What are all the things that we would talk about? For example, what is your target customer? How many customers do you have to get to make a profit? How much do you have to charge? What if your landlord increases your rent? Those are things that help you understand what makes it a really good business versus what defines a bad business. The more you understand business, the easier it is to make a decision about stock. And so that's why we're excited to have you guys be part of this.

MORGAN: Okay, so what's the next step?

MAURY: We would love for you to be involved, but you guys don't have to do anything on the investment side right away.

MORGAN: No, no, no, I wanna be involved. I wanna know more, but like I just don't know.

MATT: Just listening and talking to me about it because, you know, a lot of times it's when you guys ask me questions, it helps me become better. It is one of the greatest things that I've enjoyed with Neeraj. He asks me questions on these stocks, challenging my ideas and information. He forces me to have to go back and revisit my own thought process. It can be frustrating at times, but it really makes me a much better investor. For you guys, I would love for you to review my ideas, and we can talk through any of the stories.

PIERCE: Can we use the rest of our portfolios to invest in the same stocks?

MATT: Definitely, but the $10,000 we gave you was also your opportunity
to learn on your own in companies you find interesting. One of the
reasons we have not pushed you one way or the other is I really want you
guys to learn from the investing process. The more that you invest, then
you identify what worked and what didn't. That's the learning process I
want you guys to have so that you can develop your own style.

The idea of developing their own style grabbed the girls' attention. They
started to debate the various stocks in the coffee can, even declaring their personal favorites.

PIERCE: Rentokil. It was really easy to understand the value Rentokil
provides. I know that I will want to keep out rodents and bugs from
my house. What struck me about the company was how long they
can continue to grow by simply buying up many of the small Mom
and Pop pest control businesses. And that doesn't even include the
hygiene business.

MORGAN: Bio-Techne. I am learning about enzymes and antibodies in
school right now, and I love that they are figuring out how to test for
new drugs and interactions without doing it on animals or humans.

PEYTON: Bentley Systems. I like that it was a family of brothers that did
it together, plus having nine out of ten of the horizontal infrastructure
projects in the US created on their software is really amazing.

These were the kinds of conversations Matt and Maury were hoping the girls
would have. Instead of talking about extravagant things they wanted to buy
someday (literally not once), the girls were talking about the attributes of great
companies they wanted to personally invest in. And with more exposure to the
decisions made within the family's coffee can as well as other investments, they
would get more financially sophisticated over time. But there was one last thing
Matt and Maury wanted to hammer home—the responsibility they have to lift
up others along the way.

MAURY: We want you to know how to look at stocks, who you should seek
counsel from, what to ask, where to look, but also how to use money.
Because our greatest gift, if this money turns into half a billion dollars—

which is more money than you guys can spend, or your kids could spend—will be our ability to help others even more.

MATT: The idea is we'd like you to give back to society as well. This money can have a huge impact on other people's lives. Philanthropy should be a big part of how we think about it, because when you get to a certain level, you want to be able to give back to society. You want to be able to help your fellow citizens. We have our time and our resources, right? For me, time is by far so much more valuable than money. If you can figure out how best to use your time in the highest use with what you have, then you can actually give back to society in multiple ways. And so that's one of the things that mom and I have talked about wanting to do more is opportunities to give back. When I was growing up, around Christmas my dad and I would deliver popcorn balls and candy to friends and elderly people in the area. We'd go for an entire day starting at like 8 o'clock in the morning, we would visit twelve, fifteen people. As a teenager, I could never understand why we couldn't just give them this stuff and then walk away. And then I realized, these people only cared about the time we spent with them. They just wanted to talk to somebody. So, we'd spend forty-five minutes to an hour with each of them, sitting down and talking. Often, we'd hear the same stories over and over, but they just wanted to spend time with us. They were so happy to be able to talk to somebody. Plus, my dad always scheduled the last two visits with his best buddies, so he could have a drink with them and then I could drive home.

MORGAN: Ha! Clever guy!

Everyone erupted in laughter. And then the girls turned their nervous energy about their inheritance into proactive ideas about how they could contribute to the family's philanthropic goals. Financial investing was something they would learn over time. Ideas for how they could help people was something they could do right now! Peyton suggested helping people who need therapy but can't afford it. Morgan discussed the idea of helping teens with acne problems pro bono. Pierce and her dad talked about helping entrepreneurs without connections launch start-ups. They then asked their parents what they wanted to do to help others, if they had a plan? Matt and Maury talked about their donations to charities and how the coffee can would generate even more dollars for future giving as well. On the donating time side of the equation, Matt said he enjoyed teaching and mentoring kids at the University of Missouri Kansas City as well as St. Mary's Academy (where two of the girls went to high school while in Denver) and wants to do more of it.

> **MATT:** One of the things that I have really enjoyed is mentoring young people. For example, I mentored Ian over the summer. I really enjoy helping them because if they can be successful, I know that's the compounding effect that I can create with my knowledge and skills. If Ian, whether he chooses to continue in investing or he goes on to do something else, I hope that I have helped put him on a higher trajectory.

Peyton loved the idea of mentoring and then suggested to her dad that it would be cool if he started a nonprofit classroom that taught students—that applied and got in—about business and investing so that they could eventually pay back their student loans. He liked the idea and said he would consider how best to amplify his efforts with young people. He then shared what he and Maury were thinking about in the immediate future. He explained that they had met with leadership at their Methodist church and were working on a way to "adopt a family" this Christmas. From food and gifts to time and counseling for this family, everything was on the table for discussion. The girls were excited about contributing as well.

Matt and Maury were thrilled with the outcome of the meeting, and after Thanksgiving dinner they walked down to the Plaza, fifteen blocks of shops and eateries inspired by Spanish architecture and known for its statues, fountains, and art fairs. Each year on Thanksgiving night, families across Kansas City head there to participate in the annual Christmas lighting ceremony. As they stood outside in chilly twenty-degree weather, the Ankrum family counted their blessings and said how grateful they were for each other (figure C.2). Matt and Maury felt very fortunate that their girls really understood what they were trying to do. No one changed their stated ambitions. If anything, the girls were more excited about their individual plans. But they knew they had each other. They were one family with shared values, on a mission to continue to learn and grow together and help those around them.

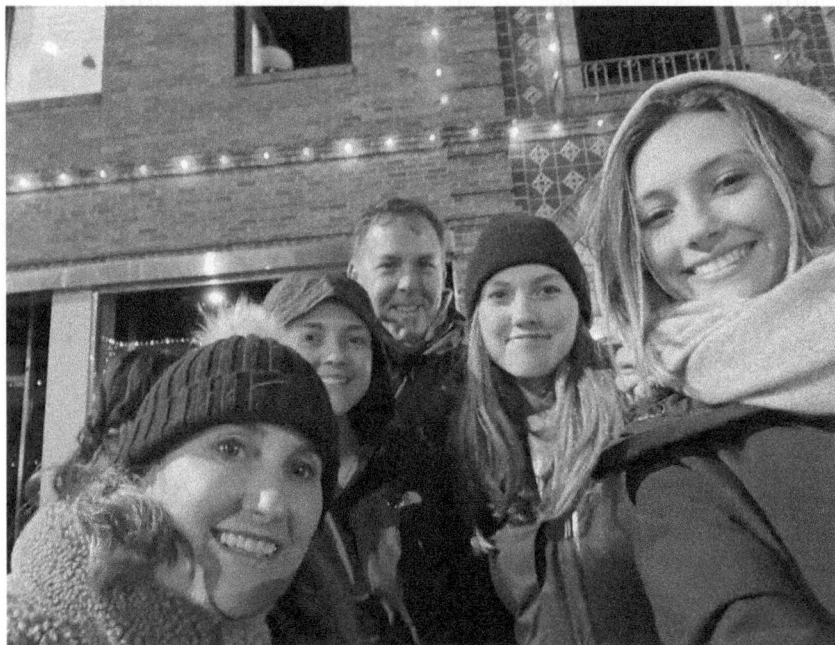

C.2 The Ankrum family on Thanksgiving night at the Christmas lighting ceremony at The Plaza, Kansas City, 2024.

In New York, a similar story was playing out at the Khemlani household. My wife Heather and I had decided to invest in all the stocks as well. And we, too, chose that weekend to tell our kids about *their* coffee can.

Ian and Samantha were both back home from college. On Thanksgiving morning, we all took a carful of food we made and solicited from wonderful neighbors over to a teenage runaway safe house that my wife was working in. You see, in addition to writing her fourth book—this one about a historical investigation into one of largest government boarding schools founded to erase Native American identity— Heather was also studying to get a master's degree in social work. She was putting her skills to work at the safe house.

As we walked in, the girls at the shelter were so happy to see Heather—and possibly even happier with the two kinds of mac and cheese she made, one with breadcrumbs and one without. And Ian, Samantha, and I were deeply impressed by what Heather was doing to help change young lives one at a time. Later that day we had celebrated Thanksgiving in two different locations, dinner with my side of the family and then dessert (including Samantha's decadent white chocolate ganache and caramel pumpkin pie) at our house with Heather's family. There was too much family in town to do it all in one location.

The next day we reserved a cozy table for just the four of us at a nearby Thai restaurant, a place we have been going to for years, and usually the restaurant of choice for celebratory occasions for our nuclear family. None of us ever had to look at the menu. The waitress knew what we wanted: Thai sausage salad, papaya salad, ginger chicken, grilled shrimp, heaping portions of Chinese broccoli, and mango and sticky rice for dessert.

Ian and Samantha were already aware of Matt's coffee can for his children. With writers for parents, they usually got a healthy dose of where we were in the creative process at any given dinner. Plus, Ian had helped research NICE, the Israeli customer service company, for Matt. He also had just made a detailed presentation of the company at his university's investment club (which blew me away because of the sheer amount of financial detail he had come to master). Samantha was a fan of Bio-Techne, given her desire to do medical research. But what they weren't expecting was that we would also make a coffee can portfolio for them. When they found out, they were flabbergasted. After the initial shock, they, too, readily accepted the invitation to help steward its growth. And instead of being demotivated, they saw the shared effort around investing as an accelerant for their own interests (figure C.3). Ian even asked if we should make some long-term investments in real estate. "One investment book at a time," I said jokingly. And when it came time to discuss philanthropy, like Matt's kids they lit up. Samantha wants to build mental health infrastructure in rural Asia, and Ian, still inspired by his trip to Denmark's seaweed farms, started to spell out ideas in the environmental space. Heather and I smiled at each other as we left dinner, knowing that our kids had become adults, well-adjusted and happy, taking nothing for granted, savvier than we were at their age, full of boundless energy and potential, with dreams to make an impact on the global stage.

I called Matt when I got home to compare notes about our respective family meetings. We had known each other for a very long time. Even though we worked in completely different professions, came from completely different worlds, we had somehow found each other in Denver decades ago thanks to my wife. And every year we said to each other that we needed to do something together. Well, we finally did it. This book was buttressed on a mutual admiration for

C.3 The Khemlani family, 2024.

B2B companies, essential products, and finely constructed business models by operating teams that create real value for shareholders. It also embraced the wise and timeless teachings of Warren Buffett, Charlie Munger, and so many other investment legends. But it was really built on our mutual trust and respect for each other, our combined desire to learn new things every day, and a desire to contribute to the financial literacy of the people around us.

As parents, we hope we will be able to do something big to contribute to the long-term financial security of our families. Throughout the process, we found willing partners in our spouses, and we have had a chance to rediscover our kids all over again as they embark on their own journeys. We have realized that they are remarkable, responsible, and incredibly capable of being long-term stewards of our coffee can investments as well as our values. And we learned, frankly, that inheritance was something they had never even considered. They simply desired to succeed on their own. And all they ever really wanted from us was love, support, and wisdom along the way. In the end, as much as we thought we were going to give our children the ultimate lottery ticket, we learned we had already won the jackpot.

ACKNOWLEDGMENTS

Standing up a book like this requires a powerful group effort.

I'd like to thank Maury for sharing her husband and the Ankrum girls for sharing their dad with me for years.

I want to thank Brian Smith for his deft editing and helping me to find the right balance of personal stories and financial explanations throughout the book. He and his team have and continue to be champions of my efforts to surface unique and accessible investment stories.

Also at Columbia University Press, I want to thank the editorial and faculty committees for their guidance and contributions. I am grateful for the entire publishing team's tireless work to produce and promote this book—from design, copy editing, and typesetting to marketing and publicity.

I had the privilege of receiving valuable feedback from a strong peer review committee who provided both business and journalistic perspectives. You know who you are!

I'd also like to call out Anand Kini (CFO and COO of Versant) and former *60 Minutes* producer Ira Rosen for their advice along the way.

To all the companies covered in this book, I hope you find the descriptions and Matt's assessments to be fair. I am grateful to the Investor Relations and Public Relations teams at all the companies that helped with access and photography.

I want to also thank in advance all my mentors and colleagues that I have worked with in media over the years for their support of long form journalism and ongoing efforts to promote this book.

And, last, thanks to my family for their support and involvement in this book. This project is as much yours as it is mine!

NOTES

1. THE BOY FROM BELOIT

1. Kerry A. Dolan and Andrea Murphy, "America's Richest Self-Made Women," *Forbes*, May 28, 2024, https://www.forbes.com/self-made-women/?sh=76e37fe96d96.

2. COFFEE CAN INVESTING

1. Laurent Dangeard, "24h of Le Mans 1979," *24h-en-piste*, February 16, 2024, http://www.24h-en-piste.com/en/AfficherDetails.php?Type=Course&Annee=1979&Numero=73.
2. Myrna Oliver, "Robert Kirby, 80; Helped Analyze 1987 Market Crash," *Los Angeles Times*, April 20, 2005, https://www.latimes.com/archives/la-xpm-2005-apr-20-me-kirby20-story.html.
3. Robert Kirby, "The Coffee Can Portfolio," *Journal of Portfolio Management*, Fall 1984, https://www.scribd.com/document/381312005/the-coffee-can-portfolio-pdf.

3. THE EIGHTH WONDER OF THE WORLD

1. goodreads, "Poor Charlie's Almanack Quotes," from *Poor Charlie's Almanack: The Wit and Wisdom of Charles T. Munger*, by Charles T. Munger, https://www.goodreads.com/quotes/310173-in-my-whole-life-i-have-known-no-wise-people.
2. goodreads, "Poor Charlie's Almanack Quotes," from *Poor Charlie's Almanack, The Wit and Wisdom of Charles T. Munger*, by Charles T. Munger, https://www.goodreads.com/quotes/1402049-spend-each-day-trying-to-be-a-little-wiser-than.
3. "Thomas W. Phelps, 90, Ex-Investment Counsel," *New York Times*, November 5, 1992, https://www.nytimes.com/1992/11/05/obituaries/thomas-w-phelps-90-ex-investment-counsel.html.
4. Thomas W. Phelps, *100 to 1 in the Stock Market: A Distinguished Security Analyst Tells How to Make More of Your Investment Opportunities* (McGraw-Hill, 1972), 14, 20.
5. Christopher W. Mayer, *100 Baggers: Stocks That Return 100-to-1 and How to Find Them* (Laissez Faire, 2015).
6. Thomas W. Phelps, *100 to 1 in the Stock Market*, 373.

7. Rebecca Lake, "What Is the Average Stock Holding Period?," *SmartAsset*, April 20, 2022, https://finance.yahoo.com/news/average-stock-holding-period-121123957.html.

8. "How Much Does a Grain of Rice Cost?," *Answers*, November 27, 2024, https://www.answers.com/grocery-stores/How_much_does_a_grain_of_rice_cost.

9. goodreads, "Albert Einstein," https://www.goodreads.com/quotes/76863-compound-interest-is-the-eighth-wonder-of-the-world-he.

10. Jeannine Mancini, "Charlie Munger Says, 'The Big Money Is Not in the Buying and the Selling But in the Waiting'—High Returns Don't Actually Require High Effort," *Benzinga*, October 9, 2023, https://finance.yahoo.com/news/charlie-munger-says-big-money-173549307.html.

11. Dillon Jacobs, "Warren Buffett's Net Worth Over the Years," *Finmasters*, December 2, 2024, https://finmasters.com/warren-buffett-net-worth/#gref.

4. MATT'S 100-BAGGER STUDY

1. Warren Buffett, "Discover Good and Great Business in Warren Buffett Way," *Fortune*, October 7, 2014, https://www.youtube.com/watch?v=pjP709i6OGE.

2. Charles T. Munger, "Wise Words from Charlie Munger," *Novel Investor*, November 29, 2023, https://novelinvestor.com/wise-words-from-charlie-munger/.

3. Abram Brown, "The 47,500 Percent Return: Meet the Billionaire Family Behind the Hottest Stock of the Past 30 Years," *Forbes*, January 13, 2020, https://www.forbes.com/sites/abrambrown/2020/01/13/heico-mendelson/.

4. Caleb Naysmith, "Warren Buffett Just Bought a $185,373,840 Stake in This Little-Known SpaceX Competitor," *Globe and Mail*, October 31, 2024, https://www.theglobeandmail.com/investing/markets/indices/SRCS/pressreleases/29331445/warren-buffett-just-bought-a-185373840-stake-in-this-little-known-spacex-competitor/.

5. Chris Gallant, "How an Economic Moat Provides a Competitive Advantage," *Investopedia*, October 18, 2024, https://www.investopedia.com/ask/answers/05/economicmoat.asp.

6. Steve Slaggie, "Fastenal History," 1994, 4:41, https://www.youtube.com/watch?v=AMbzeSrMfc4.

7. Reuters Staff, "Fastenal Q3 Results Beat Market Estimates," *Reuters*, October 12, 2010, https://www.reuters.com/article/business/fastenal-q3-results-beat-market-estimates-idUSSGE69B0EN/.

5. SHIBBOLETH

1. Steve Swartz, "Annual Letter from Steve Swartz," *Hearst News*, February 14, 2024, https://www.hearst.com/-/annual-letter-from-steve-swartz-2.

2. Sara Fischer, "Majority of Hearst Profits Now B2B, CEO Says," *Axios*, November 26, 2024, https://www.axios.com/2024/11/26/hearst-media-profit-b2b.

6. DIWORSIFICATION

1. Pieter Slegers, "How to Outperform the Market by Nick Sleep," *Compounding Quality*, December 1, 2022, https://www.compoundingquality.net/p/how-to-outperform-the-market-by-nick.

2. Nick Sleep and Qais Zakaria, *The Full Collection of the Nomad Investment Partnership Letters to Partners*, 2002–2014, https://igyfoundation.org.uk/wp-content/uploads/2021/03/Full _Collection_Nomad_Letters_.pdf.

3. Clay Finck, "The Best Investor You've Never Heard Of," *We Study Billionaires*, November 7, 2022, 39:33, https://www.youtube.com/watch?v=YJQaKHnurpo.

4. Kate Taylor, "Costco Is Inspiring Tech CEOs like Jeff Bezos and Mark Zuckerberg in One Key Way," *Business Insider*, April 11, 2018, https://www.businessinsider.com/costco -inspires-mark-zuckerberg-jeff-bezos-2018-4; Saul Hansell, "A Profitable Amazon Looks to Do an Encore, *New York Times*, January 26, 2002, https://www.nytimes.com/2002/01/26 /business/a-profitable-amazon-looks-to-do-an-encore.html; and Tom Huddleston, "Cost-co's Founder Met Jeff Bezos for Coffee—His Advice Helped Turn a Near-Death Amazon Into a $2 Trillion Business," *CNBC*, November 17, 2024, https://www.cnbc.com/2024/11/17 /jeff-bezos-costco-founder-coffee-meeting-helped-revive-amazon.html?__source =iosappshare%7Ccom.apple.UIKit.activity.Mail.

5. Ben Thompson, "The Relentless Jeff Bezos," *Stratechery*, February 3, 2021, https:// stratechery.com/2021/the-relentless-jeff-bezos/.

6. Finck, "The Best Investor You've Never Heard Of."

7. Bill Gurley, "Uber's New BHAG: UberPool," *Above the Crowd*, January 30, 2015, https:// abovethecrowd.com/2015/01/30/ubers-new-bhag-uberpool/.

8. Morgan Housel, *The Psychology of Money* (Harriman House, 2020), https://www.goodreads .com/quotes/10933182-at-berkshire-hathaway-shareholder-meeting-in-2013-warren -buffett-said.

9. Robert Stephens, "Charlie Munger on the Dangers of Diworsification," *Gurufocus*, April 29, 2021, https://www.gurufocus.com/news/1410400/charlie-munger-on-the-dangers -of-diworsification.

10. Bill Stone, "Berkshire Hathaway's Third Quarter 2024 Portfolio Moves," *Forbes*, November 16, 2024, https://www.forbes.com/sites/bill_stone/2024/11/16/berkshire -hathaways-third-quarter-2024-portfolio-moves/.

11. Hardika Singh, "It's the Magnificent Seven's Market, the Other Stocks Are Just Living in It," *Wall Street Journal*, December 17, 2023, https://www.wsj.com/finance/stocks /its-the-magnificent-sevens-market-the-other-stocks-are-just-living-in-it-5d212f95.

12. Faizan Farooque, "Magnificent Seven Stocks Dominate S&P 500 Gains in 2024," *Guru Focus*, January 6, 2025, https://www.gurufocus.com/news/2794322/sumitomo-sbi-throw-support -behind-fpts-nvidiapowered-ai-expansion.

13. Phil Rosen, "Big Tech Is So Dominant the Stock Market Would Have Been Flat for 2 Years Without It," *Inc.*, January 6, 2025, https://www.inc.com/phil-rosen/stock-market -outlook-sp500-investors-economic-fed-rate-cut-magnificent-seven/91103119.

14. Sean Williams, "Billionaire Warren Buffett Has Purchased $77 Billion of His Favorite Stock, Which Is More Than Double What He's Spent Buying Shares of Apple, *The Motley Fool*, July 22, 2024, https://finance.yahoo.com/news/billionaire-warren-buffett-purchased -77-092100281.html.

15. Johnny Rice, "Warren Buffett's Billion-Dollar Dividend Duo: Apple and Coca-Cola Account for Over $1.6 Billion a Year in Income for Berkshire Hathaway," *Benzinga*, October 20, 2023, https://finance.yahoo.com/news/warren-buffetts-billion-dollar-dividend-115512368 .html#:~:text=People%20know%20Apple%20for%20its,million%20a%20year%20in%20dividends.

7. FLUGELBINDERS

1. "CADEYE for Colonic Polyps: Eluxeo Meets Artificial Intelligence," *FujiFilm*, https://asset.fujifilm.com/www/uk/files/2021-05/8fbe51b9718df4e16e3e3a545fa5593a/ELUXEO_CADEYE_Brochure.pdf.

2. Charlie Huggins, "Diploma: Specialized Distribution," *Business Breakdowns*, June 15, 2022, https://www.joincolossus.com/episodes/53165581/huggins-diploma-specialized-distribution?tab=transcript.

3. "Full Year Results for the Year Ended 30 September 2024," *Diploma PLC*, November 19, 2024, https://www.diplomaplc.com/media/cvpbhtt3/fy24-full-year-results-presentation.pdf.

4. Tom Dines, "Diploma's New Chief Buys In," *Investor's Chronicle*, https://www.investorschronicle.co.uk/Standard-Articles/2019/03/05/diploma_dd_05032019.

5. "Investor Seminar 2023," *Diploma*, 35:45, https://www.diplomaplc.com/investors/investor-seminar-2023/.

8. THE NEW MAGICIANS

1. Mathew Di Salvo, "The Real Story Behind the Origins of Globant," *Nearshore Americas*, September 25, 2019, https://nearshoreamericas.com/the-real-story-behind-the-origins-of-globant/.

2. Martin Migoya, "Charting the Cognitive Revolution with Globant's Martin Migoya," *Inside the ICE House*, November 5, 2018, https://podcasts.apple.com/us/podcast/inside-the-ice-house/id1684241594?i=1000610408802.

3. Migoya, "Charting the Cognitive Revolution with Globant's Martin Migoya."

4. Jason Bloomberg, "Digital Influencer Martin Migoya of Globant: Reinventing Marketing with Consumer Journeys," *Forbes*, February 5, 2016, https://www.forbes.com/sites/jasonbloomberg/2016/02/05/digital-influencer-martin-migoya-of-globant-reinventing-marketing-with-consumer-journeys/.

5. Georgina Portas Ruiz, "Globant Timeline: 20 Years of Expansion and Growth," *Globant*, September 19, 2023, https://stayrelevant.globant.com/en/culture/globant-experience/globant-global-expansion-and-growth/.

6. Kurt Badenhausen, "Formula 1 and Globant Partner to Enhance F1 Digital Capabilities," *Sportico*, May 2, 2024, https://www.sportico.com/leagues/motorsports/2024/formula-1-globant-partner-digital-1234777574/.

7. Jon Wertheim, "Ballmer's Ballgame," *60 Minutes*, October 13, 2024, https://www.cbsnews.com/video/steve-ballmer-60-minutes-video-2024-10-13/.

8. "Globant Partners with the Metropolitan Police to Transform Public Online Access to Police Service," *Globant*, May 14, 2020, https://www.youtube.com/watch?v=kTfFiDoVf2Q.

9. "Globant Partners with the Metropolitan Police."

10. Steve Jobs, "Great Idea Doesn't Always Translates Into Great Product," *Investors Archive*, https://www.youtube.com/watch?v=Qdplq4cj76I.

11. Jobs, "Great Idea Doesn't Always Translates Into Great Product."

12. Martin Migoya, "Globant CEO Migoya on Grabbing Market Share," *Bloomberg Intelligence Tech Disruptors*, April 4, 2024, https://podcasts.apple.com/us/podcast/globant-ceo-migoya-on-grabbing-market-share/id1621165150?i=1000651424013.

13. Georgina Portas Ruiz, "Bob Iger at Globant Converge: Connecting the Past, Present, and Future of Innovation," *Globant*, November 15, 2022, https://stayrelevant.globant .com/en/culture/great-new-things/bob-iger-disney-digital-transformation-converge -lessons-insights/.

14. Migoya, "Charting the Cognitive Revolution with Globant's Martin Migoya."

15. Migoya, "Globant CEO Migoya on Grabbing Market Share."

16. Martin Migoya, "Creating Autonomy and Internal Mobility for Employees: Insights from the CEO of Globant," *Future Ready Leadership with Jacob Morgan*, June 10, 2019, https://podcasts.apple.com/us/podcast/future-ready-leadership-with-jacob-morgan /id907990904?i=1000441029291&r=941.

17. Stephanie Vozza, "This Is How to Know if an Employee Is Thinking of Quitting," *Fast Company*, May 8, 2019, https://www.fastcompany.com/90342802/this-is-how-to-know -if-an-employee-is-thinking-of-quitting.

18. "Market Opportunity Map: Digital Technology and Business Services Worldwide," *Gartner Research*, January 17, 2024, https://www.gartner.com/en/documents/5111931.

19. "Forecast Analysis: Digital Business Implementation and Refinement Services Worldwide," *Gartner Research*, September 5, 2023, https://www.gartner.com/en/documents /4709499.

20. Charles Newberry, "Globant Sees 'Big' Pipeline of Potential Acquisitions—CEO," *Latin-Finance*, November 5, 2023, https://latinfinance.com/daily-brief/2023/11/05/globant-sees -big-pipeline-of-potential-acquisitions-ceo/.

21. Thomas Dohmke and Martin Migoya, "AI, the Future of Work, and Its Impact on the Technology Industry," *Globant*, May 9, 2023, https://www.youtube.com/watch?v =dWzNQ1nTN1M.

9. DEATH AND TAXES

1. Jay Jackson, "From Policy to Profit: Unlocking the Hidden Value of Life Insurance, Jay Jackson," *Wealthion*, February 6, 2024, https://wealthion.com/from-policy-to-profit -unlocking-the-hidden-value-of-life-insurance-jay-jackson/.

2. *Grigsby v. Russell*, December 4, 1911, https://tile.loc.gov/storage-services/service/ll/usrep /usrep222/usrep222149/usrep222149.pdf.

3. Jackson, "From Policy to Profit."

4. Jackson, "From Policy to Profit."

5. Jackson, "From Policy to Profit."

6. Jackson, "From Policy to Profit."

7. David DeStefano, "How to Become an Intelligent Enterprise: Vertex at SAP TechEd 2018," *SAP TechEd*, https://www.youtube.com/watch?v=dYy5SwicnjI.

8. "Payments, Assistance & Taxes," City of Philadelphia, https://www.phila.gov/services /payments-assistance-taxes/taxes/business-taxes/business-taxes-by-type/philadelphia -beverage-tax-pbt/#:~:text=How%20much%20is%20it%3F,of%20raw%20syrup%20or%20 concentrate.

9. Vertex, "William Blair 44th Annual Growth Stock Conference," June 2024, https://ir .vertexinc.com/static-files/021ac00e-4f2d-4798-8b8e-26e4ff925795.

10. NICHES MAKE RICHES

1. Ed Chung, "The Platform Podcast, Episode 200," June 28, 2022, 5:20, https://www.youtube.com/watch?v=SkWMwXso9nM.
2. Chung, "The Platform Podcast, Episode 200."
3. "City of Newcastle," *TechnologyOne*, November 1, 2023, https://www.technologyonecorp.com/resources/case-studies/city-of-newcastle.
4. Stuart Bromley, "Should You Buy, Hold or Sell TechnologyOne Shares?," *Money*, April 24, 2024, https://www.moneymag.com.au/should-you-buy-hold-or-sell-technologyone-shares.

11. NICE GUYS FINISH FIRST

1. Curt Schleier, "How a 'Lazy' Student Became CEO of a Multibillion-Dollar Firm," *Investor's Business Daily*, November 11, 2021, https://www.investors.com/news/management/leaders-and-success/nice-ceo-tapped-military-experience-to-lead/.
2. Barak Eilam, "Workforce Continuity as Competitive Advantage," *Managing the Future of Work*, Harvard Business School, November 3, 2021, https://www.hbs.edu/managing-the-future-of-work/podcast/Pages/podcast-details.aspx?episode=21034067.
3. Julie Hyman and Josh Lipton, "How NICE Is Using AI to Change the Customer Relations Game," *Yahoo! Finance*, February 23, 2024, https://finance.yahoo.com/video/nice-using-ai-change-customer-213040646.html.

12. BOURBON AND OTHER STUNNING APPROACHES TO POLICING

1. Rick Smith, "Axon CEO Rick Smith at Singularity Summit 2017," *Axon*, February 28, 2019, https://www.youtube.com/watch?v=EjOZxQS-GAA.
2. Peter Eisler, Jason Szep, Tim Reid, and Grant Smith, "Deaths Involving Tasers," *Reuters Investigates*, August 22, 2017, https://www.reuters.com/investigates/special-report/usa-taser-tracker/.
3. Smith, "Axon CEO Rick Smith at Singularity Summit 2017."
4. Anna Ashcraft, "SDPD First in County to Upgrade to Latest TASER 10, Giving Them Further Range with Less Voltage," *FOX 5 KUSI News*, June 7, 2024, https://fox5sandiego.com/news/local-news/sdpd-first-in-county-to-upgrade-to-latest-taser-10-giving-them-further-range-with-less-voltage/.
5. Randall Stross, "Wearing a Badge, and a Video Camera," *New York Times*, April 6, 2013, https://www.nytimes.com/2013/04/07/business/wearable-video-cameras-for-police-officers.html?_r=2&.
6. Axon Enterprise (Axon), "Q2 2024 Earnings Call Transcript," *Motley Fool*, August 6, 2024, https://www.fool.com/earnings/call-transcripts/2024/08/06/axon-enterprise-axon-q2-2024-earnings-call-transcr/.
7. Danielle Menichella, "Axon: Stunning the Competition," *Business Breakdowns*, July 24, 2024, https://podcasts.apple.com/us/podcast/axon-stunning-the-competition/id1559120677?i=1000663179877.
8. Nate Rosenfield, Brian Howey, and Sarah Cohen, "Where the Police Used a Taser on a Bible-Reading Great-Grandmother," *New York Times*, January 14, 2025, https://www

.nytimes.com/2025/01/14/us/abuse-and-injury-result-from-uneven-rules-on-police
-taser-use.html?smid=nytcore-ios-share&referringSource=articleShare.

9.   CNN Newswire, "Bodycam Maker Unveils New Features It Hopes to Curb Police Offi-
     cer Misconduct," October 28, 2020, https://abc7.com/body-camera-police-bodycam
     -officer/7422266/.

10. CNN Newswire, "Bodycam Maker Unveils New Features."

11. Smith, "Axon CEO Rick Smith at Singularity Summit 2017."

13. DON'T LET THE BED BUGS BITE

1.   Andy Ransom, "Rentokil Initial CEO: Pest Control, AI and Dealmaking," *In Good
     Company with Nicolai Tangen*, February 6, 2024, https://podcasts.apple.com/us/podcast
     /in-good-company-with-nicolai-tangen/id1614211565?i=1000644432730.

2.   "Over 100 Years of Service," *Rentokil*, https://www.rentokil-initial.com/about-us/our
     -story-so-far.aspx.

3.   Sumathi Reddy, "The Risk of Mosquito-Borne Illnesses Is Rising. How to Protect
     Yourself," *Wall Street Journal*, September 6, 2024, https://www.wsj.com/health/mosquito
     -season-longer-warmer-diseases-5819c29c.

4.   United States Department of Agriculture, "What 'Wood' a Termite Prefer to Eat?," *AgRe-
     search Magazine*, November 2015, https://agresearchmag.ars.usda.gov/2015/nov/termites/.

5.   "Fascinating Facts About Termites," *Termidor*, https://www.termidorhome.com
     /abouttermites/termitefacts.html.

6.   "Climate Change Indicators: West Nile Virus," *United State Environmental Protection
     Agency*, https://www.epa.gov/climate-indicators/climate-change-indicators-west-nile
     -virus#:~:text=Studies%20show%20that%20warmer%20temperatures,the%20disease%20
     within%20a%20mosquito.

7.   Heather Whitney, "The Role of Climate Change in Bed Bug Proliferation," *Medium*,
     July 6, 2024, https://medium.com/@ms.heather.whitney/the-role-of-climate-change-in
     -bed-bug-proliferation-c0c98b7a8bcb.

8.   Aayushi Sharma, "Is Increasing Termite Activity a Consequence of Climate Change?,"
     Climate Fact Checks, January 2023, https://climatefactchecks.org/is-increasing-termite
     -activity-a-consequence-of-climate-change/#:~:text=The%20research%20revealed%20
     that%20as,release%20carbon%20into%20the%20atmosphere.

9.   Ransom, "Rentokil Initial CEO."

10. Ransom, "Rentokil Initial CEO."

11. Leke Oso Alabi, "Rentokil Takes on the World's Rat Problem with Facial Recognition,"
     Financial Times, January 20, 2023, https://www.ft.com/content/641036f1-acbb-409b
     -9b78-e63c04bdf4e7.

12. Frances McKim, "Rentokil Now the Largest Pest Control Company in India," *Pest*,
     March 15, 2017, https://www.pestmagazine.co.uk/news/companies/rentokil-now-the-largest
     -pest-control-company-in-india.html.

13. Bojan Popovski, "A Bullish Perspective on Rentokil Initial plc (RTO)," *Insider Monkey*,
     August 14, 2024, https://finance.yahoo.com/news/bullish-perspective-rentokil-initial-plc
     -174225016.html.

14. Zack Fuss, "Cintas: Rags to Riches," *Business Breakdowns*, July 10, 2024, https://podcasts .apple.com/us/podcast/cintas-rags-to-riches/id1559120677?i=1000661752700.

15. Cristina Gallardo, "Rentokil Shares Plunge After Profit Warning," *Wall Street Journal*, September 11, 2024, https://www.wsj.com/business/retail/rentokil-initial-warns-on -profits-as-u-s-sales-slow-1dfdac22?st=g2fhdifp4n55m6r&reflink=article_email_share.

16. David Senra, "#364 Nick & Zak's Excellent Adventure: How Nick Sleep and Qais Zah-aria Built Their Investment Partnership," *Founders*, September 9, 2024, https://podcasts .apple.com/us/podcast/founders/id1141877104?i=1000668959994.

17. Ransom, "Rentokil Initial CEO."

14. DAD'S NOT PERFECT

1. Roger Federer, "2024 Commencement Address by Roger Federer at Dartmouth," Dart-mouth, June 9, 2024, https://www.youtube.com/watch?v=pqWUuYTcG-0.

2. Charlie Munger quote available on https://novelinvestor.com/quote-author/charlie -munger/, accessed September 4, 2025.

15. THE ROAD TO SUCCESS IS ALWAYS UNDER CONSTRUCTION

1. "We Are Bentley Systems, the Leading Provider of Infrastructure Engineering Soft-ware," *Bentley Systems*, https://www.bentley.com/company/about-us/.

2. "Bentley History," *Bentley Systems*, 2:03, https://www.bentley.com/history/?

3. "Bentley History," *Bentley Systems*, 2:32, https://www.bentley.com/history/?

4. "Bentley History," *Bentley Systems*, 2:37, https://www.bentley.com/history/?

5. "Bentley History," *Bentley Systems*, 2:45, https://www.bentley.com/history/?

6. "Bentley History," Bentley Systems, 1:30, https://www.bentley.com/history/?

7. "Bentley History," *Bentley Systems*, 3:25, https://www.bentley.com/history/?

8. "Bentley History," *Bentley Systems*, 4:40, https://www.bentley.com/history/?

9. "Bentley History," *Bentley Systems*, 5:00, https://www.bentley.com/history/

10. "Bentley History," *Bentley Systems*, 6:08, https://www.bentley.com/history/?

11. Keith Bentley, "Looking Backward with Tech Experts Keith and Greg Bentley," *Engineering News-Record*, 5:20, https://www.youtube.com/watch?v=KlrrFTpBu4A.

12. "Bentley History," *Bentley Systems*, 7:45, https://www.bentley.com/history/?

13. "Wounds of Layoff Remain Fresh for Bentley Systems CEO," *Science Center*, April 8, 2010, https://sciencecenter.org/news/wounds-of-layoff-remain-fresh-for-bentley-systems-ceo.

14. "Bentley History," *Bentley Systems*, 7:45, https://www.bentley.com/history/?

15. "Bentley History," *Bentley Systems*, 8:00, https://www.bentley.com/history/?

16. "Bentley History," *Bentley Systems*, 8:10, https://www.bentley.com/history/?

17. Karen Moltenbrey, " Bentley Redefines the Meaning of Family Business," *Jon Peddie Research*, July 14, 2023, https://www.jonpeddie.com/news/bentley-redefines-the-meaning -of-family-business/.

18. "Bentley History," *Bentley Systems*, 8:24, https://www.bentley.com/history/?

19. "We Are Bentley Systems, the Leading Provider of Infrastructure Engineering Soft-ware," *Bentley Systems*, https://www.bentley.com/company/about-us/.

20. "We Are Bentley Systems."

21. "We Are Bentley Systems."

22. Greg Bentley, "Digital Twins Executive Interview—Greg Bentley of Bentley Systems— ARC Industry Forum 2019," March 14, 2019, https://www.youtube.com/watch?v =KqXaAerjB00.

23. Greg Bentley, William Blair Growth Stock Conference, June 4, 2024, https://investors .bentley.com/static-files/a8ec9afd-83eb-4c40-9739-8beaa51227dd.

24. George Lawton, "A Legacy Built on 40 Years of Trust—Learnings from Greg Bentley as He Steps Down as CEO of Bentley Systems," *Diginomica*, March 25, 2024, https:// diginomica.com/legacy-built-40-years-trust-learnings-greg-bentley-he-steps-down-ceo -bentley-systems.

25. James McBride, Noah Berman, and Anshu Siripurapu, "The State of U.S. Infrastructure," *Council on Foreign Relations*, September 20, 2023, https://www.cfr.org/backgrounder/state -us-infrastructure.

26. "Bridge Report," American Road & Transportation Builders Association, February 16, 2024, https://artbabridgereport.org.

27. Andrew Birmingham, "Ex-Google Chief Eric Schmidt Says AI's Impact Over Two Years Will Be Profound. But He Warns 'There's Not Enough Electricity in the US' to Meet OpenAI's US$300bn Investment Ambitions," *Mi3*, September 9, 2024, https:// www.mi-3.com.au/09-09-2024/eric-schmidt-who-built-google-global-powerhouse -says-ais-impact-over-2-years-will-be.

28. "Founders' Perspectives: Letter from Greg, Barry, Keith, and Ray Bentley," *Bentley*, https://investors.bentley.com/static-files/53fc3910-1b81-4584-9e6b-145ccobc192b.

29. Mike Ettore, "Why Most New Executives Fail—And Four Things Companies Can Do About It," *Forbes*, March 13, 2020, https://www.forbes.com/councils/forbescoachescouncil /2020/03/13/why-most-new-executives-fail-and-four-things-companies-can-do -about-it/.

30. Lawton, "A Legacy Built on 40 Years of Trust."

31. "Bentley History," *Bentley Systems*, https://www.bentley.com/history/?

32. "Nicholas Cumins Takes Charge as CEO of Bentley Systems, Ushering in a New Era," *Bentley Systems*, July 1, 2024, "https://www.bentley.com/news/nicholas-cumins -takes-charge-as-ceo-of-bentley-systems-ushering-in-a-new-era/.

16. SOMEWHERE, SOMETHING INCREDIBLE IS WAITING TO BE KNOWN

1. "Gene Therapy," *Mayo Clinic*, https://www.mayoclinic.org/tests-procedures/gene-therapy /about/pac-20384619, February 16, 2024.

2. Aylin Sertkaya, Trinidad Beleche, and Amber Jessup, "Costs of Drug Development and Research and Development Intensity in the US, 2008–2018," *JAMA Network*, June 28, 2024, https://jamanetwork.com/journals/jamanetworkopen/fullarticle/2820562.

3. Dhruv Khullar, "How Machines Learned to Discover Drugs," *The New Yorker*, September 2, 2024, https://www.newyorker.com/magazine/2024/09/09/how-machines-learned-to -discover-drugs.

4. Google DeepMind AlphaFold team and Isomorphic Labs, "AlphaFold 3 Predicts the Structures and Interactions of All of Life's Molecules," *Google The Keyword*, May 8, 2024, https://blog.google/technology/ai/google-deepmind-isomorphic-alphafold-3-ai-model/#life-molecules.

5. "Reputation of Quality: The Bio-Techne Brand Story," *Bio-Techne*, February 9, 2018, https://www.youtube.com/watch?v=-lVIi3JddVI.

6. "Bio-Techne Announces Investment in Wilson Wolf," *Bio-Techne*, March 1, 2023, https://investors.bio-techne.com/press-releases/detail/356/bio-techne-announces-investment-in-wilson-wolf.

7. Johan Skog, "Johan Skog: Exosomes—The Future of Diagnostics, Back of the Napkin—Inspiring Stories from Biotech Pioneers," June 10, 2024, https://podcasts.apple.com/us/podcast/back-of-the-napkin-inspiring-stories-from-biotech-pioneers/id1690601747?i=1000658509966.

8. Nick Paul Taylor, "Bio-Techne Closes $250M Exosome Diagnostics Takeover," *MedTech Dive*, August 3, 2018, https://www.medtechdive.com/news/bio-techne-closes-250m-exosome-diagnostics-takeover/529287/.

17. NETWORK EFFECTS TIMES TWO

1. William Brian Arthur, "Network Effects, Origin Stories, and the Evolution of Tech," *A16Z*, May 16, 2018, https://a16z.com/podcast/a16z-podcast-network-effects-origin-stories-and-the-evolution-of-tech/.

2. Emily Curran, "#159—EDI 101: Emily Curran, SPS Commerce," *The Startup CPG Podcast*, September 3, 2024, https://podcasts.apple.com/us/podcast/the-startup-cpg-podcast/id1509862352?i=1000668129178&r=729.

3. Curran, "#159—EDI 101: Emily Curran, SPS Commerce."

4. Christian Hassold, "E17: Deal Report: SPS Commerce $206 M Acquisition of SupplyPike," *In/Organic Podcast*, August 25, 2024, https://podcasts.apple.com/us/podcast/in-organic-podcast/id1710070954?i=1000666558930&r=612.

5. Ed Ryan, "Descartes Evolution 2015: Conversation with Ed Ryan, CEO at Descartes Systems Group," *Talking Logistics*, July 9, 2015, 4:37, https://www.youtube.com/watch?v=NT50GbFNUow.

6. Ryan, "Descartes Evolution 2015," 7:00.

7. Ryan, "Descartes Evolution 2015," 11:38.

8. Ed Ryan, "Descartes (DSGX) CEO on Maintaining Profit and Utilizing A.I.," *Schwab Network*, September 9, 2024, https://schwabnetwork.com/video/descartes-dsgx-ceo-on-maintaining-profit-and-utilizing-a-i-.

18. DRIVE TIME

1. Githesh Ramamurthy, "Githesh Ramamurthy, Chairman, CEO, CCC Intelligent Solutions," *The Future of Insurance*, October 4, 2022, https://www.youtube.com/watch?v=dV1qNxgkOKQ.

2. "Nvidia Earnings Call Transcript Q1 2024," *Alpha Spread*, https://www.alphaspread.com/security/nasdaq/nvda/earnings-calls/q1-2024.

3. Marc Fredman, "Applying a Platform-Based Approach to Data, Technology, Ecosystems, and AI," *Moor Insights & Strategy*, June 4, 2024, https://moorinsightsstrategy.com/mis-insider-podcast/applying-a-platform-based-approach-to-data-technology-ecosystems-and-ai-mis-insider-podcast/.

4. Ramamurthy, "Githesh Ramamurthy, Chairman, CEO, CCC Intelligent Solutions."

5. Lurah Lowery, "CCC: Number of Claims Rebound, Driving Up Cycle Time & Increasing Need for AI," *Repairer Driven News*, August 3, 2023, https://www.repairerdrivennews.com/2023/08/03/ccc-number-of-claims-rebound-driving-up-cycle-time-increasing-need-for-ai/.

6. Ramamurthy, "Githesh Ramamurthy, Chairman, CEO, CCC Intelligent Solutions."

7. Fredman, "Applying a Platform-Based Approach to Data, Technology, Ecosystems, and AI."

8. Githesh Ramamurthy, "CCCS Investor Overview," December 13, 2024, https://ir.cccis.com.

9. "CCC Intelligent Solutions Investor Presentation," October 28, 2024, https://ir.cccis.com/static-files/180c214c-95c0-4ea9-83a5-5b685860440a.

10. Fredman, "Applying a Platform-Based Approach to Data, Technology, Ecosystems, and AI."

CONCLUSION: HAPPY THANKSGIVING

1. Max Ehrmann, "Desiderata—Words for Life," https://allpoetry.com/desiderata---words-for-life.

INDEX

GPSR Authorized Representative: Easy Access System Europe, Mustamäe tee
50, 10621 Tallinn, Estonia, gpsr.requests@easproject.com